Our Mother Earth

– OF THE FURROW BORN –

SILVERWEED OR 'FOOTSEASE'
The late Hilda Smith of Wickham St. Paul's recalled that her Father put, "'Foots-
ease' in the soles of his boots if he had a long way to walk"; Bert Surridge of
Gestingthorpe similarly remembered old men putting the soft, springy leaves of the
plant in their boots when ploughing, "as it helped to keep their feet cool".
The plant grows quite naturally along the Suffolk-Essex border.

Cover Picture: Hedingham Castle with an early 'seed drill' in the foreground, October 1786. The author is constantly intrigued by the logistics of obtaining the flints in the keep's massive walls. The 'seed drill' however testifies to the more usual 'crops' which have been harvested from 'Our Mother Earth'.

OUR MOTHER EARTH

– OF THE FURROW BORN –

(Heart of our History, Volume Two)

BY

Ashley Cooper

BULMER HISTORICAL SOCIETY

By the same author:

The Long Furrow
The Khyber Connection
Tales of Woodland and Harvest (fiction)
Heart of Our History

Published by Bulmer Historical Society 1998

©Ashley Cooper
Hill Farm, Gestingthorpe, Halstead, Essex, CO9 3BL

ISBN 0-9524778 2 3

Illustrations by Benjamin Perkins

Design by Colin Freeman
Printed in Great Britain by The Five Castles Press Limited, Ipswich

FOREWORD

You have toiled on this land before us,
As you ploughed your 'acre a day',
As you pitched the sheaves in harvest fields,
And led the waggons away.

You have told of the hardship and backache,
– But also the moments of mirth,
As you sowed and garnered these fields,
As you worked on Our Mother Earth.

*   *   *

To you in the future – whose past I am,
We commit these stories of yore,
That you may yet know how once it was
– From those who have gone before!

This Countryside

Dedicated
in grateful respect
to

ADRIAN CORDER-BIRCH

past chairman of Halstead and District Local History Society,
for the limitless help he has given to this – and so many
other local publications;

to

JOHN WASPE

of Whatfield near Hadleigh

– last of the 'Tithe War' heroes–

and to

BARTHOLOMEW AND JOSIAH MINTER

of Bulmer Brickyard

born 1990 and 1992 respectively – in the hope that some of what is
written herein, will preserve for their generation,
an element of the country lore so beloved by their Forefathers.

ACKNOWLEDGEMENTS

I would like to express my most sincere gratitude to Geoffrey Jackson of Cavendish for allowing me to borrow John Row's Farm Diaries for a protracted number of years and for permission to publish extracts from them. They have been an invaluable and richly stimulating source for both this book and lectures, and I am deeply grateful to him.

I must similarly thank Peter and Robin Rowe for allowing me to read their grandfather's recollections of Bulmer and for Robin's permission to quote extracts from them in Chapters Two, Thirteen and Eighteen.

My debt to Adrian Corder-Birch has already been recorded but I would again like to thank him and also Peter Minter, Dr. Arthur Brown and Witgar Hitchcock for checking portions of the text despite their own very busy schedules.

Additionally, I would like to thank Marion Smith for making available her copious – and excellent – researches on Wickham St. Paul and particularly for introducing me to the farm diaries of William Porter from the early nineteenth century. The fruits of Marion's research have now been published under the title, 'Land of My Fathers: Wickham St. Paul 1750–1850', printed under her maiden name of Marion Turp.

I am also sincerely grateful to Edith Freeman for sharing with me her extensive knowledge of Thomas Gainsborough and eighteenth century Sudbury; Hugh Belsey the curator of Gainsborough's House; Lavender Hawkins for providing a copy of the Andrews family tree; Rosemary Meekings for information on George Washington Brownlow and Barry Wall for his enthusiasm and support in historical matters generally. Finally, my thanks to Anne Legg and her staff at Sudbury Library for their willing assistance in obtaining obscure research material.

*　*　*　*　*

Once more I have been privileged to spend some wonderful afternoons recording the memories of local people whose recollections are the core of this work. Sadly many have passed away during the protracted period of research and writing. To those who remain – and to the families of those who have suffered bereavements – I offer my sincerest gratitude for both the welcome I received and for the humour and frankness with which the past has been recalled:

George Alderton, the late Claude Alleston; Brian Ambrose; Frank Billimore; Tom Bird; the late Ida Bird; Tom Black; Mary Brook; Bunny Brown; Willie Brown; the late Jim Bryant; Fred Chatters; the late George 'Jute' Chatters; the late Hazell Chinnery; Vera Chinnery; Gertie Coe; the late Cecil Cook; Harold Cooper; John Cooper; Dorothy and the late Jack Cornell; Ken Day; the late Percy Darlington; Doreen Desmond; Geoffrey, Hilda and Tony Dixey; Les Downs; Horace Elsey; the late Alf and Maggie Finch; the late Dick Finch; the late George 'Rover' Finch; Maurice Findlay; Edith Freeman; Alan Frost; the late John Frost; Gillman Game; the late Harry Gilbert; Tom Gilbert; Chris Glass; Cyril and Phyliss Golding; Kathleen Grimwood; Dick Halls; Lily Harrington; the late Douglas Hasler; Jim Hastie; Gordon Hastie; Dennis Holland; Canon Trevor Howard; Fred Hunt; David Jackson; the late George Jackson; Sid Knott; Peter Lawson; the late Philip Lawson; the late Ernie Lott; Charlie Martin; Peter Minter; Tony Minter; the late Daisy Nice; Frank Nice; Tom Nott; Cecil Pannell; Doris Pannell; Edwin Partridge; the late Cyril Philp; the late Muriel Pickering; the late Bob Pinhey; Oliver Prentice; Evelyn Reeve; John Riches; the late Dennis Rippingale; the late Reg Rippingale; Peter Rowe; Tom Rowe; the late Bert Surridge; David Taylor-Balls; Jimmy Theobald; David Tuffin; Eddie Tuffin; the late Frank Turner; the late Wally Twinn; Alf Weavers; the late Jack Wallace; John Waspe; Jim Waters and the late Bill Yeldham.

The extracts of poetry from 'This Countryside' *are by the present author.*

The section with the colour plates may one day be published as a separate booklet.

CONTENTS

PART ONE: Our Mother Earth: Surviving on Local Resources

Prelude 13

1. Brickyards and Brickmakers: *Local homes from local clay* 18
2. Chalk, Limekilns, Claypits and Sand: *The White Cliffs of Sudbury*...35
3. Local Pot Works: *Gestingthorpe and Castle Hedingham* 57
4. Hops, Teasels and Flax: *The Hedinghams, Maplesteads, and Stowmarket* 68
5. Cheesemaking, Tanning and Stockmen's Memories....................76
6. Straw Plaiting and Hay Trussing..86
7. Light and Water: *Well diggers' memories* 98
8. Herbal Remedies, Wildlife and Woodlands: *Two Local Apothecaries* 108

PART TWO: People on the Move – and Rural Rebellion!

9. John Row's Farm Diaries 1888–1899: *Long Melford and Foxearth* .127
10. Emigrations: *The Countryside abandoned* 146
11. Immigrant Farmers: *A Scottish, Cornish and Cheshire Invasion!*.......164
12. The Tithe War: *The Farmers Revolt!* 184

PART THREE: 'Of the Furrow Born'

13. Reaping Machines and Horse Ploughs: *Local Inventors and Farmworkers' Memories*...208
14. Steam Cultivation and early Tractors: *A Remarkable Lady*............223
15. Windmills and Water Mills: *Borley, Belchamp Walter, Henny and Halstead* 234

PART FOUR: 'More of the Long Furrow'

16. Further Diaries of John Row 255
17. Some Creatures Great and Small: *Stockmen and Shepherds: Veterinary Memories* 267
18. Harvesting Techniques: *The Sickle, Scythe, Reaper and Binder*........278
19. Threshing Machines and Traction Engines 290
20. Seedtime, Ploughing and Combine Harvesters 313
    Epilogue: Farm Diaries 1983–1998...313
    Appendix: Farming Immigrants to Essex-Suffolk Border 318
    Bibliography..322
    Index..325

(continued over)

Contents – *continued*

DISCUSSION ON PAINTINGS (in centre of book)

Building Gestingthorpe Church Tower i
John Morley of Halstead's Herbal Remedies............................... ii
Wild Flower Enthusiasts, 1738 iv
Gainsborough's Puzzling Farming Painting................................. vi
Thomas Gainsborough . . . and Harvest Mysteries! xii
A Famous Visitor Measures Trees at Bulmer.............................. xvi
A Farming Blunder in 1786! xx
Lewis Majendie's First 'Seed Drill' xxii
'Mole Draining' at Little Maplestead with Eighteen Horses! xxvii
The Straw Plaiters... xxix
Bulmer Street in the Late Nineteen Twenties xxx
The Tithe War.. xxxii

Publication Acknowledgements

I would like to thank Arthur Brown for permission to use the extracts drawn from *Meagre Harvest*, (published Essex Record Office, 1990), Adrian Corder-Birch for references drawn from *A History of Little Yeldham* (published by Halstead and District Local History Society), Robert Whitehead for an extract from *Garrett Diesel Tractors* published R. A. Whitehead and partners and Cynthia Brown for material drawn from her article, *'Drovers, Cattle and Dung'*, published in the Proceedings of the Suffolk Institute of Archaeology and History, Vol. XXXVII, Part 4, 1996.

I am sincerely grateful to Sarah Thomas for the use of her article entitled, *'Orchids from the Eighteenth Century Herbarium of Joseph Andrews'*, published in the Botanical Society of the British Isles News in September 1997, and to Jim Waters M.R.C.V.S. for allowing me to use stories from his autobiography *Animal Crackers* (published by St. Andrews Church, Halstead).

Finally, I would like to acknowledge the courtesy of the National Gallery in London for permitting the reproductions of Thomas Gainsborough's painting, *Mr. & Mrs. Robert Andrews* and Curtis Lane & Co. Commercial Photography for their assistance with the other colour paintings.

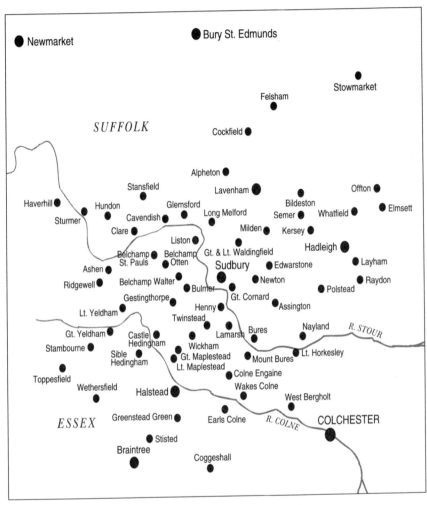

Newmarket

Bury St. Edmunds

Stowmarket

Felsham

SUFFOLK

Cockfield

Alpheton

Stansfield

Lavenham

Offton

Haverhill

Hundon

Glemsford

Bildeston

Elmsett

Long Melford

Semer

Whatfield

Sturmer

Cavendish

Milden

Clare

Kersey

Liston

Hadleigh

Belchamp St. Pauls

Belchamp Otten

Gt. & Lt. Waldingfield

Ashen

Sudbury

Edwarstone

Layham

Ridgewell

Belchamp Walter

Newton

Raydon

Bulmer

Polstead

Gestingthorpe

Gt. Cornard

Lt. Yeldham

Henny

Assington

Twinstead

Nayland

R. STOUR

Gt. Yeldham

Castle Hedingham

Lamarsh

Bures

Stambourne

Wickham

Lt. Horkesley

Sible Hedingham

Gt. Maplestead

Mount Bures

Toppesfield

Lt. Maplestead

Colne Engaine

Wethersfield

Halstead

Wakes Colne

West Bergholt

ESSEX

Greenstead Green

Earls Colne

R. COLNE

COLCHESTER

Stisted

Braintree

Coggeshall

'Our Mother Earth'

ABBREVIATIONS

References to the *Victoria County History of Essex* have sometimes been credited as *V.C.H.*

The local expression 'Gestup' (for Gestingthorpe), has sometimes been used when quoting contributors.

Driving the cattle from Station Road into Friars Street, Sudbury, on their way to Bulmer in 1936.

On 10th May, 1893, the Suffolk Free Press recorded another incident involving cattle droving. "On Tuesday afternoon", the paper reported, "a cow was being driven down Friars Street by a boy, when it ran onto the pavement next to Mr. Hills's jeweller's shop. The boy tried to guide the cow away, but swinging round, it smashed a large square of plate-glass." A large stock of watches and jewellery were in the window, a silver watch was damaged and much work was involved effecting repairs and re-fitting. (From Sudbury and District News 1875-1930 *by Stephen Bixley.)*

PART ONE

MOTHER EARTH

– THE GREAT SUSTAINER –

See the rectory's white brick face,
Or red brick porch of Churching place.
And sunshine's sweeping silver glint,
On rising towers and walls of flint.

See cottage there of plastered lath,
Whose 'jettys' overhang the path;
For weavers', horsemen's, yeomen's homes
Were built of nearby trees and loams.

Then see the laughter and the tears
Of those who dwelt here o'er the years.
What secrets do these walls confide?
About these homes - this countryside!

This Countryside

Prelude

A WET SATURDAY
– HILLY FIELD, BULMER –

The Belchamp Brook Valley lies between Sudbury, Little Yeldham and
Belchamp St. Pauls. It is typical of many that dissect the rolling
countryside of the Suffolk-Essex border. A gentle stream meanders
between rising hillocks - which have surprisingly steep gradients.
In fine weather they also provide stunning, beautiful views.
But on the rain-drenched October afternoon with which this book
begins it was anything but pleasant . . .

"Why the devil can't it stop raining?" I muttered irritably. I was
trudging across the sodden, clay 'seed bed' of Hilly Field, Bulmer –
which slopes down from the Gestingthorpe-Bulmer road to the
Belchamp Valley.

It was like walking on wet, yellow-brown pug with each footstep
accumulating a greater weight of tenacious mud. "And so much for
the damned weather forecast!" I grimaced crossly. In front of me
stood the rain-lashed seed-drill and almost sixty acres of unsown
'heavy' soil, that was puddled down now with rain-pocked pools of
water. The storm was getting heavier. I was soaked through and for-
lorn. In front of me was the worst soil of all – that was 'cultivated fine'
– ready for sowing but was now a mass of doughy, unworkable mud.

It would take days of dry weather before we could resume drilling
again. In despair I decide to devote the afternoon to researching the
history of local farming. (Somehow it seems easier than the real
thing!).

Six miles from my Gestingthorpe home is the village of Foxearth
(pop. 211). It was here that I journeyed on that damp afternoon,

14

through narrow lanes with overhanging boughs and rivulets of running water. Eventually I emerged on the higher plateau near Huntsman's Farm – with its wide, extensive views to Bulmer and beyond. I had come to meet retired farmworker Jim Hastie, who, together with his brother Gordon, also knows Hilly Field, Bulmer, for in the late 1930's, their Father was stockman on the farm.

Jim – like Gordon – worked for the same family, the Brands at Foxearth, for many years. Additionally he is a stalwart of Bures Agricultural Society, the local Farm Machinery Preservation Society, and is a past member of Foxearth Cricket Club. Gordon is passionately interested in local history and has done valuable work in recording the memories of local people.

One would imagine that their ancestors have dwelt in the area for generations past. But there is a twist.

For the Hastie family hail from Scotland. As do SCORES of farming folk along the Suffolk-Essex border.

"My Father was a stockman for Coll Bain of Castle Douglas in Kirkcudbrightshire," explains Jim (b.1927), "But in 1936 Bain moved south to Goldingham Hall, Bulmer. However Bain also brought his livestock. So father came down with him. 'Course for us children it was a wonderful adventure!

"But why did Mr. Bain want to bring his livestock?"

"Because his cattle were the oldest 'tuberculosis free' herd in the country – and he wanted to keep them intact. So he hired a special train. Then once we'd arrived at Sudbury the 'milkers' were taken by Cyril Cornell's lorry to Goldingham. But the young stock and younger cows were 'walked up' to the farm. In fact I went with them! Spencer Coe and Freddy Hunt helped us. We drove them from Sudbury Station along Friars Street, round by All Saints Church, through Ballingdon, up past Batt Hall to Bulmer and then on to Goldingham Hall."

"It was quite a human migration as well," I observed.

"There were NINETEEN of us who moved!" exclaims Gordon (b.1929). "And it wasn't just Mr. Bain's family and ours. Because my grandfather also came – and he was well into his seventies! Then there was the ploughman, Jimmy Wilson, who came with his family

– together with another young Scot called Bob Shields. But do you know what the biggest shock of all was?

"There was no sanitation or modern services in Bulmer! EAST ANGLIA WAS PROPERLY BACKWARD! Just an old-fashioned lavatory pail in the toilet. And there was no running water or electricity like we had on the farm in Scotland. In fact Jimmy Wilson went back to Scotland after a while. His family went by train. But he biked the *whole way* and slept in the woods as he went!"[*]

We have written this prelude to introduce the reader to Hilly Field, Bulmer – since it will reappear in a later Chapter. Additionally, we wanted to show how farming and rural memories combine to shed light on the overall 'social history' of our area. For, although this book is based on agrarian reminiscences and research, its scope goes wider. As indicated above, the fluctuating population of our villages, and the area's depressed, neglected status in the early twentieth century are also investigated. Farmworker's daughter, the late Ida Bird (1895-1993) of Wickham St. Pauls provides a typical memory:

"When I was young there was hardly any work around here at all. Dozens of girls like me had to leave home to get jobs 'in service'. I even went up to London for a while – before World War One – as did lots more girls as well."

* Shortly before going to print, Gordon discovered an article in *The East Anglian Daily Times* describing the event. The train Mr. Bain hired, records the paper, consisted of TWENTY ONE vehicles, and had left Castle Douglas at about 4p.m. on Thursday September 24th, arriving at Sudbury some fourteen hours later. The animals, consisting of 45 Friesian cows, 40 young stock and three horses travelled in eleven waggons and a horse box. Arriving at Sudbury Mr.Bain was greeted by both a representative of the E.A.D.T. and Sudbury Station Master, Mr. P. Grimes. The latter's wife who also "served tea to the passengers and crew, was heartily thanked by Mr. Bain for her kindly thought."

Not only was there little work, but numerous houses were deserted, land went derelict and farms were abandoned.

Fred Chatters of Borley (b.1906) paints a vivid picture of the Suffolk-Essex border during the great depression of the nineteen thirties.

"There were two abandoned cottages on the edge of Goldingham Wood, Bulmer and there was another between the Deal Nursery and Bulmer Brickyard and that was all overgrown with Old Man's Beard! Then there was a row up Edeys Lane in Gestingthorpe, whilst in Belchamp Walter the cottages at New Barns were deserted – as were those at the bottom of Forty Acres!

"Empty houses! Cuh! There were scores of them! Just tumbling down with the doors swinging loose and the rooves caved in, and bellbine growing all over the windows."

"At Lower Houses, Bulmer," comments another source, "you could see daylight right through one of the cottages it was in such a poor state – and I don't think any of them sold for more than fifty pounds!"

But as the quest continued and the human memories of bygone life came forth, the 'trail' led to a larger – more self-provident concept of our local history. It was started by Colne Engaine engineer, John Hadley, who exclaimed one afternoon at the Hadleigh Show:

"I know EXACTLY where the bricks came from that built my house. From the clay pits of Pudney's brickyard – two hundred yards away!"

In our first chapters then, we look at local brickyards, potteries, limekilns, tanneries and cheese makers. We record memories of the mighty corn mills that were driven solely by wind or water. And we explore the utilisation of our natural resources – and in particular the soil – our Mother Earth – that has been the 'great sustainer' of the Suffolk-Essex border for millennia past.

Chapter One

BRICKYARDS AND BRICKMAKERS

Sudbury, the Hedinghams, Gestingthorpe and Bulmer

"When I was a lad father didn't just farm at Water Houses, Lower Layham, but also had a brick kiln as well. One year he had a terrific trade for these bricks. He made ten kilns of 30,000 – and sold the great majority to East Bergholt – which in those days was a real growing place!. . . He had a van pulled by a pair of horses and a 'one-horse-cart' and they used to go twice a day taking these bricks to Bergholt. But when the First World War came on, all this brickwork got stopped."

Edwin Partridge
*Farmer of Raydon and Layham, near Hadleigh, Suffolk
and World War One Veteran, 1892-1993*

It was an autumn evening many years ago. Adrian Corder-Birch, the past Chairman of Halstead and District Local History Society, was due to visit me.

Whilst pouring him a glass of beer, I asked what had initially inspired his interest in local history.

"Oh everything," he replied keenly. "But particularly bricks – they are such interesting things."

I stared dumbly. Bricks being interesting!

"In fact my forefathers actually ran a brickyard at Sible Hedingham. In this area brickmaking was a really important local industry in the last century."

"Was it?" I murmured mildly.

"And it tied in so well with the navigation of the River Stour! You see the barges took bricks and chalk from Sudbury – and brought back coal to fire the kilns. Later of course there were special brick trains. In fact," continued Adrian, "many of the bricks in the Albert Hall, Liverpool Street Station and the South Kensington Museums were made at Ballingdon near Sudbury."

"Were they?"

"And one Hedingham brickmaker actually supplied the bricks for SIXTEEN London churches – and another one exported them as far away as Ireland and Egypt."

"Really."

"And by 1901 some thirty to forty truck loads of bricks were being despatched by rail from Hedingham every – single – day."

"Every day!"

"Yes, the Hedingham brickyards were producing seven to eight MILLION bricks a year! And, even though some brickyards only employed ten to fifteen people, it's been estimated that at the turn of the century the Hedingham brick industry was employing up to FOUR TO FIVE HUNDRED PEOPLE 'in the season' . . . Anyway," he continued, "I'm sure you know all this already, Ashley."*

"Yes, yes," I murmured with restraint, when what I really meant was 'No'. I had never realised that here – along our Essex-Suffolk border –

Adrian is also the author of A History of Little Yeldham, A Pictorial History of Sible Hedingham, A Centenary History of Halstead Hospital 1884-1984 and A History of Great Yeldham, (all published by Halstead and District Local History Society). His ancestors' principal brickyard was at Southey Green, Sible Hedingham but they also owned others at Potters Hall, Great Yeldham and Park Hall Road, Gosfield. Additionally they managed the brickyard at Brick Kiln Hill, Castle Hedingham. Over twenty members of the Corder family were brickmakers, tile makers and potters for four generations. Today Adrian continues this interest as the Hon. Auditor of the British Brick Society.

was an industry which had once supported scores of families in our erst-
while villages – and was entirely dependant on our local Mother Earth."

After I had collected a biro and notepad – and by now sitting keenly on the edge of my chair – Adrian explained that following the
decline of the Roman Empire, the art of brickmaking was lost in
Britain until about 1170 A.D. Then, monks from the Low Countries
had revived it on the edge of our area – at Coggeshall – in North
Essex. By 1220 they were receiving commissions from the great
Abbey at Bury St. Edmunds.

Over the following three centuries the use of brick slowly
increased. By Tudor times they were being utilised in magnificent
mansions (such as Gosfield, Kentwell and Long Melford Hall). And
local churches began to construct brick towers and porches, e.g:

Castle Hedingham:	*Tower about 1616.*
Chilton near Sudbury:	*Brick tower – probably sixteenth century.*
Colne Engaine:	*Brick top added to flint base of tower and south porch 1509.*
Gestingthorpe:	*Porch built about 1500; tower approximately c. 1520–1530.*
Gosfield:	*Chancel 1560.*
Hadleigh (Suffolk):	*The famous 'Deanery Tower' built in 1495, was reputed to have inspired Cardinal Wolsey when building Hampton Court.*
Helions Bumpstead:	*Tower early nineteenth century.*
Liston:	*Brick tower – early sixteenth century.*
Long Melford:	*Brick tower erected early eighteenth century (encased in flint 1898 – 1903).*
Pebmarsh:	*Porch early sixteenth century.*
Polstead:	*Very early brickwork inside church, some believe 12th or 13th century.*
Stoke-by-Nayland:	*Brick north porch. Magnificent 120 foot tower contains brick together with flint, septaria and freestone. Both porch and tower are described as Tudor.*
Sturmer:	*Brick porch – early sixteenth century.*
Tilbury-juxta-Clare:	*Tower built 1519.*
Toppesfield:	*Tower 1699.*

Twinstead: *Nineteenth century church.*
Wickham St. Paul: *Tower built 1505 for £20.*

CHURCHES WITH BRICK TOWERS OR PORCHES

More churches have brick towers in Essex than in any other county in England. Locally, many also have Roman brick and tile mingled in with the flint and mortar of earlier walls.

"But how," I was bursting to know, "did they manage to convey the bricks around at a time of such poor transportation?"

"They didn't." explained Adrian. "Almost certainly the bricks were made 'on site' by journeymen brickmakers."

"And did this process of local brick-making continue for long?"

"Oh yes. In the days of horse-drawn transport delivering them ten miles – instead of five – DOUBLED their cost. Farmers and estate owners would open a brickyard for one specific project until the late nineteenth century. (Hence the number of 'Brick Fields' or 'Kell' Fields on old parish maps). But so too did the engineers of the Colne and Stour Valley Railways. Think of the bricks they needed for bridges, stations and viaducts!"

"So the bricks in the viaduct at Chappel, were actually made nearby?"

"Yes! All **SIX MILLION** of them! At a brickworks within a mile of the site – and from local clay. But so too was the viaduct at Haverhill – which you drive under as you enter the town."

Testament to our local Mother Earth. Our illustration shows the viaduct at Chappel crossing the main road between Colchester and Halstead. However, it actually has thirty-two arches and is 350 yards long!

"But what of the lovely 'Suffolk Whites' that one sees in the country rectories and Georgian houses of the area?"

"They are actually harder than reds," continued Adrian, "and were often used as floor bricks or 'pamments'. The whites obviously require different clay but sometimes pockets of both are found quite close together."

"Are there any local examples?" I asked keenly.

"Yes, Gestingthorpe! In fact the pits for the red and white bricks were only a couple of hundred yards from each other! (Near 'Pot Kiln Chase' and at Delvyns 'Clamp'). But red and white bricks were also made at Ballingdon and Great Yeldham. Many yards actually produced a complete range – including drain pipes, paving bricks, 'pamments' and roof tiles. In fact the best roof tiles in Essex were actually reputed to come from Gestingthorpe!"

The brickyards were of such obvious local importance that with Adrian's help we have prepared a provisional list.

BRICKYARDS IN THE SUDBURY–HALSTEAD AREA c.1895

LOCATION	COLOUR OF BRICK	PROPRIETOR
Ballingdon-cum-Brundon		
'Victoria Works' (Brundon Lane)	Red/White	Edward Charles Gibbons
Ballingdon; The Grove	Red/White	Robert A. Allen & Sons
Bulmer; Hole Farm	Red	George English
Bures Hamlet	Red	Robert A. Allen & Sons
Castle Hedingham; Brick Kiln Tomas Moy (Manager: Hill)	Red	Robert Corder
Castle Hedingham; Maiden Ley	Red	William Rayner & Son
Cavendish	Red	William Bird
Chilton; Alexandra Brickyard	Red/White	Edward Charles Gibbons
Clare; Cavendish Road	Red	William George Jarvis
Colne Engaine; Abbot's Shrubs	Red	Pudney & Son
Colne Engaine; The Croft	Red	Pudney & Son
Earls Colne; Tey Road	Red	Zackariah Rogers
Gestingthorpe; 'Clamp'	Red	Mrs Elizabeth Rayner
Gestinghtorpe; Pot Kiln Chase	White	Mrs Elizabeth Rayner
Glemsford; George Savage Gosfield; Park Hall Road	Red	William Corder
Gt. Yeldham; Potters Hall	Red/White	William Corder
Halstead; Brook Farm	Red	Alfred & Joseph Blomfield
Little Cornard	White	Arthur Grimwood – trading as Cornard Brick & Tile Company. Joseph Seagrave, listed 1883).
Long Melford; Rodbridge Hill	Red	Byford
Sible Hedingham; Langthorne, Wethersfield Road	Red	Mark Gentry (trading as Hedingham Brick & Tile Works
Sible Hedingham; Southey Green	Red	William Corder
Sible Hedingham; Tortoise, Wethersfield Road	Red	Eli Cornish
Stambourne	Green	Farm Red George Ruffle
Sudbury; Waldingfield Road	White	'California' Brickworks owned by Allen family.

| Sudbury; Waldingfield Road | White | (Began 1900) Arthur Grimwood (trading as Sudbury Brick Company) |
| Sudbury; (Between Cats Lane and the Cornard and Waldingfield roads: | Red/White | 'Chilton Brickworks' (advertised for sale in 1884 with a capacity of $1\frac{1}{4}$ million bricks per annum. Not definitely known if working in 1895 – but probable. |

Others – as Adrian has previously indicated – had been started in earlier decades by the railway engineers. Moreover, as Peter Minter points out, "There still were around EIGHTY brickyards in Suffolk and a HUNDRED in Essex before World War Two!"

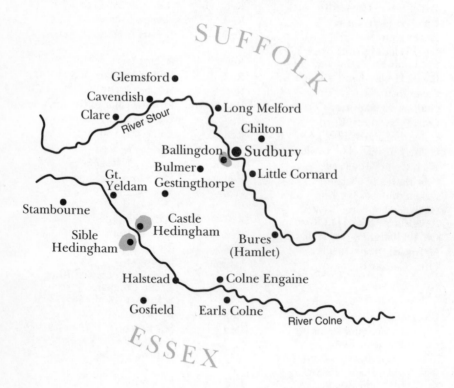

A FORGOTTEN LOCAL INDUSTRY:
Brickyards in the Sudbury-Halstead area in 1895.

Yet this is still only a fraction of those which once existed in our parishes. For initially not even a kiln is required – since the bricks *could* be fired in a simple 'clamp' – covered with nothing more than a canopy of sods and branches. One extraordinary memory comes from Bulmer craftsman the late Philip Rowe (b.1900):

"During the nineteen thirties I found myself out of work for a while. So what I did was this. I started a 'one-man brickyard'! Anyway I spent the winter digging clay, and then I fired about 12,000 bricks in the bank of the lane near Upper Houses. 'Course I hadn't got any kiln or anything! I just covered them up with reject bricks and sods of earth and so forth! Well they turned out all right, but the depression was on. Times were hard and I couldn't sell many. To tell you the truth, I was the worst bloke I ever worked for!"

In earlier times many similar 'clamps' had become established brickyards and the owner's name was stamped into the 'frog', (or hollow), of their bricks. Indeed, by examining a 'frog', many readers of this book can ascertain exactly where the clay came from which made the bricks of their houses. Some of you are dwelling – literally – inside the Mother Earth of the parish in which you live.

Next time you attend your parish church the likelihood is that you will stand inside walls whose flints were picked from parish fields, whose mortar of lime and sand was extracted from nearby pits, and whose roof of tile is surely local. Similarly if you visit Sudbury's Quay Theatre – once 'ye great granary', you will see bricks almost certainly made, "just over the river and across the meadows" – at Ballingdon Brickyard.

The point is brought home by Little Yeldham market gardener Tom Gilbert:

"I'll never forget the day my father built his greenhouse. The bricks came in a horse-drawn tumbril from 'Rayners' at Gestingthorpe – two or three hundred at a time. But they were still hot! I was only a boy at the time and it was my job to dip them in water so that they'd 'take' the cement better. But my goodness – they just gobbled up the water!"

The Rayners were undoubtedly the 'great' family of Gestingthorpe brickmakers. Today, one of their descendants is the parish's history recorder – and secretary of the 'Over Sixties Club' – Dorrie Pannell.

"I've searched back and my Rayner ancestors made bricks in the village – at the 'Clamp yard' – for SIX generations and at least TWO HUNDRED years. In 1881 when Elizabeth Rayner was proprietor, she was advertising a tremendous range, including;
'Plain Tiles, Pan Tiles, Red Bricks, Best White Paving Bricks, Coping Bricks, White Bricks, Arch Bricks, Pamments and Drain Pipes – made of the *best white earth* and all fourteen inches long!'"

"And do you know of any local houses that were built from Rayner bricks?" I asked Dorrie.

"Yes! THIS ONE! (The Firs). But one of my grandfathers also managed the 'bottom yard', (near 'Pot Kiln Chase'). And we've still got an old letter he wrote in 1868."

Carefully unfolding it, I was staggered by the scale of Gestingthorpe's brickmaking industry. For on the faded paper was written:

"Fired three kilns with 90,000 of goods (bricks) Most will be in London in ten days' time."

But what of our other human memories? Close to the last overgrown remnants of Gestingthorpe's erstwhile 'bottom yard', lives Dick Finch, who was born in 1910 in the nearby 'Homestead'. (The latter incidentally was built entirely of Bulmer Bricks – as were 'New Cottages', and Laurel Cottage!). Humorous, wry, kindly and constantly observant, Dick was not only a farm and brick worker, but one of our most helpful and encouraging contributors:

"I can remember when there were at least twelve men working at Rayner's brickyard here – and do you know – at least seven of them were Finches! But my father didn't only make bricks. He also made tiles. And that's a lot more skilful! The other thing he made were 'pamments' – and they were about a foot square. Now Father was a strong man – but you wanted to be strong to do that job! The thirst he worked up! Cuh! He drank enough beer to float the Queen Mary on! The sweat just ran off him! But every single time I go past 'Long Acre', (near the *Pheasant*), I think to myself, 'my father made all the bricks in that house – and ol' Ernie Taylor made all the tiles!"*

Farmworker Bert Surridge (b.1907) tells of Gestingthorpe's 'bottom' brickyard where the superior white clay was obtained:

"I've heard 'em say that digging this white clay was such fearful hard work that the men were allowed two gallons of beer."

Rather like traditional harvest work, the beer was a crucial 'food'. Adrian Corder-Birch describes the situation in Victorian times:

"At some small brickyards, the master brickmaker actually brewed all the beer himself: it was certainly the case at my great grandfather's kiln at Southey Green in Sible Hedingham. The beer he supplied to his employees was a recognised component of their wages."

Yet the references to beer – free or otherwise – should not detract from our impression of the grim, arduous exertion expended in the work. The late Jim Bryant of Middleton, bitingly declares of the Ballingdon Brickyard – where his father was employed:

"You know what it was called? The BONE YARD! No-one who worked there had much of a pod to carry about. They didn't have to worry about diets!"

Explaining that the bricks were made on 'piece-work', Gestingthorpe's Dick Finch explains:

---

*We have one especially early reference to tiles. For during the Peasants Revolt of 1381 when the mob attacked the home of Richard Lyon at Liston near Long Melford, it was recorded that they 'treasonably broke down doors, windows and walls . . . *smashed the tiles* and did much other damage'.
Two centuries later in 1595 no less than forty six 'tyle kelles' were listed in Essex.

"When I left school my father was paid 8/3d for every 1,000 bricks. It makes you wonder really. People would work like hell from 6 a.m. to 6 p.m. to get a shilling a day more than farm-workers."

Stanley Surridge, who worked at Delvyns' Farm – which surrounds the 'clamp' – confirms the general impression about brick workers' remuneration in the nineteen thirties:

"Brickwork paid better than the land – but they did more hours and jolly well did earn it too! During the season they might draw two pounds a week when a farmworker's wages were thirty shillings – and then they sorted out all the brickmakers' bonuses at the end of the season."

(Adrian Corder-Birch points out that during the 'Victorian brick boom' the disparity was greater, with brickmakers earning double the agricultural wage. However in both centuries the 'basic target' was to make a thousand bricks a day).

Yet whatever the rate of pay there were still hardships to be faced. Dick Finch continues:

"Every winter, all the unskilled chaps were stood off. Eventually we might get a little 'dole' money – but even then we had to 'sign on' three times a week!"

Retired brickworker Tom Rowe of Bulmer (b.1903) clarifies the situation:

"Brickmaking was seasonal work. Because they couldn't artificially dry the bricks – or protect them from frost – they had to be made in the summer. However they did keep the 'skilled brickmakers' on all year. After the 'season' was over they'd spend the winter digging clay – so it could 'weather'. And they could still 'fire' bricks which had dried in the summer.

"But all the other brick hands would be laid off. Some might find work in the maltings at Sudbury or Melford - which needed extra labour from September to April. Those two jobs could 'work in together' quite well."

Interviewed in his white brick cottage beside Sudbury's Newton

Road, when in his late eighties, the late Jim Bryant (b.1901) continues:

"My father was a skilled brickmaker and made 'daisies' – or decorative flower bricks. Anyway he worked for Allens at Ballingdon Grove – along the Middleton Road. But there was also a maltings there – of which my father eventually became foreman. There were twelve men in the maltings – and it was his job to keep the temperature right. He'd be there at four in the morning!

"But every year the maltings had to close for repairs – virtually from April to September. So that's when he went brickmaking."

As he spoke of those far off days I wondered if Jim – who was a gardener – had ever thought of becoming a brick worker or maltster himself?

"Not if I could help it! Both jobs were punishing – they were terribly, terribly hard work!"

Not surprisingly, resentment at the conditions sometimes surfaced. At Castle Hedingham, 'Bunny' Brown tells of a strike to get an extra halfpenny for every thousand bricks made. (The pay rise wasn't given.)

Meanwhile, Gestingthorpe's 'Rover' Finch – our oldest contributor – must be amongst many who around the year 1900,

". . . did an hour's work at Rayner's brickyard before and after school, every day, to help my uncle who was a tile maker. It was my job to put the tiles in the 'loca' or 'drying rack'."

Others recall the steady circling of the horse around the works that drove the pug mill; the filling of the wheelbarrows in the bottom of the pits; and the 'stanks' or ledges which were cut like steps into the sides of the pit – which itself might be twenty to twenty-five feet deep.

"And talk of a struggle!" declares Dick Finch, "I've dug sand out of one end of Delvyns Pit. But we hadn't got any Wellington boots that time of day and the bloomin' water ran in almost as hard as we dug the sand out! In fact it's the only time I can remember them 'finding' us beer.

"But there was one benefit. If we were digging clay we could

29

keep different types separate. The very best 'red' clay was used for ridge tiles. And the white clay from the 'bottom yard' here, was so good that they actually used to take it to Bulmer Brickyard – by horse and tumbril!"

But even when the digging was done and the bricks were fired the laborious work was not over. At his cottage near the Gestingthorpe 'Pheasant', farmworker and horseman Bert Surridge explains:

"Gussie Gooderam used to take three tumbril loads of bricks from 'Gestup' (Gestingthorpe), to Hedingham Station every day and then bring coal back for the kilns. But of course every single brick had to be loaded in – by hand. Every single one of them!"

"At Sudbury Station," records retired stockman, Les Downs of Batt Hall, Bulmer, "at least one man was employed full time – just taking bricks off tumbrils and loading them onto trains!"

Yet mechanisation was attempted.

"Some of the Hedingham brickyards," explains retired engineer Bunny Brown, "had rails, on which trolley loads of bricks could be pushed along. Others were even able to load up directly onto railway trucks left in sidings – so that made them more efficient to start with." (Examples come from Purls Hill, Maplestead and some of the Hedingham brickyards.)

In many ways it seems a shame that Gestingthorpe was not linked to the railway network. If it had been, the original brickfields would have doubtless expanded and new kilns would have been started near to the line.

The idea is not an academic one. For Gestingthorpe almost did have a railway. In 1898 a detailed proposal to link Long Melford with Hedingham was drawn up. The estimated cost of construction was £99,671. And Gestingthorpe Parish Council wholeheartedly supported the idea as being 'beneficial to the area'.

One cannot help fantasising about the sight of steam trains passing along the lower meadows of Brundon, Smeetham and Goldingham Hall, (including our 'Hilly Field'), beside the Belchamp Brook to Little Yeldham. The valley is especially lovely in all its undulating beauty – and it is difficult to decide – would the quiet chuff and billow of white smoke have made it any more endearing?

Gestingthorpe's Rector at the time, the Rev. Bromwich, was also not beyond a little humour:

"Fancy hearing the roar of the Belchamp Walter and Melford Express as it rushes on its mad career under Nether Hall Hill! We may have excursions to the Belchamp Brook proving just as popular as excursions up the Rhine!"

More seriously, he was also one of several keen advocates:

"The railway may be a great boon to us," he wrote in the Parish Magazine of July 1898. "We shall not object to coal being a little cheaper. Some say it will mean more brickyards as there is some of the best earth in the neighbourhood in this parish ... A GOOD TIME MAY BE COMING"

But the railway was never built. (Opposition from some landowners and the size of the initial investment proved insurmountable.)

Nor did the good time come. A depression in building before the First World War, the lean years of the thirties, the prohibition on some kilns being fired in World War Two and – more importantly – the overriding thrust of mechanisation spelt the death knell of this local industry. (Mechanisation took the industry to Peterborough's more 'machinable clay', whilst improved transportation – especially by lorries – enabled bricks to be purchased from cheaper and more distant producers.)

Gestingthorpe's 'white earth' yard closed in the late eighteen nineties. In the early nineteen fifties, the 'clamp' followed suit.

Almost without notice, a village's four hundred and fifty year brickmaking tradition had quietly faded away. Elsewhere it was the same. The last brickworks in the Hedinghams fired its last kiln in 1954.

The industry – locally – had all but died out. The skill and craft of hand-made bricks became a thing of the past. The laborious human input, a bygone memory. The erstwhile pits returned to rough vegetation. And the abandoned 'hacks', (drying sheds) slowly decayed in the overcast rains of passing seasons. An era – and a rich tradition – was consigned to history.

Thus we might have ended our chapter.

But not quite.

For in a low, damp dell, on the boundary of Gestingthorpe and Bulmer, one family – one family alone – had the foresight and flair, the imagination, the perseverance and the irrepressible enthusiasm to continue. They were Lawrence and Peter Minter. And against all the odds they have preserved the craft – and humanity – of a hand-made brickyard.

(Lawrence, who was Peter's father, passed away in 1974. Peter was born in 1933 and is today joined by his own sons, Tony and David – who conducted the Wildlife Survey recorded in *The Long Furrow*). Appropriately there is evidence of a medieval tile kiln, which dates to around 1450, on an adjoining field, whilst Roman tile was almost certainly made in the area.

> *Every three to four weeks as I am tractoring at Hill Farm, I see, rising from the wooded hollow of Hole Farm to the east, a rising coil of smoke – signalling the monthly kiln firing. One evening last June, I finally wandered down the ancient trackway, past Wesborough Hills to watch the stoking of the kiln with its glowing furnace and pungent smell of acrid burning. As Tony Minter (b. 1957), manfully shovelled coal into the ruddy glow of the sparking furnace, I was reminded – inevitably – of the alluring aura of steam trains and traction engines.*
>
> *Later we go outside and gaze upwards, heavenwards as smoke issues into the twilight sky.*
>
> *"It's too lazy" pronounces Tom Bird (b.1912) – a veteran of the kiln for four decades. More coal is shovelled in.*
>
> *For four days the furnace has to be fed every hour. The family and Tom take it in shifts to sleep and work.*
>
> *"Like a cup of tea, Ashley?" suggests Peter who has joined the discussion.*
>
> *I glance at my watch. Peter is unquenchably – irresistibly – enthusiastic. A 'cup of tea' in Minter parlance means two to three hours of fascinating explanations and re-interpretations of local history.*

Indoors he tells of moulds and 'shrinkage'; of the qualities of local clays; of the dating of bricks by their size and bonding, and also of the 're-use' of bricks – from one structure to another – and which frequently confuses historical analysis of old buildings. He recounts too, how the family rescued over a hundred moulds of bricks and friezes – from wanton destruction – when other brickyards in the area were closed. Many, he continues, have now been used in restoration projects on historic buildings such as Hampton Court, St. James's Palace, Layer Marney towers, Kentwell Hall and many local churches. More recently indeed, during the renovation of Dublin's barracks, bricks were ordered from Bulmer – to closely match those originally made by Mark Gentry of Hedingham a hundred years ago!

But Peter tells also of the human aspect of brickmaking in our area: of how journeymen brickmakers would look for sallow and coltsfoot to indicate good clay beneath the surface, and how chalk was often added to enhance the colour of white bricks, whilst also explaining that:

"The horses from the brickfield wore larger shoes than normal – so that they could grip as they went down Ballingdon Hill with a tumbril load of bricks behind them!"

Yet it is not just the Minter family's passion for the history of local brickmaking that appeals to me.

It is also the feel of Bulmer Brickyard itself. Mossy banks and puddled tracks lead round the yard: crack willows and ash trees overhang the buildings – almost to the exclusion of the sky. Blackthorn bushes disguise the claypit and a lethargic stream wends between the brick kiln and a meadow. Blackberry bushes, burdock and cow mumble encroach from the edges.

Indeed the atmosphere is of such tranquil leafiness that one rather forgets there is a fascinating tradition there at all. I am indeed privileged to know the Minter family, not only as friends and neighbours, but also for being able to enjoy the historical and ecological redoubt that they have so well preserved against the forces of twentieth century 'progress'.

To have adapted to society's constantly changing needs and to have kept the enterprise afloat – against all fashionable logic – is a truly outstanding achievement.

Yet it is retired Bulmer brickyard employee Tom Rowe, (b.1903), who perhaps best describes the brickyard of bygone decades – and how it has changed:

"When I was a boy the present kiln wasn't built. There were actually two small kilns on that site – which were joined together.

"Well, the owner, Mr. English done away with those two small ones. Then he built three really big kilns which each held THIRTY THOUSAND bricks. They made a terrific number of bricks for a while. There must have been at least thirty men working there at times. But then when Mr. Minter bought it the depression was on. The thirties were terrible. So Mr. Minter built a new kiln – for just 12,000 bricks . . . And now, sixty years later, Peter has just rebuilt his father's kiln again!"

✧ ✧ ✧ ✧ ✧

"At Ballingdon Grove," recalled the late Jim Bryant, "there was a channel from the River Stour to enable barges to reach Allen's brick-works and maltings before going 'under the road', to the chalk pit." Jim additionally remembers workmen walking from Sudbury to Allen's brickworks and maltings, "and crossing the river in flat-bottomed boats to get there."

Chapter Two

CHALK, LIMEKILNS, CLAYPITS AND SAND

'The White Cliffs of Sudbury'

"When I lived at Applecroft in Henny," recalls Hilda Dixey (b.1912), we used to walk down to Sudbury beside the fields and come out on the Middleton road. But when we went by the great big chalk pit, where Ballingdon Fuel are now – it was so enormous that the workmen looked right little down there!"

Beneath East Anglia is a massive 'bed rock' of one material. At Culford near Bury St. Edmunds it is 556 feet thick; at Harwich it is 890 feet thick; at Combs near Stowmarket, it is 843½ feet thick and at Sudbury, about 700 feet thick.

The material is chalk.*

The latter has actually been used in Britain since pre-Roman times. The classical geographer Strabo (b. 63 B.C.), records that our Celtic predecessors even used it to artificially increase the natural colour of their hair. "They continually soak it with 'limewash'," he wrote, "and draw it back from the forehead to the crown." Another Roman author, Cato (234-149 B.C.), described the building of a 'lime kiln' and the manufacture of lime 'wall-plaster', whilst chalk's ability to rectify acidity in farmland was also early recognised.

"When I was in command of the army . . . near the Rhine," observed Marcus Teretius Varro (116-27 B.C.), "they fertilised the

---

*From *The Geology of the Country around Sudbury (Suffolk)*, explanation of sheet 206, by Professor P.G.H. Boswell, O.B.E., DSc. His Majesty's Stationery Office, 1929.

land with a white chalk which they dug."

From the very heart of our area at Gestingthorpe moreover, comes evidence that chalking was practised here, in the centuries of imperial Roman might, when Hadrian, Marcus Aurelius and Constantine were the masters of Britain. The author's Father, farmer and archaeologist Harold Cooper, explains:

"When we were excavating the Roman site here at Hill Farm, we dug some 'trial holes' to the east of the main building – but well away from any structures. Curiously however, we noted nodules of chalk in small clusters which were significantly below our plough depth. I believe they must have been placed there many centuries before as fertiliser, since chalk is never found like that in such light, sandy soil."

As agriculture again became more productive in the later Middle Ages, the practice was resumed. In about 1800 it was observed locally by travelling agrarian writer Arthur Young, who visited many parishes in our area on horseback. "Mr. Newman of Belchamp," he wrote, "spread 160 bushels an acre of lime on a light sandy soil – and it gave a visible improvement for seven years." At Bulmer he recorded the following costs for 'improving the land' by chalking and draining:

First cost of eight waggon loads of chalk,
    containing 90 bushels each, at 9s. per load is:– £3.12.0.
To this add filling, carriage and spreading,
    and allowance for beer, 8s. per load:– £3. 4.0.
Hollow draining at a rod apart:– £2.10.0. per acre

Total: £9. 6.0. per acre.

Over two centuries later chalk is still applied to the lighter soils of Bulmer and Gestingthorpe, usually after harvest – but now at a cost of £30–£40 an acre, (for 2½–3 tons). For the author, the piles of gleaming white chalk, glistening in the summer sunshine, as it awaits the spreader, never fails to be pleasing – in an almost spiritual way. For chalk is one of the most traditional and natural means of improving land. And unlike almost everything else contains not a single added ingredient. It is utterly pure. And entirely of our Mother Earth.

However we have still only glimpsed chalk's extraordinary useful-ness to our local human existence. For below us – beneath the Suffolk-Essex border – it also serves as an enormous sponge, or 'underground reservoir'. At Foxearth, Ward's one-time brewery pro-vides a good example of the quantities that could be extracted. For in 1931, three 'artesian wells' bored into the chalk enabled the pro-duction of a staggering '400 barrels and 12,000 bottles of beer a day!*

Chalk moreover was additionally used in paints, medicinal tablets and the foundations of buildings and farmyards. Indeed, "The chalk foundations of one Gestingthorpe cottage," recalls Bert Surridge, "were rammed down so bloomin' hard that they simply couldn't touch it with pick axes. It was impossible to break it up!"

Yet after being burnt in a 'lime kiln' chalk could be used in even more processes. Food preservation was one. ("Before we had refrig-erators we used to put 'limewash' on dried hams – until there was a layer almost a quarter of an inch thick!," recalls one contributor). Additionally it was used for tanning, for limewashing walls, for clean-ing wooden utensils, as a disinfectant in poultry houses, and on dead animals which had died from contagious diseases. But possibly its most important role was as the major constituent of mortar.

The latter *preceded* cement, and is a simple mixture of *slaked lime*, sand and water. Yet it still enduringly bonds the walls of our medieval buildings, Tudor mansions and churches. In fact 'lime mortar' was used in buildings from the Roman era onwards. Quite possibly there were Roman lime kilns in our area – although they yet await discov-ery. Consequently our earliest evidence of a local lime kiln comes from the reign of Henry VI in 1425 (just ten years after the battle of Agincourt), when the tithes from a Bulmer lime kiln were appor-tioned to a newly appointed vicar.

A hundred years later we have another glimpse. For in 1536 – dur-ing Henry VIII's last years – a local controversy developed:

"The highway next to ye lime kiln between Bulmer and Gestingthorpe is damaged and dangerous," declared Gesting-thorpe's Overhall manor court on Saturday, 30th April, "By reason of digging chalk for burning on either side of the way, to the great damage and encroachment of the same way. PROTEST to be

*From *Essex Brewers* by Ian P. Peaty, Published by the Brewery Society 1997.

made to the Lord of the manor and to the Lord of Goldingham Hall." (Had the problem been exacerbated by the building of Gestingthorpe Church tower in the previous decade, we wonder?)

As noted 'mortar' consisted of sand and 'slaked lime'. But what exactly is 'slaked' lime? And how is it created – particularly in an area where there are no limestone rocks?

To answer these questions I visited Bulmer Street, where, in a beautifully restored cottage, with a preserved 'white brick' floor – lives one of our oldest – and most knowledgeable contributors. He is Tom Rowe (b.1903), who together with his Father and brothers, spent a lifetime engaged in the 'piece-work' crafts of hurdlemaking, sheep-shearing, thatching, brickmaking, building and threshing. Versatile and skilled in so many practical spheres he nevertheless thoughtfully explained:

"To 'slake' lime, you first burn chalk in a kiln. After that it was known as 'burnt lime' and often went grey. Then, if water was added the 'slaking' took place. But the thing is this. When you add the water there is a real reaction! THE LIME GETS FEROCIOUSLY HOT! You had to watch what you were doing – and be a bit careful – otherwise you'd get burnt!"

The memories of both 'slaking lime' and the local lime kilns are fast fading and I was particularly excited when a few afternoons later, retired farmworker Bert Surridge recalled:

"I'd take a horse and tumbril from Parkgate Farm, [Gesting-thorpe], and go down to the pit along Middleton Road [Sudbury] to get 'burnt' lime. But it had to be covered up with something. If not – well – if you got caught in a thunderstorm it would start to 'slack' – and get so hot that it would set the bloomin' cart on fire!"

Somewhat sceptically I later returned to Tom Rowe. "Surely it wouldn't get *that* hot?" I mused. "It jolly well would!" came the retort, "you could cook a potato on it!"

(Bert's story incidentally was repeated a few days after his funeral in January 1997, by another of the mourners, Bunny Brown of Castle Hedingham. "Although a sheet was always put over the burnt lime," he explained, "on one occasion at Pannells Ash Farm it somehow got damp during the night, and did actually burn the waggon up!")

If slaked lime is heated it begins to glow. Consequently, it was a means of illuminating the stages of early theatres. From this practice comes the expression, 'to be in the limelight'. Quicklime incidentally was also used in medieval warfare. In a naval battle of 1218 English sailors threw it into the faces of their French antagonists.

"But what were the actual lime kilns like?" I now asked, as I thought of this fundamental local industry, that had existed in several locations around Sudbury and also on my own farm.

"At the pit along Middleton Road," continues Tom Rowe, "they were about twelve feet high and bricked round the side. 'Course they were open at the top and there would be a plank up the side, where they'd push the wheelbarrows. They'd barrow in a layer of coke – and then a layer of chalk and once it was alight they'd keep it going the whole time . . . Then as it got burnt they could shovel it out from a hole or two in the bottom."

"They didn't need any bellows or air blast?"

"Oh no. Once the kiln was lit it would stay alight for as long as they kept filling it up . . ."

"Did they have to remove the coke?"

"No. Most of it burnt away – although the lime was a bit grey and there might be a few cinders in it."

After listening to Tom Rowe describing 'lime mortar', I suddenly perceived our older buildings in an exciting new light. For it is this simple blend of locally burnt chalk and sand which bonds the walls of Melford and Kentwell Hall, Hedingham Castle, mighty Lavenham Church – and ALL of our other medieval parish churches!

Another impressive example of lime mortar's durability can be seen at Colchester.

"In the eighteenth century," says Borough Guide, Colin Scrivener, "the Castle was actually bought by a demolition contractor – who wanted to cannibalise the walls for the building materials. But after he'd removed the top third – he went bankrupt! The mortar was so strong that he just COULD NOT knock it down easily enough!"

Later, as he led a party from *Bulmer History Group* around the town, we stopped to examine the ancient but enduring Roman walls. They have withstood some eighteen centuries of weathering, abuse and vibration. Yet they still stand – up to twelve feet high in places. (Here moreover the mortar was mixed with an additive – which acts as a 'hardener'. Traditionally this was thought to be volcanic ash, which was used in Italy. But it is now known that brick dust provides the same effect. And countless small red flecks can be seen in the mortar).

Yet in researching this chapter another discovery is made. It is to do with Sudbury. For the town was literally SURROUNDED with chalk pits. One colossal example was situated along the Cornard Road. Directly opposite Ernest Doe & Sons Ltd. – the Ford tractor agents.

Today, the old quarry contains a 'cul de sac' known as Lucas Road. (For some years after World War Two a Lucas C.A.V. factory was situated there). But walk down Lucas Road now. And see the huge, rising cliffs – sometimes FORTY feet high. For this massive pit cuts some 200 yards deep into the hillside, and *is still* over a hundred yards wide at its broadest point. The map reveals another surprise.

For a railway spur actually went UNDER THE CORNARD ROAD and into the pit! Equally inspiring was the publication of a delightful poem – describing the very lime kilns – in the *Suffolk Free Press* of 13th July, 1995. It was written by Mrs. Vera Chinery who adds, "I wrote the poem some time ago, after walking down the footpath between Newton Road and Cornard Road."

THE OLD LIME KILNS

Walking along a footpath high,
Peacefully watching the world go by.
Dreaming of lime kilns
That glowed in the night,
Three in a row, a wonderful sight.

Two chalk pits, one either side,
A tree-lined path, not very wide,
With railings to climb and stand and look –
It was quite as good as a story book.

A tunnel that went right under the road,
Where trains shunted in to pick up a load.
We lay on a bridge, imagined the ride
And watched as it came out the other side!

Factories now stand on this wonderland.
The rattle of trains has gone.
But I close my eyes, and it's there in a haze
Those wonderful childhood days.

Yet almost adjoining the pit in today's Lucas Road, was 'The Chilton Brickfield and Lime Works'. (The two were only separated by the narrow path described in Verse Two of Vera's poem). In April 1884 moreover it was advertised as having, "A practically inexhaustible supply of chalk . . . together with a substantial and well-constructed limekiln capable of converting 100 bushels at a burning." (The property was later sold for £1,025.)

And slowly one becomes aware that here an industry once existed of which there is now scant recognition. But arguably, was quite equal to slate quarrying – for example – in a small Welsh town. And likewise contributed *directly* to the town's prosperity. For Sudbury's chalk pits not only encircled the Victorian town – but were almost a barrier to its natural expansion.

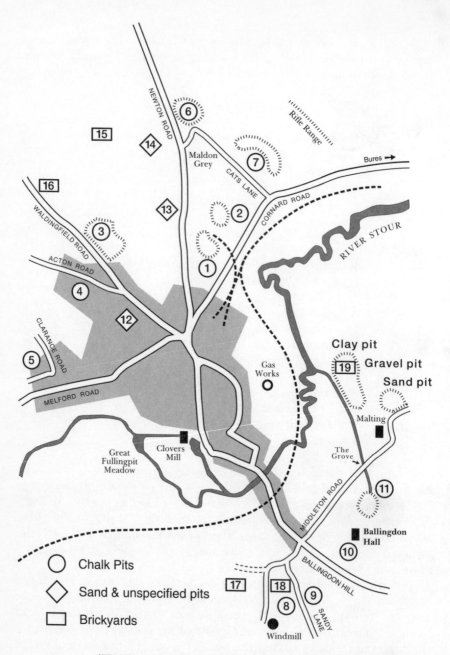

Chalk Pits

Sand & unspecified pits

Brickyards

'THE WHITE CLIFFS OF SUDBURY'

The measurements and names are taken from the twenty-five inch Ordnance Survey maps of 1886-87 and six inch maps *c.* 1905.)

1. Cornard Road Chalk pit as mentioned above, belonging to 'Allen and Boggis'.

2. 'Chilton Brickfield and Lime Works', as described above, (where 'Armes' factory is currently situated).

3. 'Jordan's Pit' along the Waldingfield Road – between Constitution Hill, Park Road and the Cemetery. Now known as Banham Drive. Chalk was extracted from approximately half the area, with the remainder producing clay. In total was over 260 yards long and between 50–150 yards wide. Officially known as the Victoria Works it contained THREE lime kilns. Today, Marlborough Drive looks over the escarpment.

4. Chalk pit with one lime kiln. Measured approximately 70m x 45m. Location is now known as 'Prince Charles Close' – which is beside Acton Lane. (The latter leads off from the Waldingfield Road, and is near today's police station.)

5. Between Queens Road, Clarence Road and Woodhall Road. A lime kiln in a chalk pit approximately 70m x 33m in size.

6. Around *Maldon Grey* Public House, (off the Newton Road). Massive, 'old chalk pit', (as described on map of 1904), together with huge embankments. In places over 150 yards long.

7. Near Cats Lane, Great Cornard. On map of 1908 termed 'Old Chalk Pit'. Approximately 180 by 200 yards in size. Now known as 'The Dell'.

8. "Old Chalk Pit" in what is now 'Bush Grove'. Measured approximately 90m x 90m. Adjoins other unspecified workings at least 140m x 70m.

9. Beside Sandy Lane. (Where Total Fuel are based, next to the District Council's 'Waste Disposal Unit'.) Yet this pit was not even begun until the late 1930's or early 40's. Indeed across this very hillside, Tom Rowe, "once cut a crop of hay." But today, look down from Sandy Lane. For at one point the road is literally on a two sided precipice, so close has the chalk been mined on either side.

10. Around the original site of Ballingdon Hall, two 'old lime kilns' are shown in a pit measuring 100m x 70m at its greatest extent.

11. Middleton Road. Here the chalk pit was connected to the navigable river by a special cut. The 1886 maps show a lime kiln and two, "old lime kilns." Both were in a chalk pit whose staggering dimensions were 300m in length and between 60–100m in width. (Where 'Balfuelco' are now based.)

UNSPECIFIED

12. Between Newmans Road, Upper East Street and Queen's Close, (off Queen's Road). A small pit is shown measuring 50m x 30m. (The material extracted is not indicated.)

SAND PITS

13. Sand pit and kiln between the Cemetery, Newton Road and today's C.A.V. car park and Alexandra Road. 50 x 40 yards. (The function of the kiln in the designated sand pit is not revealed).

14. Sand pit between Newton Road and Alexandra Brick Works. (There were further sand and gravel pits at Ballingdon Grove Brickworks, see below.)

BRICKWORKS

15. Alexandra Brick Works. Containing a 'tramway', two kilns and clay workings 120 x 130 yards in size.

16. California Brick Works (near Waldingfield Road).

17. Brundon Lane. Victoria Brick Works with clay pit measuring 60m x 20m.

18. Un-named brickworks on map of 1887 in today's Bush Grove, together with clay pit almost adjoining the chalk pit.

19. Allen's famous Ballingdon Grove Brickworks, together with extensive sand, gravel and clay pits nearby and a wharf beside the channel to the river.

Not surprisingly, Sudbury's kilns and chalk pits have stimulated many memories.

"In the chalk pits near Cats Lane," I was told, "the diggers actually worked so deep into the chalk face that there were caves big enough to get a complete horse and cart in! They dug it out like that so they could get 'dry chalk' during wet weather."

Ken Partridge and others repeated stories heard in their youth of a tramway and tunnel which reputedly connected Jordan's lime pit in Waldingfield Road, with another further away. George Alderton and Cyril Golding recall the big wooden American gantry (or bridge) which was constructed near the pit and may have been part of this link. (Photographs of the bridge exist but are rather indistinct.)

Phyliss Golding described her father, Ted Crack, (who was foreman at Jordan's Pit), standing on top of the chalk face and driving in a long 'crow bar' to prise off the chalk.

"The chalk face was like a series of steps or ledges. So as he loosened it off, the chalk would fall onto the ledge below, and then they'd take it away in wheelbarrows. But every morning Father would take a bottle of cold tea, and a hunk of bread and cheese and eat it with a penknife at lunchtime. And then after school I'd go there and play until five o'clock – because Mother was at work."

Others recall looking for shark's teeth in the sand and gravel. Additionally there were apple, bullace and plum trees, together with wild strawberries growing along the embankment. The chalk it was remembered was in layers or seams. Several contributors described the steam rising off the kilns. Retired pharmacist John Wardman believes that it caused his asthma as a child. At Long Melford Sid Knott (b.1928), provided a particularly poignant memory:

"When I was a boy," he explains, "my Father was a policeman in Sudbury. In fact I was actually born in the old Police Station! But if Father came across any vagrants sleeping rough on very cold nights, he would take them to the chalk pit along the Waldingfield Road, and put them in the shed where they kept the 'burnt lime' – which was still warm – so they wouldn't freeze to death! But the next morning he'd march them up to the top of Ballingdon Hill – so they were in the county of Essex, who then had to take care of them!"

Several contributors described the lime kilns, "glowing at night until some more chalk or coal was put in the top." Indeed it is often asserted that it was the glow from the lime kilns which led to the Zeppelin raid on Sudbury on March 31st, 1916.

By comparison in World War Two, the railway tunnel which went "under the Cornard road and into Allen and Boggis's chalk pit," recalls Noel King of Little Cornard, "was actually blocked up – and I believe used by the Home Guard and others." George Alderton (b.1924), who lived nearby continues:

"Because of Air Raid Precautions they couldn't use the lime kilns during the Second World War," he explains. "So they put a door in the tunnel, and then put some forms along the side, brought in some candles and then local families like ours used it as an Air Raid Shelter!"

"One thing I'm not clear about," I said, *"is whether the train's engine actually went 'under the road' with the trucks – or whether a horse pulled them through?"*

"No, the engine definitely went under – and the line went right down to the bottom of the pit. When we were children we used to play down there. There were no security fences or anything – I don't think they even had a gate! . . . But I was also told there had once been a tunnel from Allen & Boggis' yard to the chalk pit in the Chilton Brickworks next door."

"Was it still in full time production when you were a boy?"

"Oh yes! There were two kilns and they kept them running day and night. But I also remember how they quarried the chalk! There was about twenty feet of soil on top of the chalk, you see. So

"Dislodging the chalk on Allen and Boggis's pit beside the Cornard Road."

they had two ropes coming over the edge – which were tied onto a wooden plank about six feet wide, and a man sat on that plank with a little pick chipping away at the chalk. But it was cleverly designed, because he could lower himself down a bit further whenever he wanted!"

"And they then barrowed it to the kilns?" I asked.

"Well, there was another little track with small trucks on it, which took the chalk almost to the kilns. Then they put the chalk into wheelbarrows and pushed them up wooden planks to the top of the kilns. There were probably six or seven men working there I should think . . . But there'd also be horses and carts going there from builders' yards and local farmers, so it was quite busy."

"How did they dig the top soil off?"

"By my time they had a 'dragline' which loaded it into lorries. They were actually digging into allotments by then . . . But that pit was fifty to sixty feet deep in places . . . and down in the bottom, where the railway line went, there was a Ruston and Hornsby gas engine which they used to crush up the chalk. In fact my father used to do repairs on it."

"Where did the railway line actually go?"

"Near enough right under Doe's main showroom . . . You see the spur was on a bit of a curve so it could re-join the main line. The tunnel itself was made like an arch. But it was all *white* bricks – which almost certainly came from the nearby Chilton Brickyard."

Another enormous chalk pit was created beside Sandy Lane (No. 9 on map). Here, the overriding memory is of the colossal tonnages of chalk which were removed after the Second World War to rectify acidity on farmland. At Milden, Dick Halls vividly described, "the hundreds of lorries that went into Allen & Boggis' pit in Sandy Lane. But the bulldozer driver was on top of the chalk face – sixty feet up – removing the top soil! It was a dare devil job!" At Hadleigh, Maurice Findlay instantly recalled, "The big diesel burner that dried the chalk, the two old boys who shovelled the chalk onto the conveyor, and the lorries which came for chalk from as far away as Tiptree and

Southminster! At the busiest times of the year we did two shifts and ran from six in the morning until ten at night."

From earlier times Cecil Cook (1919–1997), of Little Maplestead, recalls one interesting character:

"I shall never forget ol' Bill Turps! He used to go down to one of the Sudbury chalk pits in his donkey cart and get a load of lime. Then he'd take it home and make it into lumps the size of footballs – before coming round the villages and selling it for whitewash!"

Others visited the chalk pit for different reasons. Christopher Hawkins of Milden told of his grandfather, Dr. Holden, searching for fossils in the Sudbury chalk pits and of finally presenting his collection to Ipswich Museum. By comparison, army cadet Gillman Game was, "marched to the Chalk Pit opposite Doe's for rifle practice in the late 1930's." Much later, "in the nineteen fifties," relates another contributor, "when the Middleton Road pit had partly reverted to woodland, with masses of wildflowers and lots of lovely bird song, a man who had suffered a nervous breakdown was ordered by his doctor to go and walk about there every day for three months – and it was such a peaceful setting that it did actually help his recovery!"

Not surprisingly there are also references to the chalk pits and lime kilns in old newspapers and histories. Allan Berry's superb vignette of local life, entitled *Eighteenth Century Sudbury*, contains three accounts of the lime-burners attempting to standardise both their prices – and the measures in which the lime was sold. In 1795 they agreed on, "Sixpence for a large bushel of eight gallons – with a penny extra for any credit, however short." Delivery charges were included for places as far off as Lavenham, Halstead and Braintree.

Inevitably accidents occurred. On Thursday 19th June, 1783, recorded the *Ipswich Journal*, "Four men were working at Mr. Warren's pit near Sudbury getting chalk, when the earth suddenly fell in and killed one of them, Samuel Cook of Waldingfield. He left a widow and eight children."* Another even more horrifying tragedy occurred at Goldingham Hall in Bulmer. Here a man was killed when he fell into the lime kiln whilst charging it† By comparison in

---

*Again drawn from *Eighteenth Century Sudbury*.
†From the diaries of Philip 'Tulip' Rowe. By kind permission of Robin Rowe.

May 1894, the *Suffolk Free Press* reported that, when the bank of the chalk pit in Cats Lane, Great Cornard gave way. "A plough and two horses were thrown into the pit, with only one horse surviving."*

Another fruit of our Mother Earth are Septaria stones. Obtained from the coast near Harwich, they were used in Roman cement, and also as a 'rock' in Colchester's Roman walls. Here several layers of Septaria are separated by four layers of Roman tile. But eight hundred years later they were again used in Colchester's famous Castle – which is actually the biggest Norman keep in England. Additionally Septaria can be seen in Framlingham Castle, Stoke by Nayland's Church tower, Gestingthorpe Church, St. Peter's Church, Sudbury and others along the River Stour. Septaria incidentally can actually be found at a depth of eight to ten feet in the current clay seam at Bulmer Brickyard).

Colchester Castle. Although largely built of septaria stones the castle's Norman builders also incorporated the pillars from Roman hypercausts into the walls. Unable however to break the Roman mortar the pillars are laid into the walls sideways – where they are still clearly visible.

*From *Sudbury and District News 1875–1930* by Stephen R. Bixley.

49

Nor should we forget flint which our Neolithic predecessors made into knives, axes and arrows and from the Roman era onwards was used in local buildings such as Gestingthorpe's Roman 'villa'. At Brandon, north of Bury St. Edmunds, moreover, the stone was still being made into 'gun flints' – for 'flint-lock' rifles and pistols until the 1920's. Meanwhile salt has been produced along the Essex coast for at least two thousand years.

Then there are Coprolites, which are found in Suffolk near Ipswich, (and are actually the fossilised excreta of prehistoric animals). However about 1843 the Rev. Henslow of Hitcham, identified their potential as a source of phosphate. So beneficial was this source of fertiliser in the nineteenth century, that the Museum of Rural Life at Stowmarket records nothing less than, "A Coprolite Mining Land Rush . . . on no less a scale than the Gold Rush in the U.S.A.!" (Up to 10,000 tons of Coprolites, explains the Museum were dug up each year with some seams being an extraordinary forty feet deep! Red Crag however had been spread in Suffolk for over a hundred years).

Indeed all manner of 'earth spreading' is recorded on East Anglian farms, in an attempt to improve fertility. These included distributing the scourings from ditches, the spreading of marl – even on 'heavy land' fields, and the BURNING OF CLODS or sods of grassland.

"Burnt earth is used on fallows at 15 to 30 loads per acre" recorded William and Hugh Raynbird in 1849. "It is also drilled with turnips, whilst a dressing of *burnt earth* is considered by some to be the best manure for clover."

Half a century earlier, Arthur Young records that at Bradfields Farm, Toppesfield:

"Mr. Edward Piper, pared and burnt an old lay in March. Before paring and burning, the poor wet pasture was worth scarcely 7s 6d an acre – but is now worth double that."

Additionally 'marl' (colloquially called 'clay'), was also applied to fields at a rate of 30 – 40 cubic yards an acre. In 1813 Arthur Young wrote that, "'clay' is thought to be nearly as good a manure for light land as heavy land." More recently, Norman Smedley surmises that 'clayey-marl' was particularly spread on pasture land which was being converted to arable husbandry. This practice he suggests

50

explains, "the large number of clay pits even found in heavy land parishes."*

LOCAL DETAIL

Farmers in the late eighteenth and early nineteenth century were experimenting 'blindly' – yet thoughtfully and determinedly. Chemical analysis had not yet been developed. However close scrutiny and observation had shown that on some fields, *certain* techniques had proved beneficial.

Arthur Young's great contribution to 'agricultural improvement' was to disseminate these localised observations – and in so doing create a wider consensus of what was genuinely effective. In the 1790's for example, he recorded that:

"At SPAINS HALL, FINCHINGFIELD, Mr. Ruggles's principal tenant, 'had made great exertions in claying'. 'From one pit alone 3,000 loads had been taken and spread at 60 loads an acre. It was a clayey-marl. But he reckons chalk more improving and values it according to its whiteness."

"At HALSTEAD, MR. VAIZEY manufactures potash, and either mixes it with yard dung or spreads it on its own at 160 bushels an acre."

"At BELCHAMP WALTER, one of Mr. Raymond's tenants forms a compost of lime and yard dung."

"Mr. DICKINSON of WETHERSFIELD manured a field for white clover with blue clay full of chalk stones."

At BORLEY, "Mr. Coker mixes dung with earth."

"MR. SPERLING of DYNES HALL in Great Maplestead has greatly improved some 'spongy sand' by laying on 60–80 loads an acre of GRAVEL' , whilst on a 'moory hop ground' he had, "spread 100 loads of whitish clay marl an acre. On some land he believes clay is better than chalk."

Yet was there any real logic to 'clod burning' or spreading of clay <u>on</u>

*From *Life and Tradition in Suffolk and North-East Essex*. The author is a retired Director of the Museum of Rural Life at Stowmarket. Might this reference to clay pits account for some of the extraordinary number of basins and holes – already referred to – in the Mother Earth of our local fields?

heavy land? _Fortunately crop agronomist Bruce Hill, who today advises many farmers along the Suffolk-Essex border was prepared to answer my questions._

"It may astonish you to know," he explained, "that a one-inch dressing of clay would have actually provided 136kg/ha (or 93 units/acre) of available potash. For crops at the time – yielding less than a ton an acre – that was the equivalent of six or seven years supply of potash."

"But I thought that 'heavy land' has inherently high reserves of potash?"

"It does. But pasture land diminishes what is available. So the claying or 'marling' would have made some sense. Additionally, the burning of clods and grass released essential nutrients. Moreover it would have destroyed insects such as leather jackets and wireworms, which cause problems to cereals after 'ploughing up' old grass land."

Our Mother Earth has provided so much. Gravel obtained beside the River Stour at Liston, Long Melford and Glemsford was used in local airfields in World War Two. 'Hoggin' is equally available, while sand which is similarly found throughout our locality had many uses.

"In my grandmother's time," reminisces Maggie Finch of Borley (b.1904), "they used to sprinkle sand over the brick floors in their cottages. In fact people used to come round and sell sand for putting on floors. I can remember her talking of it – but never known it myself."

At Bulmer, Tom Rowe provides a similar memory:

"I've heard say that about once a week, the sand would be brushed up – and sifted out and then put back again. In fact my grandmother used to draw decorations on it – although I don't suppose they lasted long!"

Yet before leaving our Mother Earth we should not overlook one of the most elementary building materials of all. For 'unfired clay' was also utilised. (Indeed Peter Minter still prefers clay as an adhesive for the 'fire bricks' of chimneys since cement can crack. Moreover at one fifteenth century farmhouse – less than two miles from Halstead – the entire internal chimney is bonded with *unfired* clay).

However UNFIRED CLAY BLOCKS were also used to make walls. Known as 'clay lump' they were used for many centuries. (There is even evidence that some of the barracks at Roman Colchester were built of them.)* More recently 'clay lump' buildings were discussed in *The Agriculture of Suffolk* by William and Hugh Raynbird in 1849.

"Throughout the heavy land of Suffolk," declared one of their contributors, the Rev. Copinger Hill of Buxhall, "cottages, farm buildings and farmhouses are very often constructed with clay walls. When whitewashed, plastered or stuccoed," he continued, "they are not only neat in appearance but also warm and durable.

"So long as clay walls are placed on a stone or brick foundation and are covered at the top, they will last a great length of time. I have seen some that have stood 50 years, with very slight repair, and which were as good as when first put up . . ." (slightly rephrased).

The clay, Messrs. Raynbird later explain, was usually mixed with a little sand and straw, and then 'trodden in by a horse', before being thrown into wooden moulds, "18 inches long, 12 inches wide and 7 inches deep." Finally the blocks were dried out by the wind and sun. "Clay walled cottages with thatched rooves," the authors emphatically conclude, "are the warmest in winter and coolest in summer, and are moreover, not liable to brick duty!" (The latter being repealed in 1850).

Yet was this form of construction still in the bounds of *local* human memory? Once more I rushed back to Tom Rowe. Could he recall any such buildings when hay cutting or sheep shearing in surrounding villages.

"There was the *remains* of one 'clay lump' cottage near Belchamp Walter Hall – at the north end of the 'Canal'," he said, "but over at Hundon, there was another. It actually looked like a 'lath and

*From *City of Victory* by Philip Crummy.

plaster' building, but where the plaster had fallen off you could see the blocks."

However Tom's most intriguing memory was to follow:

"We cut some hay at Glemsford once, for a man who had a small coconut matting factory. Anyway, he dug a well – and with the clay from that, he built a little 'clay lump' barn. But instead of using straw he actually mixed coconut fibre in the clay! It was in the street leading to Boxted. But the thing was this. So long as they were kept dry, clay lumps were practically as good as bricks."

Yet something more exciting was to follow. For speaking to the Sudbury and Melford branch of the Suffolk Naturalist Trust, I asked if anyone remembered any 'clay lump' buildings in their youth?

"Yes!" exclaimed Noel King. "Little Cornard Village Hall – and it is still there!"

Little Cornard Village Hall. The portion built of clay lump is on the left. The building however contains a number of other architectural features and both the bricks in the chimney and mullions in the windows may have come from earlier buildings.

54

Some months later I visited the building which is in Spout Lane, (just off the road to Bures), with Noel, his wife Eileen and members of the village's Conservation Society. It was built in 1854 as a school to accommodate seventy pupils. A few rows of bricks act as a barrier between the ground and the 'clay lump' blocks. However these have now been covered with metal lath and plaster – making it quite impossible to detect the true nature of the walls from outside! From the inside however the solid nature of the clay lump is quite evident.

"Some years ago," explains Noel with a laugh, "an extra 'Fire Door' had to be built into the wall – to comply with new regulations. But the builder had a devil of a job to make the hole! Because when you knock the chisel into the clay you can't smash out a large chunk – like you can with a brick or block wall! He just had to keep prising it off in small pieces!"

Within this review we have often referred to the bounty of our local Mother Earth. Yet along the Suffolk-Essex border the soils also change with extraordinary rapidity:

"At Alphamstone," records farmer Tom Nott, "there are fields where the rear wheels of a tractor can be stuck in clay – whilst the front wheels are sinking in sand!"

At Hill Farm, Gestingthorpe it is the same. When a new grain store was erected in 1971, we found solid yellow 'boulder clay' in the footings of one corner; pure white chalk in another, whilst in the third was sand so fine that it was used when plastering the walls of the new, twenty-five ton grain pit. Some years later this author was to write in his diary:

"I honestly, truly believe that the Suffolk-Essex border is like a geological – and ecological 'Garden of Eden!'. Where else in the world can you obtain sand, chalk and clay – together with flint for making razor-sharp tools and buildings – all within a *few hundred yards* of each other?" In every village between Sudbury and

Halstead you can grow *everything* from hops, flax, and grapes to greengages, walnuts or apples.

"Additionally there are rivers for transport and fishing. There are valleys for meadows and 'wet land plant life'. And there are woods and hedges which contain – quite naturally – a tremendous variety of species from 'light land' Broom to 'heavy land' Hornbeam. And ALL of this – EVERYTHING – is available within a half-hour's walk of Bulmer or Gestingthorpe church!!"

Emblazoned over the massive portal of Bury St. Edmunds Corn Exchange are the words: "The Earth is the Lord's and the fullness thereof."

What better words could possibly sum up these chapters?

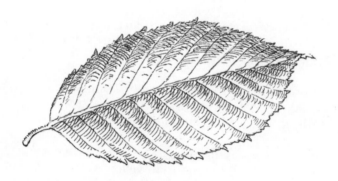

Hornbeam

Chapter Three

LOCAL POT WORKS

'Gestingthorpe and Castle Hedingham'

By tall St. Andrew's looming tower
The wintry clock marks passing hour;
As stage coach patrons urge, "Keep time!"
("Up Halstead hill? – A fearful climb!")

Though townsfolk snug in doors reflect
'Twelve months have passed – to what effect?'
- Yet others call through frosty chill
"Bring victuals – and the old jar fill!"

Thus muffled ringers shuffling cold:
Keep warm from 'Gestup' pot of old:
Til comes The Time! – And peals revere
'God Speed! Good Will! A Brand New Year!

This Countryside
('Gestup' is the colloquial term for Gestingthorpe.)

Imagine you are at Gestingthorpe Church. The latter has a mighty red-brick tower, made of Gestingthorpe clay, and walls of flint which were picked from the parish's fields. Inside, is a spectacular 'double hammer-beam roof'. On the north wall a brass memorial commemorates Antarctic hero Captain L.E.G. Oates. Beside the tower a carved plaque honours the forty-nine parishioners who served in World War One. In the graveyard lie our other local stalwarts. Those who worked the surrounding fields, turned the hay, brought home the harvest, or laboured in the brickyards of which we have written.

Six hundred yards to the east however, is a small wood. And here a rural pottery existed from *at least* the seventeenth century until 1912. (Today commemorated in a short lane named 'Pot Kiln Chase'.) And it was sometime operated by two of Gestingthorpe's oldest families, the Rippingales and the Finches.

LOCAL DETAIL

There have in fact been potteries in our area since Iron Age times – if not earlier. Certainly there were Roman potteries at Colchester, West Stow, Wattisfield, Sicklesmere, Hartest, Stanningfield and Halstead, (with others surely awaiting discovery); and Roman tile kilns at Alphamstone, Mount Bures and possibly Little Cornard. In medieval times potteries operated along the River Colne between Sible Hedingham, Gosfield and Halstead. Great Cornard has a Pot Kiln Lane whilst two 'Pot Kiln Fields' were recorded on the Tithe Map of 1839. More recently the brickyards at Bulmer, 'Southey Green' in Sible Hedingham, and Gestingthorpe's 'Clamp Yard', produced pottery from their own clay in the twentieth century. (Indeed the pottery produced at Bulmer Brickyard during and after the Second World War – especially by Sam Hailes – is now internationally acclaimed and sought after.)

By comparison, Gestingthorpe's independent pottery was a truly rustic enterprise. It operated in the most primitive conditions and in the most bucolic surroundings. It had changed little since medieval times.

"The principal poducts," wrote local historian Alfred Hills in 1944, "were latterly Glazed Dishes, Pans, Pitchers for dairies, Vessels for pickling joints of pork, Garden Ware and a few specially decorated pots and puzzle-jugs . . . In earlier times, however, the range was greater. For 'Bell-Ringers Jars' and 'Harvest Pitchers' were also produced"*.

*From 'The Gestingthorpe Pot Works', by Alfred Hills M.A., *published in The Essex Review,* Vol. LIII, pp 37 – 45, April, 1944. His invaluable article is gratefully acknowledged.

One rare 'Bell-Ringers Jar' from Gestingthorpe has actually been preserved in the belfry of St. Andrew's Church, Halstead. Dated 1658, it stands 14½ inches high and holds four and a half GALLONS!

"On New Year's Eve," explains Hills, "this imposing vessel was carried round the town from house to house, to receive a mixture of beer, wine and spirits known as 'hot pot'. It was then stood on a block in the centre of the belfry and drawn from as the occasion might require!" (Hence the verses from *This Countryside* at the beginning of this chapter.)

Yet for fear of too many intoxicated bell ringers, or discordant peals, some salutary verses were also scratched into the chocolate-coloured glaze of the jar itself. One reads:

> *As w sit by the fyre To keepe ourselves warme*
> *This pot of good liqvor wil doe vs no harme*
> *If you be wice*
> *Fil me not twice*
> *at one sitting.*

Carrying the Gestingthorpe Bell-Ringers' Jar. A similar jar made at Stock in Essex in 1685 for Braintree's Ringers can be seen in Colchester Castle.

Inspired by Hills's invaluable article I ventured to Halstead, one cold January evening, parked on the Market Hill and climbed the forty-two steps to the bell-ringers gallery in St. Andrew's Church. A small group of enthusiasts led by Tower Captain, Doreen Middleton, were preparing to practise.

Keen to swell their ranks and attract new ringers they provided an enthusiastic welcome. Confessing my real reason for attending however, they good-naturedly laughed as I looked for the Ringers Jar.

It is huge! The basic dimensions – already recorded – simply do not convey its sheer size and volume. Carefully moving it to be photographed I was also staggered by its weight – when empty! When full it must have weighed over 50 lbs (20 kgs). Intrigued, I looked at the handles which had carried the vessel's load; and at the 'finger print' indentations where they had been pressed into the main pot. Transfixed I gazed at the jar.

The glaze is dark brown. The graffiti is scrawled round the sides in large, ungainly letters. At the base is a hole for a tap or stopper . . . It is not 'spectacularly attractive'. And yet it is curiously, compellingly endearing – despite its lack of finesse.

I was enthralled to see the vase – and imagine its use! And then next morning to sit at my desk. And gaze across two fields. And see the <u>exact spot</u> where the pot was made – from the Mother Earth of this very parish – by men who lie now in the nearby Churchyard.

In addition to the Ringer's Jar, four 'Harvest Pitchers' dating from 1767 to 1803 are also in existence. Each held about 1¼ gallons and one bears the name of Joseph Rippingale, the potter. Interestingly they all have THREE handles, which Hills suggests,

"May indicate a custom of passing the vessel from hand to hand round the festive board in the manner of a 'loving cup'. Alternatively the piece may have been carried round by two servants, and tilted by means of the 'back handle' to pour out a modicum of the generous punch . . ."

But it was not just farmers who purchased the large Gestingthorpe jars for celebratory purposes. In 1807 a 'harvest gotch' which held four gallons was ordered by a maltster from Bures named William Groom. At the end of each malting season, says Hills, the latter gave a supper for his seventy employees. And the jar, which bore the pertinent inscription, 'SUCCESS TO THE MALTING TRADE', "was filled – and replenished, with the very best of Groom's products!"

(This 'gotch', together with several other Gestingthorpe pieces, are in the reserve collection at Colchester Castle Museum.)

For the pottery's output circulated beyond the immediate locality. In 1871 the proprietor, George Finch, not only employed four men, but even embarked on salesman's rounds – with a horse-drawn van – into Suffolk, to Dunmow, and to Chelmsford. (In the latter case he was actually away for two nights and three days, and is recorded sleeping in his pot cart). By then however the glaze which had previously been an orange, 'or treacly brown colour' had changed to a rich red, "the hue of juicy raw beef." Yet as Hills objectively observes:

"In the 'thrown' pieces the ascending circles of the potter's fingers are still well defined on the inside – in a way which would cause a Doulton craftsman to turn up his nose!" "Worse," he continues, "the fragile pots will crack for almost nothing. For Gestingthorpe's soil," he concludes, "yields up, not true potter's clay, but only a superior brick earth . . . It is not surprising that customers came to prefer more durable wares."

Yet from its fragile crudeness comes its inspiration. One 'harvest pitcher' for example, was sold to a Belchamp Walter farmer named Ray. Imagine then, how it was impulsively swigged at the boisterous horkey held in his barn! Picture also how the fiddlers played as the cracked glazed 'pitcher' went on its circuit, from the 'reapers' to the 'Harvest Lord' and shepherd, as young lads danced and old men pondered, while the ploughboy and the milkmaid embraced more fondly in the sinking straw of some dark corner!

Yet all is not in the distant past. For some contributors still recall using the 'big glazed pots' – which were latterly the staple of the business. "It was a regular thing," recalls Dick Finch with a warm, nostalgic smile, "People kept their water, bread or eggs in them." At Alphamstone, farmer Wally Twinn continues, "Bread kept in those pots might get a bit tough – but it wouldn't be stale – even after a fortnight!" By comparison, Hazell Chinnery (b.1892) recalls his Father obtaining "his flower pots from ol' Finch at Gestingthorpe," whilst as a child the late Emily Hearn had similarly walked from Bulmer to Gestingthorpe for water pots.

More exciting however is that two of our oldest contributors – interviewed in the late 1980's – could still, just, recall the original pot works in existence. George 'Rover' Finch (b.1895) – wizened but bright eyed – and ninety-three years old when we met in his small cottage near the Gestingthorpe *'Pheasant'*, spontaneously declared:

"I can remember him! Old 'Potty' Finch! And I'll tell you something funny about he. He always had a candle on the go! And do you know why? . . . It was to light his pipe with – because his hands got so daubed up with clay! But all he had were a few old thatched huts near the wood. There was nothing fancy at all! But that's where he made his bread bins, water jars, flower pots and all such things as that."

At Wickham St. Paul, retired farmworker Reg Rippingale (b.1900) – who was born at Gestingthorpe, warm-heartedly continues:

"I'll tell you suffen' else about old George Finch. He was very, very secretive and jealous of his knowledge. We lived at the 'Barracks', which is only a couple of hundred yards from where he worked. So we'd often play around there – or walk that way to church or school. But he regular hated us children watching him or messing about near the hut. And if anyone ever came along he always stopped work – so that they couldn't learn anything from him!"*

EDWARD BINGHAM

Although there have been pottery makers in the Colne-Stour area for at least two thousand years, it is nice to record that one at least has achieved a modicum of regional recognition. His name was Edward Bingham (b.1829). And he worked in Castle Hedingham.

*George Finch's son later continued for some while at Rayner's Brickyard near Delvyns Farm, where he also made, "decorative flower pots and the old fashioned big glazed vessels for bread and water."
In 1863 Elizabeth Rayner of Gestingthorpe was named in White's Directory as an 'Earthenware Manufacturer', whilst in 1894 she was advertising, "Milk pans, reed pans, rhubarb pots and beef pans, in addition to her extensive range of bricks, tiles and drainage pipes." Although Hills states that the independent pottery closed down in 1912, in another advertisement of 1894 Rayner announced that she, "has recently taken into her own hands the old established pottery works which she formerly let." Consequently one suspects that there is scope for further research to clarify the exact date of the pottery's closure as 'an independent business'.

Born in Blackheath near London in 1829, his family moved to Gestingthorpe when Edward was about five. Here his father – also a potter – not only made plain pottery, puzzle-jugs and garden vases, but according to Hills, "Clay cuckoos – which called 'CUCKOO' when blown through their tails!"

Three years later the family moved to Castle Hedingham. Here Bingham senior continued potting. And young Edward conceived his life's great crusade – to initiate a renaissance in ornamental pottery!

A century later Bingham's pottery is noted for its local and historical motifs or gallant attempts to re-create classical vases. Much is eye-catching and genuinely appealing.

Inevitably however, students of his output fall into two disparate camps. Either they adore it – or loathe the heavy glazes and congested, intense patterns. It is perhaps, 'an acquired taste'.

Yet in a dispassionate sense this author would argue that there is something far more interesting than the actual pottery. It is the character of Bingham himself. The individualistic underdog who possessed not just an extraordinary vision – but also the rugged, unremitting, lifetime's adherence to it. As one observer put it:

"I'm completely indifferent to his pottery. And that's a euphemism! But Bingham! His life story really *is* an inspiration!

The prospects for Bingham to achieve his 'renaissance' could not have been less auspicious. At the age of thirteen the young village boy had to select a trade. Already he wished to be nothing less than a decorative potter. Sensibly his parents insisted he be trained in some other 'more reliable' craft.

Reluctantly he became an apprentice bootmaker for six months of each year. In the remaining time he learnt potting. In 1846, aged just seventeen, he began independently making shoes at home. But he also had an unquenchable thirst for knowledge. In the same year then, dissatisfied with boot making, he went to help his uncle, who was the master of the, 'College for the Deaf and Dumb' at Rugby. But 'his dream' could not be suppressed. It was again on a half-yearly basis. Six months as an assistant school teacher. Six months potting at home.

This arrangement continued until his twentieth year. Returning home, he now divided his time between working as an auctioneer's clerk, (for Balls & Savill who had an office in the village), teaching at the Sunday School, and his other 'great mission' of potting.

In about 1852, he opened a small shop to sell his wares in Queen Street, Castle Hedingham. The following year he received his first order from London. Possibly success was near! Encouraged, he married his teenage sweetheart, Eliza Ruffle, a local miller's daughter. The ceremony was conducted at Castle Hedingham's Independent Chapel. He was twenty-four years old.

Then demons struck. He had problems with damp kilns. The pottery declined. By 1856 he needed to supplement his income. Consequently he opened a small school. Although very successful, (at one time attracting some thirty-nine pupils), the liftime's compulsion would not subside. Busy teaching by day, he potted at night. He worked in an upstairs garret. It was lit by candles. To increase illumination, they were placed next to large jars filled with water. All this – the compromise and dogged persistence – was to be the pattern of his life.*

"Bingham potted by candlelight. . ."

*The material on Bingham is drawn from three excellent and invaluable articles in *The Connoisseur* by R. J. Bradley, and *The Discovery of Britain* by Jack Lindsay, published by The Merlin Press 1958.

Due to competition from the new National School in Castle Hedingham, he closed his own establishment in 1864. Temporarily he resumed full time potting. But demand continued to fluctuate. Repeatedly he had to revert to 'plain ware'. Soon he again needed to bolster his income. Now he became the village's sub-postmaster. For seven years he once more persevered with two occupations. Eventually, in 1876 he felt that prospects had improved. He resigned as sub-postmaster. And assisted by his son, returned to full time potting.

How he pursued his dream! How tenaciously he battled on! A mass of lavishly decorated material was produced with historical or mythological themes. These include his most ambitious work, 'The Porsena Vase', (example in Colchester's Hollytrees Museum), and his famous 'Essex Jugs'. (The latter displays aspects of the county's history and agriculture – such as Colchester oysters and scenes of Boudicca fighting the Romans. Each moreover was originally accompanied by a hand-written explanation of the various historical depictions.)

Undoubtedly he built up a local reputation. Occasionally, as he received orders from London exhibitions he might have thought that wider acknowledgement was near.

Yet, in reality, he never became established on more than a local scale. Possibly tastes change over the decades. Today his work may appear over-indulgent and too exuberant of form. Maybe we have come to prefer simpler designs and less involved motifs . . . And yet when placed in a human context, as we imagine his lofty ambitions and the doughty battle he fought in such primitive conditions – their charm indubitably grows.

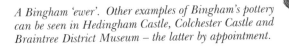

A Bingham 'ewer'. Other examples of Bingham's pottery can be seen in Hedingham Castle, Colchester Castle and Braintree District Museum – the latter by appointment.

Yet Bingham was more than an obsessed potter challenging impossible odds. He was a respected, knowledgeable and well-liked member of the community. He was known for – and lived by – his strong religious convictions. (The pot works had numerous Biblical texts pinned to the walls, whilst he regularly walked the five miles to Halstead to worship with the Plymouth Brethren.)

But for this author, he was something still more. Quite simply, Bingham was a pioneer amongst genuine local historians.

At a time when most 'antiquarians' derived from the wealthier or professional echelons of society, visited archaeological sites abroad or researched the ancestry of manorial families, Bingham was different. He kept 'an ear to the ground', recorded the memories of older people, noted interesting discoveries, and then disseminated his findings to a wider audience. His reminiscences of straw-plaiting and hop-growing are quoted at some length in the 'Victoria County History of Essex'. And his lifetime's study of Castle Hedingham is preserved, for posterity, in a fascinating document entitled, 'Castle Hedingham in Olden Times'. It was compiled following a Public Lecture in the village in 1894. Here,

Using pottery to illustrate local history. Bingham's 'Lavenham Plate' (on the left), has the De Vere and Spring family badges around the edge with the 'Town Cross' in the centre. The 'Halstead Jug', (opposite), stood some fifteen inches tall and was similarly embellished with historical details about the town.

Bingham's ware commands reasonable but not exorbitant prices. If readers discover examples in upstairs attics they will certainly find it worthwhile to show it to a reputable dealer. (Bingham's 'trade marks' include depictions of Hedingham Castle, his name or initials, on the base of the piece.) At the time of writing the Lavenham Plate above, might perhaps fetch between £150-£200 at a local auction.

Bingham not only described the traditional agriculture and older houses of the parish, but also its field names, archeological finds and 'human history' as well.

To some extent all of us who follow along the path of local studies, tread in Bingham's worthy and dedicated footsteps.

Yet irrespective of this personal eulogy, let us leave it to another craftsman, Gestingthorpe's wrought-iron blacksmith, Frank Nice, to provide his own tribute:

"I really do admire Bingham. He's been a real inspiration to me. I mean he tried so hard. He never gave up and he never lost hope. And he'd do anything – however menial – to try and achieve his ideals. He was fascinated by history and archaeology and I think he wanted to use his art to help educate people. He was only a village potter's son who left school at thirteen. And then he took on the world of 'established ceramics' – from his lowly sheds in Castle Hedingham."

Halstead Jug

Chapter Four

HOPS, TEASELS and FLAX

Stowmarket, Castle Hedingham, The Maplesteads and Long Melford

> *"The culture of hops at Hedingham is perhaps as famous as in any part of England; the quality of those at Farnham are superior, but the cultivation at Hedingham is allowed, by all who have viewed them, to be managed to great perfection."*
>
> Annals of Agriculture Volume 18, 1792

Hops are one of the most interesting crops to have been grown in our area. However, although indigenous they were not commercially cultivated in England until about 1524. Thereafter their addition to ale produced a clearer, more drinkable beverage – which became known as beer. Initially however there were some reservations. King Henry VIII, for example, actually forbade hops to be used in his own household's ale. Yet irrespective of the monarch's private inclinations, beer's popularity continued to increase – and consequently the acreage of hops.

Soon they were being grown in Essex and Suffolk. At Castle Hedingham, 'the Lord's Hop Yard' is marked on a plan of 1592, whilst at Belchamp Walter two areas of hop ground are recorded in the meadows beneath the Church, on a map of 1605.

At Sible Hedingham hops are recorded in 1643, when the parson, John Jegon, was accused of being, "a prophaner of the Sabbath Day – and one day left his wife and servants to bag hops when he himself went to evening prayer!"*

*From the *Investigation into Scandalous Ministers*. In reality it was often those who had Royalist or High Church tendencies during the Civil War.

By the eighteenth century, hops had become such a valuable crop in our Colne-Stour countryside, that an annual 'Hop Fair' (or sale) was held at Castle Hedingham. One agreement between local hop growers and Lewis Majendie, the Lord of the Manor, "for a fair to be held in the village on Monday 25th October, 1790", is still preserved at the Essex Record Office, in Victoria Road, Chelmsford.

Many of the growers who signed the agreement have names with strong local connections:

B. Myall	James Hardy	Wm. French
Isaac King	Edmund Bunn	I. Branwhite
Sam Cooke	James Finch	Richard Moss
John Rogers	Rick Myhill	Ambrose Myall
Wm. Stammers	Tho. Eley	Joseph Myall
Nath. Long	John Rust	
H. Sperling	George Firmin *	

LOCAL DETAIL

If the signatures seem numerous, the reason is simple. In about 1790 the Hedinghams had some TWO HUNDRED AND THIRTY ACRES of hops. At the same time there were 125 acres in Wethersfield, seventy in the Maplesteads, forty at Earls Colne, twelve in Stisted and about ninety in other parishes near the Hedinghams.†
At Belchamp Walter there were two oast kilns for some ten acres of hops, whilst in 1767 there had been thirty eight acres in Colne

LOCAL NAMES

*SPERLINGS were an important Maplestead family living at Dynes Hall, FINCH was exceptionally common in Gestingthorpe and the Hedinghams, (e.g. Dick Finch and Rover Finch who are contributors to this book), RUSTS still live in Wickham St. Paul, FIRMINS farmed in Bulmer in the nineteenth century, BRANWHITES still farm in Belchamp Otten – with ancestors who farmed in Gestingthorpe and others who were millers in Long Melford, whilst KING sometimes became a joint Christian-Family name, e.g. King Viall or King Downs at Gestingthorpe.

†The reference to hop grounds in Castle Hedingham and Belchamp Walter come from The Victoria County History (V.C.H.) and Essex Record Office respectively.

Engaine. In Great Maplestead hops were grown until at least 1870 – when the hop kiln at Lucking Farm was still in use, whilst the remains of oast houses can still be seen at Blackmore End in Wethersfield. (Over 300 fields from all over Essex have names which indicate how widely the crop had been grown in earlier times – with examples from almost every single parish in our area. Gestingthorpe alone, for instance, has no less than five 'field name' references).

Hops. At Castle Hedingham, recorded potter Edward Bingham, the hops were often picked by straw plaiters, who regarded it as, "a kind of outdoor holiday. Each," he continued, "got about ten day's work at seven pence a day, with half a pint of beer all round on Thursdays." (Slightly rephrased from the Victoria County History of Essex.)

There is something quietly appealing about the concept of growing hops. The pleasing fragrance of the fruits, the steady outdoor work on the hop bines, and the more recent recollections of Londoners picking hops in Kent combine to make the crop of particular 'human interest'.

Thus we can picture the bygone labourers as they hoed, and tied, and picked, within our erstwhile hop gardens in the lower valleys of our local countryside – where wild hops still grow today. And perhaps too, we can imagine their conversations as they paused to mop their brows or 'have a blow', and betimes passed comment on Oliver Cromwell, Charles the Second – and his mistresses – or the later great events of Trafalgar and Waterloo!

By the late eighteenth century, however, almost the entire Essex hop growing industry was concentrated around the Hedinghams, Maplesteads and Wethersfield. Very few were now grown elsewhere in the county.

For the crop demanded extremely fertile, rich, well-watered meadowland. When Lewis Majendie purchased *two-thirds of an acre* of hop ground in Castle Hedingham at an auction in about 1792, it cost him a staggering ONE HUNDRED AND TWENTY POUNDS!! (He actually purchased, "two roods and twenty five perches." Then considered to be the highest price ever attained for farmed land in England, it equates to £182 for a full acre). Rental values for hop grounds similarly reflect the premium commanded by Castle Hedingham's soil at the time.*

RENTS PAID FOR HOP GROUND PER ACRE, circa 1790

	£	s	d
Castle Hedingham	3	0	0
Wethersfield	2	0	0
Gt. Yeldham	1	11	6
Bulmer			
Earls Colne			
Gt. Henny	1	10	0
Halstead			
Lt. Maplestead			
Pebmarsh	1	0	0

Across the border in Suffolk, hops had similarly been widely grown. Indeed the Tithe awards of 1838–40 reveal five fields whose names record the crop having once been grown in Little Cornard, with four fields in Glemsford, three each in Lavenham, Chilton and Great Cornard, and two in Edwardstone with other references from

*From Mr. Vancouver's table of produce later printed in Arthur Young's *General View of the Agriculture of Essex*, published in 1813. The acreage from Stisted comes from the *Annals of Agriculture*, Volume 3. Other material comes from *Essex Brewers* by Ian P. Peaty, published by The Brewery Society, 1992; and *The Maplesteads; Then and Now*, published by Maplestead W.E.A.

Long Melford, Stoke by Nayland, Great Waldingfield, Kersey, Cavendish and Brent Eleigh.*

By the nineteenth century, however, the Suffolk crop had also become concentrated in one specific locality – around Stowmarket. In 1803 Arthur Young recorded 186 acres in the following villages:

Stowmarket	50 acres	Onehouse	20 acres
Combs	30 acres	Shellan	5 acres
Newton	20 acres	Buxhall	15 acres
Dagworth	8 acres	Stowupland	10 acres
Finborough	20 acres	Haughley	8 acres

Yet what were the financial returns from the crop? In 1769 Young recounted that around the Hedinghams, a "middling crop yielded 6½ hundredweight an acre, and that an average price of £5-10s a hundredweight" produced a gross return of £35-15s-0d an acre. Expenses, he said, amounted to £19 9s 0d, producing a profit of £13 6s 0d an acre.

Yet the hop growers produced some intriguingly disparate figures. Although a similar profit was again recorded from the Hedinghams in about 1790, a Wethersfield farmer calculated that his own profit over the seven years ending 1791, was just £5-10-1¼d an acre. By complete comparison, Mr. Barker Myhill of Hedingham stated that his profit per acre between 1785 – 1792, was nothing less than £38-5-0d!

Yields and prices however fluctuated wildly. At Blamsters Farm, Halstead, Mr. Vaizey grew two acres of hops. But between 1790–1801 his yields ranged from under one hundredweight an acre in the poorest year, to eighteen hundredweight in the best. At Stowmarket, Mr. Rout had experienced similarly polarised yields. Additionally, he revealed the cost of establishing a hop ground. In 1803 it was a staggering £91 an acre – with the poles alone costing £57-0s-0d. Not sur-

*From *Dr. Bisbie's Diaries* edited by Arthur Treece, published in the Newsletter of the Long Melford Historical and Archaeological Society; *Great Waldingfield* by Louise Kenyon; and *Nayland: Town and Village* by D. J. Halliday and others, together with research into the Tithe Awards at the West Suffolk Record Office.

prisingly Arthur Young repeatedly questioned the 'true profitability' of hops. Some growers claimed, and possibly made, exceptionally large profits from the crop – yet the acreage grown slowly declined. Possibly, like potatoes or sugar beet today, they produced very good returns in the very best years – on the very best soils.

But hop growing, in our area, is now beyond living memory. Although an annual Hop Growers' Dinner continued to be held at the Castle Hedingham 'Bell' until at least the 1860's the village has not commercially grown hops since 1887.

Hops were not the only intriguing crop to be grown in our local 'Garden of Eden'. Teasels, coriander and caraway were also farmed. In a will of 1631 for example, James Mountecute of Edwardstone bequeathed to his wife Mary:

"... all my taysell growing in Groton on the land of Mr. Thomas Gostlyn of Groton Hall."

Yet something far more remarkable was to be discovered. For teasels, coriander and caraway were sometimes PLANTED TOGETHER! To do this required exemplary husbandry. Indeed Arthur Young declared that, "Essex farmers are remarkable for their triple production." Additionally he included the technique of one local landowner named John Sewell – who farmed in the heart of our area – amongst the gentle hillocks and delightful views of Little Maplestead Hall. For in a letter dated, 10th July 1792, Sewell explained:

"About the beginning of March, plough some old pasture land. Mix together 10lbs of coriander, 12lbs of caraway and 12lbs of teasel seed an acre. Sow it directly after the plough and harrow well ...
"The coriander is fit to cut about the beginning of July ... The caraway is then harvested in the second year, the teasel in September, but some plants do not perfect their heads until the third – or even fourth year."*

Mr. Sewell's field of caraway, coriander and teasel, together with his hop-growing, livestock and mixed rotational farming repeatedly stimulate this author to think of the husbandry involved with both wonder, admiration – and some envy.

For in the transformed agriculture of contemporary times, the present writer in 1998, has only as many crops on his <u>entire farm</u> as Sewell had on just one field, some two hundred years ago!

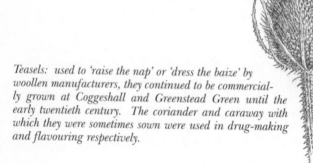

Teasels: used to 'raise the nap' or 'dress the baize' by woollen manufacturers, they continued to be commercially grown at Coggeshall and Greenstead Green until the early twentieth century. The coriander and caraway with which they were sometimes sown were used in drug-making and flavouring respectively.

Whilst teasels and hops can still be seen growing wild in local hedgerows, the processing of another crop is commemorated at Long Melford, in the name of a fashionable restaurant, not far from the church. Today it is known as *Scutchers Bistro*. Originally however it was a public house. *The Scutchers Arms*.

The crop it commemorates is flax – which was used to make linen. Initially however, the tough stems had to be 'scutched' or processed. Indeed, as early as 1222 a manorial record from Wickham St. Paul records the importance of flax to our erstwhile villagers. For it acknowledges their right to,

> "dig the land for flax, collect the flax, put it in water, pull it out and carry it home," (abbreviated) *

*From the Domesday of St. Paul 1222, printed by the Camden Society. Translated at private expense.

So crucial was flax for linen that three centuries later in 1533, Henry VIII's government decreed that, "all persons occupying sixty acres of land . . . should sow not less than a quarter of an acre with flax seed to promote the manufacture of linen cloth within the realm." (This Act and another of 1563 which increased the proportion to a full acre were finally repealed in 1593), (V.C.H).

But flax was not the only crop to provide material for clothes from our Mother Earth. Hemp, (which was also used for ropes), was similarly grown in north Suffolk until the early nineteenth century. In 1813 Arthur Young noted that hempen clothes were "a general wear for husbandmen and servants", and that he had been shown hempen "sheets and table linen that is now quite good after TWENTY YEARS' WEAR." (My capitals).

Yet the importation of cotton led to the demise of hempen garments. Now, however, both hemp and flax are being investigated again – partly to provide alternatives to synthetic materials. Flax, in fact, has been spasmodically grown locally during the nineteenth and twentieth centuries. whilst at Long Melford a Flax Factory was opened in 1874. Several contributors moreover recall harvesting the crop 'in the old-fashioned way' – before mechanisation.

"We had to pull it out of the ground BY HAND!" recalls Twinstead's Dorothy Turner, "Then we had to bundle it up into little sheaves and tie them up. But it was wiry ol' stuff! It did make your hands sore! You had to put something on them!

"But later, when it was grown again during the Second World War, a 'flax puller' and tractor came from Bures to do it, and then it was taken to the factory at Glemsford."

Flax. Grown in our area for centuries past it was again grown during the Second World War for army kit bags, canvas tents and fire hoses, etc. It has in fact been used for making textiles for at least 6500 years whilst it is believed that the Romans introduced the crop to Britain.

Chapter Five

CHEESE MAKING; TANNING AND STOCKMEN'S MEMORIES

At the time of the *Domesday Book* in 1086, the following cattle were recorded on the Mother Earth of our local manors:

Ballingdon 33	Long Melford 30
Kersey 10	Pentlow 24
Lamarsh { 10 cows / 8 calves	Ridgewell 22
	Wickham St. Paul's 4

These cattle not only provided meat and milk but also hides for leather – which were processed by tanners along our Suffolk-Essex border. Sible Hedingham for example, records tanyards from at least 1340 – which were owned by the father of the famous soldier of fortune, Sir John Hawkwood. Medieval Ipswich had no less than twelve tanneries; in 1590 even Belchamp Walter had two tanners, whilst Halstead's tannery, which traced its origins to 1573, continued to supply leather to London's West End, for use in hand-made shoes until it finally closed in the late nineteen fifties.*

Another tanners yard to continue into the twentieth century was situated near the River Stour at Bures.

"But did it STINK!" exclaims Claude Alleston of the tanyard where his grandfather once worked. "It reeked to high heaven! I've even heard my grandfather say that if it was a warm day, he'd

---

*For more on Halstead's tannery see *People at Work in Halstead and District*, by Doreen Potts, published by Halstead and District Local History Society.

sometimes come home by simply swimming across the river – and getting cleaned up at the same time!"

Collecting the oak bark for the tanners, itself became an industry:

"The barking season had just commenced," wrote Thomas Hardy in *The Woodlanders*. "What Fitzpiers heard was the tear of the 'ripping-tool' as it ploughed its way along the sticky parting between the trunk and rind."

But can Hardy's comments on rural Wessex find parallels from amongst the Colne-Stour countryside? Intrigued I turned to the farm diaries of William Porter of Park Farm, Wickham St. Pauls. And again they proved invaluable.

For in 1811, one of his employees, Jeremiah Warters, was actually 'peeling bark' for no less than sixteen days during late April and May. Later the bark was sold, and on June 3rd, Porter methodically noted:

"James Riglyn carted load of bark from Stones Farm [Wickham St. Paul] to Halstead."* (Was it delivered to the town's famous tannery, we wonder?)

From Bulmer we actually have first hand memories of the job:

"I can remember my father 'barking' some trees near 'Brakey Hill'," declared the late Philip Rowe (b.1900). "He had a special tool, and did it in the spring time when the sap was rising . . . Then, later on, he took it to the tanners yard at Bures." (Other 'bark peelers' are also remembered at Twinstead and Elmsett, whilst from Wethersfield's woods the Gilbey family took bark to the Halstead tannery).

We are deviating from the cattle who actually provided the hides to be tanned. For the cows also produced milk – which could be made

*From *Land of My Fathers* by Marion Turp. (The book is a superb account of Wickham St. Pauls between 1750–1850.)

into butter and cheese. And what of the latter? Did it rank beside the great regional cheeses like Cheddar, Cheshire or Stilton?

Apparently not. In his oft-quoted doggerel, the sixteenth century Essex agriculturalist Thomas Tusser, humorously laments of our local cheese:

> *"Those that made me were uncivil.*
> *They made me HARDER than the devil!*
> *Knives won't cut me, fire won't light me*
> *Dogs bark at me – BUT CAN'T BITE ME!"*

In *The Agriculture of Suffolk*, (published 1849), Messrs. Raynbird coyly repeat another 'well-worn' anecdote:

> "A story is told of a parcel of Suffolk cheese being packed up in a chest and put on board a ship to the East Indies. The ship's rats allured by the scent, gnawed a hole in the chest – but could not penetrate the cheese!"

Yet the question must be asked: *Why did our local cheese develop such an unenviable reputation?* Or are we just repeating the well-worn clichés of earlier writers and other historians?

One clue can be found in *The Farmer's Boy*, by Suffolk poet Robert Bloomfield, (1766-1823), who was born at Honnington. After mentioning London's increasing population – and burgeoning demand for meat and butter – he evocatively describes dairy produce from East Anglia, "passing through every town," and "thronging the Eastern road,"

> *"Delicious veal and butter every hour*
> *From Essex lowlands, and the banks of Stour:*
>
> *. . . Hence Suffolk's dairy-wives, RUN MAD FOR CREAM,*
> *And leave their milk with nothing but its name;*
> *Its name derision and reproach pursue,*
> *And strangers tell of 'THREE-TIMES SKIMM'D sky blue,'*
> *to cheese converted . . ."* (my capitals).

In other words, to produce enough butter to satisfy the growing metropolis, Suffolk's milk was skimmed 'THREE TIMES'. Only the weakest residue was left for cheese making – which doubtless accounts for the latter's impenetrable reputation. (Nevertheless some

78

985 tons of Suffolk cheese and 56,703 firkins of butter were still exported to the capital in 1730!)*

In earlier centuries however – before London's demand for butter consumed almost every fleck of cream – the county's cheese had enjoyed a very different reputation. Camden's *Britannia* (published 1607), records that, "great stores of Suffolk cheese are vended into all parts of England, nay into Germany, France and Spain," whilst in 1662, Dr. Thomas Fuller wrote in his *Worthies of England*:

> "Most excellent cheeses are made therein (Suffolk) . . . I remember when living in Cambridge the cheese of the county was preferred as the best."

Despite the clouded historical picture, one thing is certain. Cheese was produced in every parish, on the farms of our Suffolk-Essex border for many centuries. Nor should we forget its crucial importance in the bygone domestic economy. For when milk yields fluctuated wildly between summer and winter, and before the age of refrigeration, cheese was, quite simply, STORED MILK. By converting the summer surplus into cheese it became a crucial, 'all year' source of nutrition. References to its local production can be found in wills and tithe awards.

In 1632, for example, when Margaret Barret of Cavendish passed away, she left her daughter:

> ". . . the shelves in the milk house, the cheese press and forms in the dairy, with my great tub etc."†

Eleven years later the Rector of Little Cornard is recorded "collecting his tithe cheeses," whilst when Jeffrey Ruffle of Wickham St. Paul's Hall died in 1757 his estate included:

*From *The English Dairy Farm 1500-1900* by G. E. Fussell, published London, 1964.
†From *Wills of the Archdeaconary of Sudbury* by Nesta Evans. For Jeffrey Ruffle's will which follows I am again indebted to Marion Smith and the University of Reading where a copy is now deposited.

In the Cheese Chamber:
        150 cheeses @ 14lb per cheese.
        Valued @ 2½d per pound . . . £21.17.6d*

It is easy to miss the significant statistic. But Ruffle had nearly a TON of cheese in his chamber! (actually 2100lbs or 950kg). How this stimulates our imagination. For now we can picture 'WICKHAM ST. PAUL CHEESE', actually being made.

Imagine then, the bonny milkmaids carrying wooden buckets of milk into the dairy at Wickham Hall, (which itself adjoins the parish church). Next picture the gentle skimming and stirring of the milk in big wooden vats until the rennet and starter were added – by a more matronly worthy – possibly Mrs. Ruffle herself. Later the 'whey' would be poured off and the 'curds' ground up, until the latter were squeezed in the cheese press. Meanwhile cheeses which had already been made were 'turned over' on their oak shelves.

Milking Ruffle's cows with Wickham St. Paul's Church in the background. (The red brick tower incidentally was built following a bequest of twenty pounds in 1505.)

*Again from Land of My Fathers by Marion Turp.

80

Today, we can still picture Ruffle's 'milche' cows grazing beside the church, on pastures beside the village green and on the lower meadows that descend to Bulmer Brickyard. In those days they were probably an amalgam of unspecified cross-breeds – although the Suffolk Dun may have begun to predominate.

How long cheese production lingered in the Hadleigh-Sudbury-Halstead area is unknown. Although a twentieth century 'processed' cheese factory existed at Bures, one suspects that as a genuine farm-house operation, it largely died out between 1750 – 1850. Nevertheless, in 1791 the rector of Chelsworth was still expecting to receive his due of 'tithe cheeses'*. The following year a visitor from Kent to Bradfield Combust, glowingly described the dairy of one of Arthur Young's neighbours, before adding: "The butter and cheese made here is sold in waggon loads at a time at fairs in the autumn."† However there was a steady decline. In 1815 farmer William Porter of Wickham St. Paul was 'buying in' cheese rather than making his own, whilst a few years earlier Arthur Young had similarly observed:

"The area around Steeple Bumpstead which was formerly very famous for the production of cheeses . . . has generally given place to the suckling of calves for the London market. Cheeses," he explains, "can now be conveyed to market by water carriage," (i.e. the increasing network of canals and navigable rivers).

Some cheese production did however continue in north Suffolk into the nineteenth and even early twentieth century. Nevertheless in 1849 Messrs. Raynbird stoically observed that, "although a few cheeses are still made around Debenham and Earl Soham, they are not sufficient for local consumption . . ."

As already mentioned butter was also produced in our area. Here however there is no embarrassment with its reputation. For Suffolk's butter was eulogised and exalted!

*From *Chelsworth* by Geoffrey Pocklington, new revised edition by Bernard Quinlan.
†*Annals of Agriculture* Vol. 19.

"It has been 'pickled and barrelled up', and sent to the West Indies," recorded Daniel Defoe in about 1720, "and has been brought back again – as perfectly good and sweet as at first!"

Butter making moreover has none of the mystery attached to cheese production. Numerous contributors made it during the Second World War, "by saving the cream every morning and then adding a pinch of salt and shaking it in a jam jar for Sunday tea." It can still be made in exactly the same way. And for generations it was made on farms throughout our area with the farmer's wife or dairy maid slowly rotating a wooden churn.

"At Lamarsh Hall," recalls retired shepherd Eddie Tuffin (b.1903), "Bob Pinhey's father had about eighteen Red Poll cattle and his mother made butter from the cream. And when I was a boy it was my job to walk there before breakfast to collect our milk – and sometimes some butter as well!"

However we should not forget those who milked the cows, by hand, in dimly lit cowsheds on cold winter mornings. Someone who vividly recalls the days before electricity or modern 'milking machines' is the retired rector of Bulmer, Belchamp Walter and Belchamp Otten, the Reverend Trevor Howard. As we enjoyed a 'Harvest Lunch' in Bulmer Village Hall some years ago, he reminisced of his youth in that steady, reassuring, voice that has been so well appreciated in his pastoral life:

"Sometimes if you were milking on a very cold day, a guinea fowl would come in from the farm yard and sit on the cow's back to keep warm. And you'd put your own head against the cow's side – as you milked her – for exactly the same reason! In fact that is why milkmaids had very fair skin years ago – because they often caught cow pox – which was a mild inoculum to smallpox."

Often in his services, Trevor alluded to traditional farming with real feeling and frequently used agricultural analogies to illustrate his sermons.

"Whenever you call cattle in from a meadow," he recalled at one Bulmer Festival, "there will always be one cow who leads the way and be the first to come towards the gate. Well, St. Andrew – the

82

patron saint of our Church was the first as well . . ."

But as we finished our lunch on that late September Sunday, he gave me a slightly wistful look, hesitated for a moment and then laughed quietly:

"When we used to milk by hand there was always one particularly awkward old cow. Either she'd keep swishing her tail in your eyes and over your shoulders – or she'd stand on your toes and fidget about and be really difficult and troublesome. But on one occasion when I milked her, everything went really well. She wasn't a problem at all. I was just thinking how good she was – and that it was probably my 'calming influence', when she suddenly picked up her foot and stamped it right in the pail of milk. Oh! I was cross! Perhaps I shouldn't tell you this – but I was so angry that I threw the entire bucket of milk right over her!"

Trevor's memories of traditional farmsteads with their hen houses and pig sties, stables and cowsheds, with all the attendant grunting, champing and lowing, reminds us also of the skill of the older stockmen who took care of their charges and administered their own potions and concoctions – discreetly preserved and passed down – in a time when veterinary science was still in its infancy.

"If you had a calf which scoured," recalls Wethersfield farmer the late Jack Wallace (1894 -1986), "get some cobwebs and mix them up with a hen's egg – together with the shell – and then roll them up into a ball and make the calf swallow it. The mixture," he explained, "was meant to soak up the acids in the stomach."

Eddie Tuffin tells of sheep, which would 'blow' especially if they ate too much white clover:

"Of course they could be punctured – or sometimes a couple of men could pump the gas out of them by working their legs. But there was an old man round here who made up his own special mixture – and that would release it better than anything – but he'd never tell anyone what it was!"

(Thomas Hardy provides a graphic illustration of sheep being punctured in *Far From the Madding Crowd*). In a similar vein, farmer

Dennis Holland of Lavenham, was told by an old horseman, "Cut a horse's tail into hundreds of small pieces. Then, feed it to the horse a little at a time, and it will stop the horse getting worms!"

From 'elsewhere' comes a comment on the mysterious powers of certain of the old horsemen.

"I've been told – by one of them that know," revealed my source, "that if a ferret's muck and smell was rubbed onto a gate post, a horse would simply NOT go past it. But if that post was then wiped with vinegar – well the smell was removed – and the horse would carry on past."

Corroboration comes from John Cooper, (b. 1916), from the isolated mid-Suffolk village of Elmsett, about four miles from Hadleigh.

"Years ago there was an old horseman by the name of 'Flasky' Cousins in this village. He was a proper old character! He had a great white beard and lived well into his nineties – being born about 1835. But I've heard it said that he could stand at the top of the Bramford Road, (into Ipswich), and he'd say, 'that horse will stop' – when it gets to a certain point – and it would! He'd put some scent on the gatepost or something, but no one knew what it was!

"But I've also heard that he always had a little bottle of 'Oil of Fennel' with him. Apparently he would put a little on his handkerchief to 'call' horses with. Another old custom was to mix up horse chestnuts and eggs. It was reckoned to make the horses' coats shine."

At Gestingthorpe, lifelong farmworker, Bert Surridge (b.1907) relates:

"An old horseman I knew years ago would dig up the root of bryony. Then he'd rub it over a nutmeg grater, and put a little in the bait – and he reckoned that improved the horse's coat."

By comparison, the late George 'Jute' Chatters, (1910–1995), of Belchamp St. Pauls, recalled that, "wild wormwood was also reckoned to be good for making the coats shine."

Recording memories of the secretive knowledge that certain old horse keepers had acquired – in a lifetime's work with their charges, is always an exciting challenge. But as I sat in the warm sitting room of Jute's house – with its views over the surrounding countryside that he knew so well – there was a moment's pause. And then his twinkling eyes and warm, friendly face suddenly lit up, as he exclaimed:

"I'll tell you something about old Will Hart though! He had the knackers yard at Brook Farm, Walter Belchamp. Now he was a master chap with horses. One of them that could do anything with them! Like when they had the farm sale at Bevingdon. Two ol' horses had been sold – but they *would not* go in the lorry – and no-one else could get near them. To tell the truth we were half afraid of them. But ol' Will Hart just said, "Leave 'em till tomorrow." So we did! Next day he came back and sized up the situation. And then he just, 'put his smock on' – and do you know – those two horses followed him in like magic!

"But he could go in a field, and jump on a horse, and put a halter on as it was running! And the other thing was this. You'd see a horse being a bit of a nuisance. And that old man would just, *'take his hanky out'* – and wave it. And they'd smell it. And I've smelt it too in the blacksmiths! And then they'd quieten right down for him!"

Chapter Six

STRAW PLAITING and HAY TRUSSING

"Don't think you're inventing anything by researching uses of straw. When I was a boy every single bit was used – every single bit of it!"

Harold Cooper (b.1918)

Of the crops and by-products so far discussed most involved men. Yet there was one which produced vital work for the women of many local villages in the nineteenth century. As such, it filled a vacuum created by the decline of 'cottage spinning'. Like spinning however, it could also be undertaken at home, whilst the 'raw material' was originally obtained from the nearby fields of 'Our Mother Earth'.

It was the 'plaiting of straw' – an industry of immense consequence in the villages of north-east Essex. At Belchamp Walter in 1871 for example, (population then 735), no less than ONE HUNDRED and SIXTEEN women earned their principal income from this single activity.

The work itself was generally straightforward – if fiddly and tedious. By using a sharply honed splicer, (called a 'splitting engine'), wheat straw was split and the narrow strands then 'plaited' together into bands. Finally the woven fabric was purchased by local dealers, despatched to Luton and made into straw bonnets and boaters.

That straw could be plaited at home was obviously an attraction to remote rural villagers. Yet in the tiny cottages where the large farm-workers' families lived, conditions in the winter must have been unpleasantly cramped.

One pertinent reminiscence of the activity was provided by an elderly Earls Colne contributor to the *Halstead Times* of January 31st 1903:

"I have seen a whole family in their only living room with sheaves of straw, selecting and rejecting individual straws. The floor of the room was like a disordered stackyard!"*

The bonnets which were eventually produced from plaited straw are described in some of our most famous literary classics. In *A Tale of Two Cities*, for example, we first meet the heroine, Lucy Manette, as a young lady, "of not more than seventeen . . . holding her straw travelling-hat by its ribbon," whilst in *Oliver Twist*, the less reputable Nancy, leaves Fagin's den of thieves:

"With a clean apron tied over her gown, and curl-papers tucked up under a straw bonnet – both articles of dress being provided from the Jew's inexhaustible stock . . ."

But how, it might be asked, was straw plaiting developed in our area – if the manufacturers were based at Luton?

The answer derives from Gosfield Hall. (The latter lies about three miles from Halstead, and was sometime owned by the Marquis of Buckingham). In about 1790, however, the Marquis perceived that the decline of 'cottage spinning' was causing great hardship in the area. Consequently he attempted to introduce straw-plaiting as an alternative.

Initially however his good intentions were received with sceptical reserve.

"To make the first miserable coarse-bangled hats was a great effort," recorded Arthur Young in 1807, "and as nobody would wear them, Lady Buckingham decorated one with a ribbon and wore it in sight of the whole village. The Marquis went to church in another and laid it during the service in full sight of the congregation."

For some eight decades thereafter, plaiting was to be a fiscal lifeline to the residents of our rural parishes. For the latter were experiencing staggering increases in population, and also desperate

*From Dr. Arthur Brown's excellent book, *'Meagre Harvest'*, (E.R.O. publication no. 106), which explands further on rural hardship, whilst also supplying much additional background material for this chapter.

87

unemployment – which by the 1820's was manifest in the rick burning and machinery breaking of 'Captain Swing'. Within their reduced circumstances, straw plaiting had a dual advantage. It was an additional source of income. And as 'piece work', did not interfere with traditional rural activities – such as gleaning, stone picking or hop gathering. Children could also assist. We recall, from *Heart of our History*, the plaintive remarks of Little Yeldham's School teacher in 1877:

> "Kate Mitson sent home for doing her straw plait . . . I find the straw work a great nuisance in the school" *

In 1839, the Rector of Ashen similarly wrote of the village's 'school':

> "Reading is very little attended to. The great object being to learn the straw plaiting for bonnets which is the universal employment for children of both sexes in this parish."

One such establishment was vividly depicted by a local artist – the illustriously named George Washington Brownlow (1835-1876). The latter was patronised by the Raymond family of Belchamp Walter and examples of his work can still be seen in the parish Church and in Sudbury Town Hall. But he also undertook a touching, charming portrayal of the village's children, fresh-faced and innocent as they learn the rudiments of this skillful craft – in a beautiful picture appropriately entitled *The Straw Plaiter's School*. (See our alternative on centre page xxix.)

The industry was however, *particularly* localised. Those giving their profession as 'straw plaiter' in the 1871 census are listed below. The parishes are deliberately arranged in *ascending* numerical order.

*From *A History of Little Yeldham* by Adrian Corder-Birch, published by Halstead and District Local History Society.

HINCKFORD HUNDRED 1871

	Total Population	Principal Income straw-plaiting (almost all women)	% of Population
Henny (Gt & Lt)	379	19	5.0%
Alphamstone	303	28	9.2%
Wickham St. Paul	445	45	10.1%
Castle Hedingham	1235	128	10.3%
Great Maplestead	444	37	12.1%
Foxearth	423	56	13.2%
Twinstead	204	28	13.7%
Bulmer	780	110	14.1%
Gestingthorpe	766	112	14.6%
Belchamp Walter	735	116	15.7%
Belchamp St. Paul	836	146	17.4%
Lamarsh	307	54	17.5%
Sible Hedingham	2097	388	18.5%
Ridgewell	839	181	21.5%
Pentlow	379	83	21.8%
Belchamp Otten	389	86	22.1%
Stambourne	577	134	23.2%
Tilbury juxta Clare	288	77	26.7%*

Even here, we can see a definite concentration on the 'heavy land plateau' in the parishes between Sible Hedingham, Ridgewell, and Pentlow.

*The definition of 'profession' is somewhat elastic – and should be regarded as 'principal source of earned income'. A mother of eight children with only an hour spare each afternoon might possibly describe herself as a 'straw-plaiter' – as might a solitary widow of fifty-five. Conversely a child of eight or nine would be listed as 'Scholar' whilst probably doing some plaiting as well.
The figures of straw plaiters in Essex parishes are again drawn from *Meagre Harvest* by Dr. Arthur Brown. In the same work he also reveals that in the 1871 census of Essex some 2889 people were recorded as straw plaiters. Revealing just how concentrated the industry was, 1846 of them are listed in our parishes here . . . As always my sincere thanks to Arthur for so illuminating this phase of social history.

Many readers of this book will live in the villages above – some even in traditional cottages with 'wattle and daub' walls or thatched rooves. It is in these houses – your houses – that the straw plaiting took place; where mothers and unmarried daughters split and spliced the wheat stalks, and where too, on summer afternoons they sat outside on simple chairs and carried on their industry as infant children romped around them.

Today, as one drives through these villages, with their winding lanes, and scattered hamlets one can say with certainty, "Here they plaited straw!"

In neighbouring Suffolk, however, the figures are significantly different.

	Population	Straw Planters	% of Population
Acton	548	0	–
Chilton	260	0	–
Great Cornard	877	3	0.34%
Little Cornard	429	15	3.5%
Elmsett	425	0	–
Hartest	720	0	–
Hundon	1116	3 men)	2.24%
		22 women)	
Kersey	570	0	–
Poslingford	398	1	
Stoke by Clare	867	1	
Little Waldingfield	391	0	–
Wixoe	170	3	1.76%

Yet it was not just the *rural* families of north Essex for whom the plaiting brought some alleviation of poverty. In 1844 Halstead had three 'straw plait' dealers, and EIGHT straw hat makers; at Sudbury there was a 'straw plait manufacturer' and four straw hat makers, whilst three 'straw hat makers' were listed in Clare with no less than SEVEN in Hadleigh.

However the meagre few shillings of income which had been so valuable to the village plaiters were not to continue. Between 1879–81 the plaiting industry underwent great change, due to mechanisation, whilst cheaper imports of an improved plait reached England, largely from Belgium. Within two years, this crucial local industry had all but died out.

A 'straw plaiting engine'. Edward Bingham of Castle Hedingham recalled that labourers made the 'engines' from 'beef-shank bones'. Apparently produced in 'sets of six or seven', each had a different number of wings to enable the straw to be split into anything from four to ten strips, depending on the fineness required. A good workman, he said, "could make three or four engines in an evening, which sold at a penny or three-half-pence each." (From the Victoria County History.)

Throughout the author's farming career he has either burnt the straw that follows his harvests of wheat and barley, or since about 1984 chopped the straw as it leaves the combine before 'ploughing it in'. Within the contemporary East Anglian 'Grain Belt', wheat straw is almost worthless, whilst barley straw is only of use to the few remaining livestock farmers, or in occasional years when some is exported to the West Country.

Yet traditionally the straw of our Mother Earth was of *inestimable* value – and had a multitude of applications such as thatching rooves, as a constituent of wattle and daub, and as elementary beds and mats. (In *A Tale of Two Cities*, for example, Dickens describes Mr. Lorry emerging from the 'Dover Mail', "in chains of straw rather like a larger kind of dog.") Lewis Majendie similarly described 'straw ropes' being used in land drains, whilst 'straw ropes' were also employed to lag water pipes and to insulate glass 'carboy' acid containers. Wheat straw moreover was also used for packaging fragile goods – and not merely glass and porcelain.

"Even bricks had to be packed in straw years ago!" exclaims Tom Rowe. "On a windy day a building site was more like a stackyard – with all this bloomin' straw blowing about!

Yet undoubtedly straw's most fundamental role was in the littering of livestock – which boosted the supply of farmyard manure. So important was straw to the process that Arthur Young vehemently railed against the introduction of the Brick and Tile Tax – because it encouraged people to use straw for thatching rooves!

"There can be no more pernicious custom," he passionately declared in 1784, "than that of covering farm houses, barns, offices and cottages, etc. with thatch: IT ROBS THE DUNG HILL EXCESSIVELY . . . and prevents every year a large extent of land from being manured . . . To give a bounty upon substituting [thatch] with tiles would be a very good policy; and next to it would be that of laying a tax upon thatch, . . ." (My capitals. *From Annals of Agriculture – Volume Two*).

In addition to a farm's requirement, straw was also needed by many villagers until quite recent times:

"Take Saturday afternoon!," exclaims one source, "I bet you'd see at least one man trudging through Gestingthorpe with a great truss of straw on his back. He'd have been to somewhere like Hall Farm and bought a bit of straw, and he'd be carrying it back to his cottage because his pig was about to farrow – and that was an important thing in those days!"

Additionally – and crucially – straw was required to thatch the corn and hay stacks.

"Every year after you'd done threshing," explains one retired farmer, "you had to keep back a decent sized stack of wheat straw to thatch the hay stacks with – and all the stacks you expected to build from the corn harvest as well!"

Yet hay and straw also had an 'exportable value' – especially to Victorian London – with its thousands of horses used for riding, or pulling drays, carriages and Hansom cabs. Indeed with the coming of the railway, at least two local merchants, Whitlocks of Great Yeldham, and C.J.N. Row of Long Melford, became well known for arranging this trade.

Initially however, the hay or straw had to be 'trussed' – to enable its conveyance in convenient sizes. And 'trussing' reminds us of one of Thomas Hardy's most flamboyant and colourful characters – the heroically doomed 'Mayor of Casterbridge'.

The latter begins life as an itinerant 'hay trusser'. In a drunken fit he 'sells his wife'. Subsequently shamed, he renounces alcohol. By dint of obsessive, hard work he slowly prospers – becomes a success-ful grain merchant, a pillar of the community, and eventually the

Mayor. But his fortunes crash following erratic dealing. He resumes hay trussing but dies penniless, unloved and abandoned.

With such a character from Enlish literature to inspire me, I was especially anxious to see if any recollections of hay or straw trussing could still be recorded from our Sudbury-Halstead area! And once again, it is our great 'practical all-rounder', Tom Rowe of Bulmer, now in his ninety fifth year, who was able to oblige.

Initially he explained how to make straw trusses, (or 'bundles' as they were known in Bulmer), before describing their dispatch from the isolated farms of our area to Sudbury or Long Melford Railway Station.

Making 'straw bundles'. When made from wheat straw, explains Tom, they would be, "about five feet long, 2'6" wide and 1'9" high". Two bundles were then laid onto two straw ropes (or 'scuds'), pressed down as shown in the illustration and then bound up with the scuds. (The second scud is just visible on the left).

During World War One the straw trusses which the family made were taken to the Sudbury Quay, (now Theatre), cut in half, put in a mechanical press, and once compressed, sent to France.

"If we were making 'trusses or bundles' from wheat straw," he recalled, "we usually had to do them in lots of seventy two – which was one 'railway truck load'. Then the man we contracted for – Charlie Row of Long Melford – would get them taken to the station by horse and waggon. It took thirty six 'straw bundles' to make a horse 'waggon load'. So he generally sent the waggons out in pairs – so the men could help each other load up. Barley straw of course was different. The bundles were shorter and fatter. We reckoned on eighty four to a railway truck load."

"Did the 'straw bundles' or trusses have to be any particular weight?"

"Oh yes! They had to average about 36 pounds each (16 kg). In fact we weighed them every now and then to make sure we were roughly right."

"Was making the trusses hard on your hands?" I asked after Tom had explained that the straw was first 'fingered out' into 'yellms' – similar to those used in thatching.

"Was it! Think of it – making all those yellms! By night-time the ends of your fingers would be right raw! And if there were a lot of THISTLES IN THE STRAW – yes! You certainly knew about it!"

As mentioned, our local hay was also exported to London. One of our most authoritative and helpful of all local farming contributors – the late Cyril Philp (1899-1993), of Kirby Hall, Castle Hedingham – describes the process:

"Round Yeldham way, Whitlocks would buy a stack of hay off a farmer, and then bring a horse-drawn press to bale it. But at Poole Farm , Great Yeldham, they had a big vertical boiler and if they ever got any rough – or slightly mouldy stuff – they'd put it in there, and turn the steam on, and it became lovely – much better than when it went in!"

"It must have been quite labour intensive," I mused.

"It was! I can remember them employing over THIRTY men in the hay and straw business! In fact they actually had two waggons, which did nothing else other than go from Poole Farm to Yeldham Station – to put it on the train for London!*

To learn more about the self-employed 'journeyman's' work of cutting the hay stacks – and then 'pressing' the hay into bales – we return to Tom Rowe. And if we describe the technicalities in detail the reason is this: quite simply we are on the verge of losing all such recollections for ever. Now however, let us imagine him as a young man again, bicycling from farm to farm, along rutted country lanes, with a little food and a bottle of cold tea, to refresh him during the long day's work.

"Presumably you started at the top and worked down in layers?" I asked.

"No! Definitely not! You'd start at the end of the stack – and go right down – a bit like slicing bread."

"Why was that?"

"In case it came on to rain! The rest of the stack would still have a thatch on! 'Course when you got close to finishing you had to cut it down in stages – otherwise the stack would topple over. But some of the hay at the bottom – which had had the whole weight of the stack on it – well that would be suffen tight. IT WAS LIKE CUTTING THROUGH BRICKS! You knew what hard work was then! Some of it hardly needing pressing!"

"Did you ever work on stacks that had got hot and were in danger of catching fire – because the hay hadn't been properly 'made'?" I wondered. (Farmers often pulled a bag of straw up the centre of hay stacks when building them – to provide a hole for the heat to escape).

*Adrian Corder-Birch whose book, A History of Great Yeldham, includes further details of Whitlocks hay and straw business, believes that just before the First World War over seventy people were employed in their forage activities. Today the industry is still commemorated at Poole Farm, where a brick plaque records the erstwhile chaff works.

Pressing hay – by hand. The press was taken to the farm by the merchant. After being cut out of the stack the hay was placed in the frame and compressed by pulling the long lever down. As Tom Rowe exclaims, "There were no hydraulics! You were the power! And every truss had to weigh 56 pounds – half a hundredweight each!" Both hay cutting and pressing were considered to be two of the most strenuous manual tasks.
Tom is also keen to point out that the hay in the press would have had perfectly straight sides, having been cut out with a hay knife. "The hay bale was shaped like a matchbox – about three feet long, eighteen inches wide and 12 to 14 inches thick."

"We cut a stack of hay for Mr. Gardiner at Little Yeldham once – and that had got hot – but it hadn't burnt because it couldn't get any air. But parts of the inside had all gone like ashes. There was any amount of them! It was a huge stack too, but most of it was no good. Ol' Mr. Gardiner was a good farmer too. We were surprised to find it on his farm! Another time Albert Rowe carted some hay from Peoples Park in Sudbury – and that had got so hot that they had to cut a hole in! But you had to be careful then. Because that's when it might combust!"

The 'harvest pitcher', above, was made at Gestingthrorpe Pot Works in 1776. The vessel had a third handle at the rear.
(Paul Matthews: Photographic Partners.)

Discovered by landlord of the Belchamp Otten 'Red Lion' David Howard, this jar bears the words "J. MILLS: HALF MOON, BELCHAMP, SEPTEMBER 30, 1822". We wonder where it was made?

The enormous 'Bell Ringers Jar' at St. Andrews Church, Halstead, was made at Gestingthorpe in 1658. Some of the church's current ringers are seen around it. Back row: Clive Todd, Trevor Smith, Stephen Hardy, Nina Smith, Charlotte Berry, (and Norman Wiseman who is invisible!) Front row: John Daly, Judith MacFarlane, and Tower Captain Doreen Middleton.

The lime kiln and chalk pit beside the Middleton Road, Sudbury (where Balfuelco are today). For more on 'The White Cliffs of Sudbury' see Chapter Two.

Tony Minter and son Joshiah stand beside the lime kiln which Tony has just had built at Bulmer Brickyard with the help of local craftsman Chris Moulton. Once in operation it will continue a lime burning tradition in the parish which stretches back at least 470 years.

One of Sudbury's enormous chalk pits was situated in today's Locas Road (just off the Cornard road). The height of the recently built flats well indicates the depth of the working.

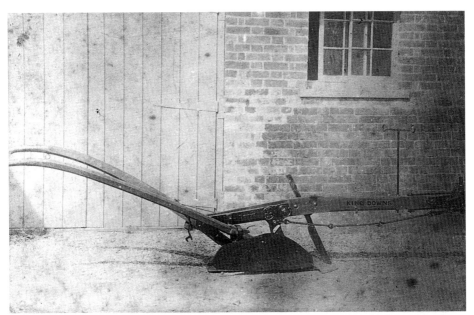

LOCALLY MADE IMPLEMENTS. Downs T.D.O. plough standing outside the Gestingthorpe Iron Foundry. (See Chapter Thirteen.)

Sudbury carpenter Brian Ambrose making a new 'beam' whilst restoring a Downs plough for the author in 1998.

'Tortoise Stove' in Belchamp Walter Church, made by Portways of Halstead. (Alastair Tuffill Photography.)

Alan Dixey of Bulmer with his collection of bricks – many of which come from the different makers who once operated along the Suffolk-Essex borders.

Our extraordinary Mother Earth. Pure sand Ⓐ and stiff 'chalky boulder clay' Ⓑ were found within just a few yards of each other on this field in Bulmer.

Local botanical wonders. This enormous ivy stem – which is at least 25 cm wide grows in the Belchamp Valley.

Bramble Leaves – I never fail to be amazed at their beauty in the autumn sunshine.

Beautiful Thistle Down. Very large thistles were believed to indicate good land by immigrant Scots farmers to East Anglia.

Stitchwort – known locally as 'Shirt-buttons'. A list of other nicknames for wild flowers appears in 'The Long Furrow' on page 216.

Foxearth's parish sign given by the Chapman family. Lower Hall, where John Row also farmed, is on the other side of the road.

Foxearth farmer David Jackson (b.1952), and daughter Kate studying John Row's Farm Diaries from Melford and Foxearth over a century ago. (Photographic Partners.)

Agronomist Bruce Hill with a group of local farmers discussing contemporary wheat growing on the same fields that John Row farmed at Foxearth in 1898. (Left to right: Fred Branwhite, John Brand, Colin Flux, Bruce Hill, Chris Paine and Peter Unwin.)

Gordon Hastie of Foxearth describes his family's move from Scotland to Bulmer in 1936. Gordon, who is a retired farmworker, is also a keen local historian and has spent many hours researching local newspapers.

Dick Finch of Gestingthorpe recalling the brickyards which once existed in the parish.

With Kathleen Grimwood (b.1901) after giving a slideshow in Sudbury Library. Kathleen's memories of the town in former times were undoubtedly the highlight of the evening. (Photograph by Elizabeth Wiles.)

Fred Chatters (b.1906) recalling Belchamp Walter water mill where his father worked after the First World War.

The late Jimmy Theobald (1919–1995) explains the use of a 'Mill Bill'. Borley Mill of which Jimmy had such vivid recollections, is in the distance.

(Alastair Tuffill, Portrait Photography)

Horace Elsey reminisces about ploughing with horses, steam cultivation and early tractors during his years at Jenkins Farm, Bulmer.

Another farming 'oracle'. Horseman and tractor driver the late Bert Surridge of Gestingthorpe.

Friend and countryman John Waspe of Whatfield.

Memorial to the Tithe War, on opposite side of the road to Elmsett Church.

Dennis Holland of Lavenham recalls farming during the Great Depression of the 1930's.

The late Bob Pinhey who farmed at Liston. As a young man Bob spent eleven years in Canada. His photographs – which follow – shed revealing light on the efficiency of 'praire agriculture' in the 1920s, and explains why so much land along the Suffolk-Essex border went derelict at the time.

THE BOB PINHEY COLLECTION

Illustrating the enormous difference between Canadian and Suffolk agriculture in the late 1920s. During harvest in Saskatchewan, Bob and his two colleagues camped in the enormous fields.

'Sheaf loaders' were used to mechanically pick up the sheaves.

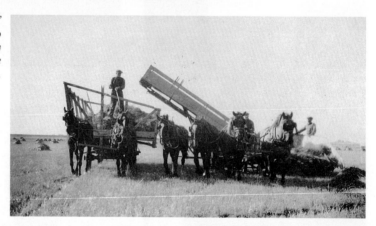

'Sheaf loader', side view.

Threshing in the fields. The sheaves are being taken directly from a trailer which avoided the need to build stacks. The dust and chaff is being blown away again eliminating labour.

Following snow the grain trailers were put onto skis.

Taken in the early 1930s, this 21 foot set of discs working on stubble would still be considered large (and very efficient) in contemporary East Anglia. (For more of Bob's memories, see Chapter Ten.)

Eight horses pull a five furrow plough in Western Australia in the late 1920's.

This huge stack of corn sacks was simply left outside after being threshed, awaiting transport.

'Clearing the virgin land. Philip's father farmed at Bradfield St. George. An older brother had preceeded Philip to Australia. Both were a part of the great migration away from our local countryside between 1880–1940.

Mary Downs (nee Oxborrow-Smith) of Halstead and friend Margaret Dick assist with the lambing during their five years in the Land Army at Armsey Farm, Bulmer.

Halstead vet Jim Waters. For more of Jim's memories of his lifetime's work with animals on local farms and his veterinary recollections generally, see Chapter Seventeen. (Photograph by kind permission of David Guthrie, Bluebridge Farm Studio, Halstead.)

'Frosts' or North Mill in Halstead.

Smythe steerage drill, working locally about 1907. (For more, see Horace Elsey's memories on page 301.)

Peter 'Pixey' Mitson of Glemsford from Ernest Doe & Sons Ltd.

Carl Potter of West Bergholt 'dressing' our seed corn on behalf of Anglia Grain Services Ltd.

THE SAGA CONTINUES!... Modern farming is a rather solitary profession and it always raises our spirits when engineers and others visit the farm.

Engineer John Scott of Greenstead Green, services the author's ageing 'seed drill'.

Apprentice Scott Mayes, Steve Lockwood and Paul Jinks from Manns of Saxham repair our Claas combine harvester.

Eric Rippingale (centre) who was born in Gestinghtorpe, setting up the author's new Simba 'Top Tilth' cultivator. Also visiting is neighbouring farmer and contractor Julian Swift (on the left).

A picture in which all our family take great pride. When the author's Grandfather purchased this Case combine in 1936, it was one of the first combine harvesters to be used in Suffolk. Driving the Lanz Bulldog tractor is Harold Cooper (b.1918), whilst his brother John adjusts the height of the 'cutter bar'. My cousin Oliver has recently restored the combine and twice demonstrated it to large and appreciative audiences. (See Page 307 .)

"How much did you try to do each day?" I asked.

"We normally reckoned on cutting and pressing THREE TONS A DAY! But some stacks of hay might by twenty tons or more! We biked from Bulmer to Ickworth, (near Bury St. Edmunds), and did some big ones there one year. But it could take a good week to do some of these big stacks! So every night – before we biked home – we had to cover up the trusses with a tarpaulin and put some straw over the stack."

The latter provides Tom with one memory that is both delightful and enduring, despite all the long hours of rigorous manual work.

"It's one of the things I'll never forget. We were working at Liston Hall, and when we 'left off' we put some straw over the bit of the hay stack we'd 'opened up'. But next morning when we came to work, we were both amazed. Because there was a robin's nest there! It wasn't actually quite finished – but even so, it had been almost completely built that morning – before we turned up!

"And the other thing was this. I never, ever saw a rat in a hay stack! And of course, you could always tell the hay that had been made from the old meadows. It was beautifully sweet!"

Chapter Seven

LIGHT AND WATER

"At Applecroft – in Henny – where I was born, there was a pump in the yard, but it wasn't very nice water, because there'd be mice and things in it! So to get nice drinking water we walked across the meadow to a spring and deeved it out with a cup and put it in a bucket – and that was lovely water! So if you wanted a cup of tea you'd have to go across the meadow first!"

Hilda Dixey (b. 1912) Bulmer Tye

How we now take light for granted! Yet in Sudbury and Halstead there are numerous three-storey 'weavers cottages' with enlarged 'middle-storey' windows – which enabled more 'natural light' to fall upon the looms.

Then there is Sudbury's Corn Exchange. Today it is the Public Library, but on entering, glance up. At that wide, expansive glass roof. But it is not just there for decoration. Rather it enabled the discerning merchants a better chance to scrutinize the samples of wheat and barley which were offered to them.

Yet natural light was also important for social functions – as Jane Austen remarks in *Sense and Sensibility*:

"(Sir John) . . . had been to several families that morning, in hopes of procuring some addition to their number; but it was moonlight, and everybody was full of engagements."

And how well – during any power cut – do we suddenly understand the full significance of the Biblical message "I AM THE LIGHT . . .", together with the Evensong Collect uttered by wary churchgoers in centuries past – before walking home along rutted tracks and overhanging lanes:

"Lighten our darkness . . . and defend us from all the perils and dangers of this night . . ."

However, there has always been *some* artificial light. When Queen Elizabeth the First visited Gosfield Hall, Long Melford Hall and 'Smallbridge' at Bures the 'torches' which her retainers carried:

"would have been made from dried cow parsley or hemlock, packed together with flax or bull-rushes which had been dipped in wax."*

Then there were candles. The latter were originally made from the tallow of sheep's fat – with a piece of flax for the wick. (Another use for flax.) But if the candle were taken outdoors, says Dorothy Hartley, "it was placed inside thin slices of cattle horn – to create a 'lanthorn' – or lantern."

With the nineteenth century came paraffin and gas lamps. Soon 'Gas Works' were being built by the owners of 'Big Houses', such as at Gosfield and Kentwell Hall, or by entrepreneurs in towns to enable street and domestic lighting.

"Sudbury's Gas Works," says White's Directory, "were erected in 1836 at a cost of £5000 – which was funded by the sale of £20 shares. Hadleigh's were built about 1834 by silk millers Brown and May. Castle Hedingham's – which lit Sible as well, commenced operation in 1862, whilst the 'Earls Colne Gas and Light Company' was formed in 1882 under the management of A. Hunt."

Fortunately Sudbury's Gas Works have been vividly recalled for us by an extraordinary *ninety-six year old lady*, who I interviewed in March 1998 in her home on Sudbury's Croft, just two doors away from the house in which she was born in 1901! Her name is Kathleen Grimwood and she is a fount of local knowledge.

*From *The Land of England* by Dorothy Hartley. This wonderful book – which reveals so much about how our ancestors lived, ate, survived and clothed themselves has been a 'Bible' for much of this section.

"My grandfather," she explains, "was the first licencee of the Gas Works and then my Father, who was born in 1875, began work there when he was fifteen. Well eventually he also became manager and remained until his retirement!"

"It must have been quite a responsibility," I ventured.

"It was! We even had a special gauge in our bathroom and if ever the 'pressure' was wrong – even if it was the middle of the night – he'd go rushing down to the Gas Works to see what the problem was. But that was the thing years ago. There was a lot more human contact – so on Christmas Eve, for example, Father would instruct the men to leave the town lights on longer so the Catholics could see to get to Church for midnight mass.

"What about the Zeppelin raid of 1916?" I wondered.

"That was awful. Several people were killed and Father had to go straight down to the Gas Works and turn off the supply. But after that the authorities wanted him to turn off the gas *immediately* there was any threat of an attack. But he refused – in case people forgot to turn it off in their own homes – and got gassed when it came back on. Eventually they reached a compromise, and he agreed to 'dip the gas' three times first – as a warning – before cutting it off."

"Where actually was the Gas Works?"

"Down Quay Lane. When it was built all the coal had to come up the river on barges you see. But I can well remember being sent down there as a child and being told to play in the oxide. We thought it was great fun – but the real idea was that the coal tar was meant to prevent whooping cough! But it was very hot work for the men. They'd be stripped to the waist raking out coke and pulling water out."

Another recollection is provided by retired stockman Les Downs (b.1916), of Batt Hall cottages, Bulmer, (which lie beside the road to Bulmer – just after leaving Sudbury).

"There was also a couple of gas 'street lamps' beside the road up

100

to Batt Hill – one at the bottom of the hill and another about half way up, and an ol' boy came round with a pole to light them. Reg Kelly was his name. He'd come and put them on, when it got dusky and then about ten o'clock at night, he'd come and put them out. They did all Sudbury like that when I was a boy."

However within 'small town life' there were always minor contretemps. The late Gertie Coe (b.1906) of Brickwall Cottages, Bulmer, recalls that on one occasion,

"Someone put CANDLES in the gas lamps around the Market Hill – because they thought the gas light was so dull! They even lit the candles as well! I think I know who did it as well! They said it was Mr. B_____ who had a sweet shop in Friars Street!"

At about the same time electricity had arrived in Sible Hedingham.

"A great character called George Bishop," recalls John Frost with a chuckle, "began to generate and sell electricity at Alderford Mill for about fifty houses in the nineteen twenties. However his customers soon realised that they could 'short circuit' his meters – and replenish their batteries free of charge! Do you know what George's solution was? He reversed the polarity and blew up their batteries!"

In rural areas, the old ways continued.

"All you had was an old candle lantern to see by, as you went along the road first thing of a morning," remembers Alphamstone stockman Eddie Tuffin (b.1903). "And when it was pitch dark in the winter that's all you had to feed the horses – or do the lambing with. I've lambed scores of sheep like that! . . . But you got used to it within a little. You didn't know any different did you!"

Of importance to all human beings is water. Yet in NINETEEN FIFTY THREE, only five parishes in the Halstead Rural District had a piped water supply.

"We had to go right up to the pump near the Maplestead *'Cock'* for our drinking water – *until 1954*," recalls Dorothy Cornell of Mosses Farm, "Oh no! You'll never hear me complain about the big water tower they built. But it wasn't many months before one newcomer did. Huh! We weren't long finding him an answer!"

"But how exactly did you manage? Did you have to get all your water from the pump?"

"Oh no. We saved the rainwater from the roof in a 'soft-water tub'. Course, there might be an old bit of moss or two in it, so I'd usually have to filter it through a stocking or something. Then we'd wash all our clothes – and ourselves – from this 'soft-water tub' – as well as using it for the 'first wash' of the vegetables. That way it saved on how much drinking water we had to carry down."

"So how did you actually get it?"

"In two buckets – and I got wet feet EVERY SINGLE TIME! But it still took a quarter of an hour to make the 'round trip'." Then she pauses. There is a mischievous twinkle in her eye . . . "That is," she exclaims, "unless there was anyone else to talk to!"

"Carrying the water sounds like hard work!"

"It was! But at least we had a pipe to take the water *out* of the house. At our first cottage in Belchamp Otten, we didn't even have a pipe *from* the sink! We had to carry *every single* drop of water into that house – and then carry it all out again! You'll never guess what our first job was after getting married . . . To get some water ready for next morning!"

Well-digging itself was highly specialised work. Retired farmworker and history enthusiast, Cecil Cook of Little Maplestead explains:

"Walter Jennings, Alf and Jack Abbott were our local well sinkers. This was a dangerous job, as most wells around here were sixty to eighty feet deep. It was also exceptionally hard work. Not only did all the soil have to be winched out, but the sides bricked round as well. The 'digger' went down in a large bucket, with two men at the top to wind the winch."

Well digging has come to fascinate this author. For it was such challenging work – yet it left so little visible result. "If you build a chimney ninety feet high, it's like a national monument," observed one contributor, "but if you dig a well that depth – whoever is there to know!"

Indeed it is the depth of these wells that is so interesting. That at New Barn, Bulmer descends for eighty feet; the one near the Bulmer 'Fox' to ninety feet; Smeetham Hall's is reputed to be, "a hundred feet or more," at Stoke by Nayland one well is allegedly, "as deep in the ground as the Church tower is high," whilst Kentwell Hall's is believed to be 120 feet deep!"

But these simple statistics do not convey the sheer skill and physical labour involved in digging the wells. For every single crumb of soil had to be both dug – and then winched out – by hand. The spoil from Bulmer Tye's ninety foot well, for example, would amount to at least seventy five tons. But not only was there hard, chalky boulder clay to pick loose, but inevitably large flints to be removed in the confined working space.

"And if they hit a seam of sand," comments Tony Dixey of Bulmer Tye, whose late Father occasionally dug wells, "They had to be even quicker with the 'bricking up' – so the sides didn't 'cave in'! And of course, *every single* brick also had to be lowered by hand!"

(Again using the ninety foot well at Bulmer Tye as an example, a staggering *seven to eight thousand* bricks would have been required. Known as 'circumference bricks' they were specially shaped to form a self-bonding circle. The well moreover was bricked in stages as the shaft was dug, using iron pegs and sometimes wooden frames to support the weight of bricks above. However there are records of older wells having *flint walls* – whilst a more modern improvement was the circular concrete ring.)

Yet the well-digger never knew how deep he would actually have to go.

"Over at Belchamp Walter – either at Springates or Newbons," continues Tony, "My Father was digging a well with his brother George when they suddenly 'hit water'. But it came in so fast that whoever was digging had to abandon their tools and be pulled out

"Before they dug the well by Bulmer Fox", relates Geoffrey Dixey, "there used to be a 'land-drain' come across the field from the wood, and into the ditch out the back here, and my Grandfather would put a bucket beneath the drain, and leave it there – and that's where his water came from!" Our illustration shows a typical well-digger's tripod which has just been used to winch up another large bucket of soil. (Some of the buckets had narrower tops to reduce the likelihood of spillage).

in a hurry! In fact the tools are still down there – at the bottom of that well!"

Invariably there were accidents. At Duff's Hill Farm, Glemsford on 29th May 1907, reported the *Suffolk Free Press*, builder Harry Debenham was being winched to the top of a ninety foot well in the bucket. When he had almost reached the top however, the rope snapped and he fell to the bottom where – fortunately – about six feet of water mitigated the effect of the descent!*

*From *Sudbury and District News 1875–1930* by Stephen R. Bixley.

In an age before safety helmets, the well-digger was particularly vulnerable to any pebble that might fall off the bucket as it was being hoisted out – or was accidentally knocked from the top.

"Just after I left school," recalls Geoffrey Dixey (b.1944), "Uncle John dug a well out the back here (at Bulmer Tye), and I had to turn the handle on the tripod to bring up the buckets full of clay. But you had to be careful at the top, when you took the bucket, because if you knocked a bit off and it fell down – well YOU WERE TOLD ABOUT IT!"

Another problem was 'bad air' at the bottom of a well.

"So when conducting repairs," explains Tony Dixey, "they'd often take the lid off a day or two before. But that is when a candle at the bottom was crucial. If it went out they knew the air was short of oxygen. You see it was quite normal to have to go down a well to replace a valve at the bottom or something. In fact when the builders finally finished digging a well they'd place wooden beams across the well at regular intervals so that ladders could be lowered down to do the repair work."

Yet despite the arduous work there were still light-hearted moments:

"When I was about seventeen," recalls Bulmer's Evelyn Reeve (b.1922), they were digging a well at Woodbine Cottage – beside the Halstead road just outside Bulmer Tye. Well I 'happened' to walk by with my step-sister Dolly Hearn, and we knew several of the men there like Pat Jennings, Jack Abbot and Bob Hearn and one of them 'dared me' to go down in the bucket. Well at that age I was game for anything – so in I got! As they were letting me down I thought this is all right – there's nothing to be frightened of at all. But there was something I didn't realise. There was a man at the bottom! The well-digger! I'd forgotten all about him! Oh! He did give me a fright! 'Pull me up!' I yelled. But then as I came up the rope started twisting round and round – and I was jolly glad to get to the top. But honestly – what a trick to play on someone!"

Some years earlier however, Evelyn had herself orchestrated a similar piece of practical joking.

"When I was at Bulmer School we used to go to Belchamp Otten once a week for cookery classes. But as we walked down the road during our lunch time, we saw a well that someone had taken the lid off to do some repairs. However there was no one there – the men had gone off for a cup of tea or something – but they'd left a candle alight in the bottom of the well. 'Course you know what we did! Quick as a flash we pulled the candle up – blew it out – and then lowered it down again! When the men came back they would have thought the air was bad – so how much more they did that afternoon, I do not know!"

Some wells had special characteristics. Ken Day recalls that:
"The water at the well at New Barns, Bulmer was always on the move – as if an underground river was down there. And the well at Batt Hall was also a bit special. You see it had two buckets on it. So as you worked the windlass one bucket went down as the other came up."

Water was of such importance that some villages are now seen in a completely new perspective after interviewing older contributors.

"People go on about Borley!," exclaims Alf Finch (1900–1996), the delightful farmworker whose memories we included in *Heart of our History*. "And drive miles to come here in the middle of the night. But I'll tell you what. It was a bad ol' place for water. That's the mystery for me!

"They were all right at the Rectory because they had their own well. But at 'The Place' (near the Church), they hadn't got any water at all, so it had to be brought up from 'The Hall' (near the river), in a big tank pulled by a horse.

"Then there was them by the cross-roads. They had to come right up to the pump on the 'green' for theirs! Poor ol' Mrs. Turp used to collect her water in a bath on wheels. And Mrs. Scrivener had a donkey cart – with a barrel in it – but if the donkey was in a bad mood it kept slopping it all about! Then there was 'Spring Road' which goes to Belchamp. But the actual spring was down near Jack Gardener's – so old Mr. Pilgrim who lived that way used to get his with a yoke and two buckets."

Sudbury octogenarian Olive Hart, tells of the water supply at the former Methodist Chapel at Smithwood Green, Cockfield:

106

"The actual building," she recalls, "was off the Bury St. Edmunds road, in the middle of the fields between Alpheton and Lavenham. Now there was an elderly lady there who always used to make the tea after the services – and it was a wonderful cup of tea as well! They had a little kitchen place where they could boil the kettles, but they always served it in the Chapel. But one day she said, 'Oh! It's been such a job to get the water today – the pond was covered with duck weed!' And I thought, 'Good Lord! We've been drinking tea made with water out of the duck pond!'"

However we should not forget the medical effects of an insanitary water supply. One time chairman of *Haverhill Family History Group*, Paul Germany continues:

"About 1870 my Grandmother, Emma Brazier of Helions Bumpstead lost three brothers. They were aged 14, 15 and 19 respectively. All had died from typhoid."

A report on, 'The Sanitary State of Helions Bumpstead, visited March 18th to 20th, 1871,' explains:

"The fever is caused by the dirty habits of the people in allowing accumulations of excreta to lie close around their dwellings. Arrangements for the removal of this are very crude ... The privys overhang a ditch, but in heavy rain the filth is carried along the ditch and flows into the roads. The children playing in the roads spread the disease ... What is wanted is a good deep well, but it would have to be 150 feet deep to reach the water table."

In Wickham St. Pauls Churchyard, a gravestone similarly records that Frederick Halstead, "Six years Police Constable of this Parish, died on September 8th, 1896, of Typhoid Fever." He was just thirty years old.

Numerous other accounts of the disease have been recorded. During 1867–8 for example, a THIRD of the inhabitants of the village of Terling, (near Witham), were affected and FORTY FOUR lost their lives*. More famously so too did Queen Victoria's husband, Prince Albert, and William Oates, squire of Gestingthorpe, (when abroad), the father of Captain Oates.

*Haverhill Family History Group, newsletter 1994.

Chapter Eight

WILDFLOWERS; HERBAL REMEDIES; WILDLIFE and WOODLANDS

Two Local Apothecaries

On 13th May, 1738 during the reign of George II and Walpole's long premiership, two men were seen walking beside 'Hilly Field', Bulmer – close to where this book began. In those days however it was known as Kiln Field – and was divided into Great, Middle and Little Kiln Fields respectively. (Due to the lime kilns which had once existed at the Gestingthorpe end of the field.)

The two gentlemen were a Braintree physician, Dr. Samuel Dale – then in his seventy ninth year – and Joseph Andrews (1688–1764), a Sudbury apothecary. Both were devoted to botany and their Herbariums have been preserved for posterity at the Natural History Museum in London.

As Dale and Andrews walked, they came to "a little hillock in the corner of a ploughed field adjoining the way leading from Goldingham Hall by the lime kiln towards Gastingthorpe" (sic). Suddenly the two men stopped and carefully bent down to examine a delicate, rare flower. Andrews had discovered the unusual specimen nine years earlier on 27th May, 1729. Unsure about its identification he had written to Dale for clarification. Now the elderly physician had come to see the plant for himself.

Two hundred and fifty years later there are only two – highly protected – sites in the whole of Great Britain where it still grows.

It was a Military Orchid. *(See painting on centre page iv.)*

LOCAL DETAIL

The *exact* location of the plant is however open to debate. Dale describes the spot as being, 'in Walter Belchamp Parish, Essex'. Yet this does not match the known geography of, "the way leading from Goldingham Hall by the Lime Kiln towards Gastingthorpe." Andrews, who had better local knowledge, described his find as being, "In a little field on the left hand of the gate that opens onto Water Belchamp Causey from Bulmer." (The 'causey' was the long reservoir that supplied Belchamp Walter's water mill.) Note however that the gate *opens onto* Walter Belchamp 'causey'. It is not necessarily in the parish. Additionally the description of 'a little hillock', again suggests the Bulmer side of the Belchamp Brook – as opposed to the Belchamp Valley 'flood plain opposite'.

The likelihood then, is that the famous Military Orchid was found just on the Bulmer side of the brook. Arguably it was at the Gestingthorpe end of our contemporary 'Hilly Field' – since it was here that 'the way' linking Goldingham Hall and Gestingthorpe actually passes. Additionally there was a historic – and long gone – route to Belchamp Walter 'causey' at this point. Finally when Andrews made another visit on 9th May, 1746, he sadly noted; "The place . . . is ploughed up and sown with oats, so I fear it is lost," which again implies that it was not on the 'water meadows' beneath Belchamp Walter Water Mill.*

Yet this is to be pedantic and diminishes our main contention. That Andrews is an unsung local hero. He was devoted to recording wild flowers in the Sudbury area, and his work sheds fascinating light on our local flora some two hundred and fifty years ago.

Today the eleven folios of Andrews's Herbarium are preserved in a small room, near the Natural History Museum's mock Gothic entrance, and famous dinosaur skeleton. Most of the 1,366 specimens that he collected, include details of their location and date of discovery. Indeed because of his research, contemporary botanists now have a superb 'data base' of what once existed in specific places around the town and surrounding countryside.

Musk Orchids for example, have probably been extinct in Suffolk for more than 170 years, yet Andrews observed them, "at BALLING-

*The information on orchids is drawn from a superb article on Andrews' Herbarium by Sarah Thomas in the *Botanical Society of the British Isles News*, September 1997, No. 76. Thomas's article – which we gratefully acknowledge – inspired this chapter and prompted my desire to transcribe more of Andrews's Herbarium.
Finally my thanks to Terri Tarpey of Colchester Natural History Society for her interest in the botany of the farm and area generally.

DON KILN YARD on 15th June 1739." *Man Orchids* – which are now very rare in Essex and Suffolk – were seen in GALLOW HILL GRAVEL PIT, (presumably near Sudbury's Waldingfield road), whilst *Bird's nest Orchid*, which is also a rare species in Suffolk, was recorded at KINGS WOOD SUDBURY on 8th May 1728.

A *Lady Orchid* was identified on 17th May, 1749, "In a field belonging to the AUBERIES, BULMUR (sic)," whilst a *Frog Orchid* was noted, "on the broad green of a field by BROOK HALL, FOX-EARTH," on 28th May, 1747. Although now scarce in East Anglia, Frog Orchids were possibly once quite common as they were also recorded at, "RAYNERS GROVE IN BELCHAMP OTTEN," and, "on pastures at Armsey from Ballingdon [Hill?] . . . a field or two from the road."

Another orchid he identified, *Common Twayblade* is however still relatively plentiful. One of those in Andrews's Herbarium came from CORNARD BRICK KILN YARD on May 13th, 1748, whilst a fortnight earlier he gathered another,

"In a boggy pasture, behind the last house on the left . . . from Milford (sic), before the turn down the road to Lavenham."

Today, this incidental description gives Andrews's Herbarium an 'extra dimension'. For not only can we imagine the more wooded and pastured scenery of our area at the time, but also see Sudbury as a genuinely small town fringed by meadows, woods, bogs, limepits and brickyards. Additionally, the years 1745 – 46, when he added the Bee and Pyramid Orchids to his collection, coincide with the famous attempt by Bonnie Prince Charlie and his Jacobite supporters to recover the throne of England from Hanoverian rule. The Pyramid Orchid obtained at 'Bulmer Limekiln' on 16th June 1746 is of especial relevance, since at the time the Prince was hiding on South Uist, shortly before making his legendary escape with Flora Macdonald, 'Over the sea to Skye'.

Unable to make the journey to London to visit the Natural History Museum myself, I was grateful when my niece Katherine Martland 'volunteered' to spend a day recording more of the Herbarium on my behalf. At lunch time she phoned up with a 'progress report'. "I couldn't believe it!" she exclaimed excitedly, "The first page I opened contained a plant picked in 'Fryars Meadow, Sudbury' – right close to where we used to live – and there are several references to the Bulmer 'Cock and Blackbirds' as well!"

Other examples follow: Punts Wood, (near Bulmer Brickyard), was the location for Mountain Speedwell, whilst at Goldingham Hall Wood, he noted Cowslip, Herb Paris, Marsh Helleborine and Broad-leaved Helleborine. Additionally Fen Violet, "was found in a lay adjoining the wood, in a moist place, where the water seems to stand in winter." (The wood was on the opposite side of the road to our 'Hilly Field' – and is the location for the opening chapter of *The Long Furrow*).

Gallows Hill, Sudbury; Cornard Mere; Link Hills, Maplestead; and Armsey and 'The Kitchen' at Bulmer all appear to have been either favourite areas or particularly rich in wildflowers. Talon-leafed Figwort, for example, was recorded, "In a moist ditch on the right hand going up Kitchen Hill, Bulmur." (Presumably near Batt Hall Cottages, since Kitchen Farm is at the top). Autumn Ladies Tresses was seen at 'Cornard Heath, Cornard Mere and Armsey in Bulmer'.

We shall refer again to Joseph Andrews's Herbarium in our projected book *Countryside Journey*. The following however are a few more selected examples of his plants and their locations:

Identifying Clary on the Sudbury Croft, June 1745.

111

Snap Dragon	"19th June 1743, in a field in Ballingdon called Lords Acre."
Water Horehound:	"In the Churrie Walk at Chilton – going to Babergh Heath."
Clary:	"In the Croft by St. Gregory's, 10th June 1745."
Dittander:	"Upon the bank of the orchard next the croft belonging to the workhouse 3 July 1739."
Scorpion Grass:	"At Hartest in Suffolk on the road side . . . where the brook crosses the road, as soon as the green, towards Brockley. . ."
Stinking Iris:	"In a little pasture on right hand as you go from Brook Street Halstead to Justice Sparrows, Sible Hedingham."
Field Penny Cress:	"Fields by Assington Street, Suffolk and Wisborough Hills, Gestingthorpe."
Strawberry Headed Clover:	"Friars Meadow, Sudbury."
Common Speedwell:	"On Link Hills, Maplestead and thereabout plentifully and in Byham Hall," (Little Maplestead).
Meadow Saffron:	"9th September 1749, in Kitchin Meadow (sic), by the Auberries, Bulmur."
Creeping Jenny:	"Banks behind Borley Mill and on Cornard Mere."
Mouse Tail:	"In field adjoining to Higham's Wood, Cornard on May 1st 1745."
Small Flowered Crowfoot:"	By the roadside between Gt. Cornard Church and the mere."

Lily of the Valley: "In a wood beside road to Hedingham in Bulmur, (Possibly Parsons Wood – where it was still growing recently).

Three of the wild flowers recorded by Joseph Andrews in the Sudbury area.
Left to right: Meadow Saffron, Lily-of-the-Valley and Stinking Iris.

As already indicated Andrews also mentions a beloved – and late lamented – local hostelry in what may be its earliest recorded reference. For on 25th May, 1746, he wrote that Creeping Brown Sedge Grass had been found, "in an old clay pitt in a pasture behind the Cock and Blackbirds in Bulmur," On 5th July 1746, Cyprus Grass and Fox Sedge were noted in the same location.

Almost all of the plants that Andrews identified in our locality appear to be within comfortable walking distance of Sudbury. (Link Hills, Maplestead; Sible Hedingham and Hartest being exceptions.) He certainly came along the road from Bulmer Tye to Hedingham as far as the 'Gestingthorpe marker post', but curiously makes no mention of having explored either of Gestingthorpe's large 'ancient woodlands'. Possibly the whole countryside was so abundant with interesting specimens that he never felt impelled to do so.

✢ ✢ ✢ ✢ ✢

Amidst our enthusiasm for Joseph Andrews we should not forget the uses and anecdotes pertaining to our local flora and fauna which we began in the 'Wildlife Survey' of *The Long Furrow*. Here Colin Ranson of the Nature Conservancy Council explained how to identify ancient woodland. Other contributors provided memories of the uses and traditions of the plants of hedgerow, woodland and meadow. Horace Elsey recalled taking faggots from Butlers Wood, Bulmer to the maltings and bakery in Long Melford with a waggon and two horses. Cecil Smith, whose father was a blacksmith at Felsham in mid-Suffolk, explained that wych elm was used for the hubs of waggons, ash for the fellies and oak for the spokes: 'Jute' Chatters remarked that holly was ideal for walking sticks; whilst the late Philip Rowe described the manufacture of whistles from both horse chestnut and wild oat stalks. In addition Hilda Smith of Wickham St. Paul's compiled a list of the local nicknames of wild flowers, husband Cecil recalled seeing "hundreds of snakes one year at Wickham Hall," David and Tony Minter from Bulmer Brickyard provided a record of birds, butterflies and moths seen on their farm, whilst the thirty year 'Shooting Diary' of Belchamp Walter's Ian Swift clearly illustrated the decline of the local partridge population.

HERBAL REMEDIES

We also discussed an eighteenth century herbalist. His name was John Morley. He lived in Halstead and about 1770 he published a book entitled, *The Nature and Cure of Scrophulous Diseases commonly called the King's Evil*.

(Scrophulous diseases were forms of Tuberculosis affecting joints and lymphatic tissues. The name 'King's Evil' originated from the belief that the illness could be cured by the Sovereign's touch. For example Samual Johnson who compiled the first English Dictionary, was actually 'touched' by Queen Anne in 1712.)

Morley had developed a series of herbal and natural cures, most of which centred on the plant Vervain and its root. (See picture on centre page ii). The latter, he says, should be,

"A fresh common purple vervain root about three or four inches long and about the size of a patient's little finger. Let the buyer take heed. Cut all the fibres off smooth but as little of the rind as possible. The root is to be worn at the pit of the stomach and tied with a yard of white satin ribbon, . . ."

Two copies of Morley's booklet are preserved in the *Essex Archeological Society*'s library in the attic of Hollytrees Museum in Colchester. Both recount his use of Vervain and other plants obtained from our local Mother Earth for healing purposes. (The tenth edition published in 1773 contains thirty five case histories. The twenty second edition dated 1783 contains thirty three more.) In the latter volume, Morley states that he could print many more 'case histories', but that to do so, "would exceed the bounds of a 12d pamphlet."

Many of his original patients had a local origin. We read of Philip Winterflood, a journeyman barber of Halstead aged 35; Deborah Alston of Henny – who had a 'running ulcer' on her thigh and left breast; Elizabeth Golden of Belchamp Walter, wife of John Golden, husbandman; and Esther Markham of Foxearth aged twenty seven.* There are other local cases.

John Butcher of Bocking Essex, for example, was a weaver aged thirty who developed, "a dashing pain and contraction in the fingers of one hand." However, he had several relatives with the 'King's Evil' – which was thought to be hereditary. Consequently Morley prescribed a vervain root. Additionally he ordered:

"A purge of rose leaves boiled in whey once a week. [Also] directed him to boil cabbage leaves bruised in water; and bathe his hand in the warm liquor morning and night . . . and then to rub all the joints after bathing with the Vervain ointment . . . The patient was cured within two months and able to rejoin the Essex militia from which he had been discharged as unfit . . ."

Amongst all of the gruesome descriptions of 'ulcers discharging putrid matter', foul or carious bones that are 'seemingly worm-eaten'; violent boils, partial blindness and disfigurations, these are some horrifyingly disturbing accounts.

*For case histories of Elizabeth Golden and Esther Markham see *Long Furrow* page 210.

CASE IX

"Robert London of Bradfield Combust, aged thirty six . . . was reduced to a mere skeleton. He was brought to me in a Cart with a Bed in it, being unable to move Hand or Foot, or to be moved without great Trouble. I went to the Cart; he looked like a dead Corpse; his Stomach was gone, and his Visage very ghastly . . . I ordered all the Sores to be gently syringed twice a Day with a strong Decoction of Hemlock.

"Milk-warm dry Lint then to be applied, and lest it should stick, Elder Ointment spread on a Rag over all. I moreover ordered him daily half a Dram of Antimony, finely powdered, with an equal Quantity of Loaf Sugar, and to wash it down with Ground-ivy Tea. I also put a [Vervain] Root about his Neck. In three Weeks Time his Stomach returned; his Sores began to heal ; and in two Months the Surgeon wrote he was quite well. This, by many, is called the Running Evil.*

"He was brought to me in a cart with a bed in it."

*Morley's case histories have sometimes had punctuation added or been very slightly rephrased.
'Manna' was the sweet juice obtained from the Flowering Ash or Manna Ash (*Fraxinus Ornus*).

Later Morley explains that elder ointment should be made:

"In the spring by boiling the young leaves in mutton suet, till the moisture is wasted, or in Pork Lard. In Winter, when ther are no leaves, take the tender Bark of the last Summer's Shoots, scrape and boil them as above, and keep for Use."

In Case Twenty Five, Morley treated Peter Raven, a labourer of Earls Colne. The latter had ulcers on his breast, deep consumption, a very bad cough and was greatly emaciated. Yet he was cured so effectively that he was able to leave the workhouse and obtain employment, get married and have a child. Here however Morley used no Vervain root, but instead prescribed:

"A dram of green hemlock leaves (morning and night), in a pint and a half of cheese whey, washing all the sores first with a strong infusion of hemlock. Then to apply elder ointment all over his breast ... After a month I added half hemlock ointment to the elder. ... The cure," he observed, "must be attributed to the Hemlock only."

In Case Twenty Six Morley again omitted the Vervain root. Here John Newton, a weaver of Halstead had an ulcer on his leg so deep that, "the bone was visible with much fungus flesh at the bottom." In this instance Morley recommended putting the leg in hot water from 'a Smith's forge', containing bruised hemlock leaves for a quarter of an hour morning and night. Next the patient was ordered to:

"Take a fresh gathered Carrot, wash and rasp it. Squeeze the Juice out with the Fingers, warm the raspings, and fill the Ulcer with it, quite down to the Bottom, and a little above the Surface of the Ulcer and Leg. Put a dry Cloth over it, bind all on with a Rowler; and repeat this Dressing – and no other – after soaking. This perfectly cured his Leg in ten Weeks, and filled the Ulcer with sound and good Flesh."*

Interestingly carrot was used by Morley in several similar situations. Yet despite the two Case histories above, Vervain Root remained a principal component of his recommendations. In Case XII for example, John Nicholls of Little Ashen near Dunmow, had a scrophulous swelling on his great toe:

117

"I gave this child a small [Vervain] Root; ordered Syrup of Roses and Manna in thin milk . . . for a gentle purge, [and instructed him] to wash his Eyes with the coldest Spring Water every Day. Also a Cataplasm of a Garden Snail out of a shell, beat to a Mash, with the same Quantity of Garden Parsley, applied to the Toe, twice in twenty-four Hours. This perfectly cured the Disorder in three Months."

Following Morley's advice . . .

Elizabeth Hart of Earls Colne had a swelling on her windpipe, "So as to cause a great difficulty in swallowing, her throat very sore within side . . . her lips often cracked and bled." Here Morley prescribed a similar concoction to the above, but also advised her:

"To bruise eight or ten Millepedes or Sow Bugs, make them into a Pill with fresh Butter and when going to Rest let it lay at the Root of her Tongue, so as to melt gradually, till the Soreness within-side the Throat was no more. These Methods in three Months removed all her Complaints."

Despite a temptation to appear conceitedly superior from our modern perspective Morley's treatments were apparently bringing a restoration of health to many suffering and unwell people. One of his most disturbing cases is described on page thirty two. For Mary Tyler, aged thirty six of Halstead, was so disfigured by:

"Monstrous swellings on her face, nose, lips and chin, that neighbours told her she ought for shame to cover her face when she went into the Street; she had many other Breakings-out of the same Kind on both Legs and Arms, which were all very much inflamed."

Morley prescribed a Vervain root, gentle jalop purges and a medicine made from boiling Ground Ivy leaves and Red Dock Roots. Further, he ordered that her mouth be:

"Washed twice a Day with an Infusion of green Hemlock Leaves, and all Scabs on the Face, Legs, and Arms, or other Places likewise. But to be careful she swallowed none, or touched her Eyes. Then to anoint with the Elder Ointment. As she lived by me, I saw her frequently, and sometimes found it proper to add Half Hemlock Ointment to the Elder. It is made by boiling the green Leaves of Hemlock, bruised in Hog's Lard, and strained: . . . She is now well, and her Face clean and smooth, and no scrophulous Symptoms. *Note.* All Ointments should be boiled in earthen Pots; for Metal is corrosive."

In addition to Mary Holmes of Monks Eleigh, Aaron Wiskey a shoemaker of Polstead, William Ardley a weaver of Coggeshall, and Joseph Traylin, a cooper from Toppesfield, Morley uses two local people to illustrate the age range of his patients. Samual Pain for example was "an infant of Clare." Whilst in Case XXXV we read of George Hoggerill a former under gardener, for Esquire Honeywood (possibly at Marks Hall, Coggeshall), who was aged eighty eight!

Yet he was also receiving testimonies from much further afield. Newmarket, Wymondham in Norfolk, Faversham in Kent, St. John's Lane, Cambridge; Maldon in Yorkshire; Godalming in Surrey, and Princes Risborough in Buckinghamshire, all provided case histories.

The aristocracy are also mentioned. Lady Rachel Austen of North Audley Street, London, recommended Michael Nail a shepherd from Wendover, Buckinghamshire to visit Morley in January 1771. The Right Honourable Countess Marchmont informed Morley of a cure effected in Scotland by a reader of his pamphlet. John Hickman, gardener to the Right Honourable Lady Bateman of Great Yeldham, wrote to Morley in February 1776 to testify that his ulcerated hand had been cured, whilst Lady Gray of Charles Street, Grosvenor Square, London provided another recommendation. In the latter case, Morley claimed he had prevented the amputation of a leg – which other doctors had deemed necessary. Similarly he had been, "fortunate to cure some scrophulated breasts deemed to be cancerous."

Unlike the treatments ordered by many of his contemporaries, Morley's cures were never extreme:

"It is gentle easy methods," he declares, "not rough prescription and painful applications that are most efficacious in this obstinate disorder."

Even though, "Some stubborn cases have not submitted to my mild and gentle treatment" he refused to use, "Dangerous methods and medicines. I dare not use," he says, "or venture on that hazardous practice of Kill or Cure."

At the end of both editions Morley summarises his treatments and guidance. He claims to have treated nearly 5000 people who have applied to him with "Scorbutic, Scrophulous and Cancerous diseases during more than twenty years practice." (Scorbutic illnesses relate to scurvey). In a table of some 2000 of his Scrophulous cases he lists 774 male and 1224 female patients. 521 were aged between ten and twenty years old. But he is approaching old age. He does not send out medicines and will only advise people who visit him. "Nor," he explains, "will my almost worn up eyes, suffice to give any directions in writing." Nevertheless,

"Persons, though ever so poor and distressed are welcome to consult me for advice in person . . . on any morning from ten to twelve, and in the afternoon from three to five of the clock, (Sundays excepted), if I am well," He repeats that he charges nothing and declares, "All that I have related in strict truth, nor do I take any money for my advice . . . Many, many guineas have been offered me; but I never take any money . . . The pleasure I take in relieving the afflicted affords me the highest (contentment), and satisfaction."

His essay is published, he states, "for the good of mankind. Particularly the common people." Undoubtedly he brought relief, health and hope to many suffering and distressed individuals. His pamphlet also sheds light on the methods of other practitioners at the time. And there is something else. His potions and ointments came almost entirely, from the gardens and the hedgerows of our local, Mother Earth.

Numerous other plants of woodland, hedgerow and meadow had uses. Bracken was utilised for littering livestock, clamping root crops and for packaging fragile goods. Locally 'Brakey Hill' in Bulmer, and 'Brakemoor Hill' in Middleton derive their names from the plant, whilst there is also a Fern Hill in Glemsford. Broom still enlivens our local 'light land' hedgerows with its spring time flowers. (And surely requires no explanation of its traditional use!). Baskets meanwhile were made from willow, osiers and bulrushes.

"It was quite a regular thing years ago," says Tom Rowe. "Farmworkers would make baskets from bulrushes to take their food in when they were working all day in the harvest fields. They called them 'frail baskets'. My Father got some from the Stour at Liston, and then another time, from a pond at the top of Bardfield Hill in Bulmer."

Even Ergot – a fungal contamination of wheat, had a purpose. Administered by midwives during difficult childbirths, "it induces contraction and eases the birth," says Dorothy Hartley in *The Land of Britain*. Yet the dose was critical. For scores of girls with unwanted pregnancies were also given ergot, by 'someone who knew', since it can further stimulate miscarriage and abortion – when convenient. (In large doses, ergot can also lead to insanity and other disorders. At Wattisham Church in mid-Suffolk, a plaque commemorates a whole family who suffered gangrene in their feet after eating ergot in their bread).

During the Second World War, bullace plums were reputedly required by the 'authorities' recalls Eddie Tuffin of Alphamstone.

"Apparently they extracted something out of them for guns or ammunition – at least that's what we were told!" he recalls. "Well in the old gardens there was nearly always a bullace tree years ago. But down the bottom of Mr. Stuck's orchard at Coppins Farm here, it was all bullace trees – and he got a Pound a bushel for them at Halstead. So one autumn we had to keep on picking them in all the cold and wet – we did days and days of it! – Huh!"

One of the 'minor wonders' of the old countryside were people who could eat bullaces without the addition of sugar.
   (It still is!)

"My wife's Grandmother did!," exclaims Eddie with a laugh. "When I was at work I'd pick a little bunch for her – and she'd sit beside the fire and eat them one by one. Cuh! It would have drawn my mouth up! But she'd have them – especially after they'd had a frost and gone a little white!"

'Maiden Hair'. So dainty was this now relatively rare plant that many older contributors recall it with great nostalgia. Sudbury's Phyllis Golding vividly describes, "a patch of Maiden Hair growing in a small meadow where there were also lots of 'peggles'. It was between the top of the Waldingfield Road and Chilton Church." (Now almost certainly part of the Industrial Estate). Kathleen Grimwood (b.1901), similarly remembers Maiden Hair on the Freemans Meadows near the River Stour, and "Harebells beneath Brundon Hall."

As a country boy in the 1930's Gestingthorpe's Dick Halls (b.1921) has an interesting ornithological memory:

"When I was about fourteen or fifteen, I was down at Rayner's brickyard, (i.e. 'The Clamp'), when I saw a *pure white* 'blackbird', singing its heart out on a willow tree! I searched about for ages to find its nest – and eggs – but I never could. Some years later however I was with Spencer Coe in his lorry taking sugar beet to Felstead Beet Factory, when I actually saw a speckled Blackbird, that was half white and half brown!"

Those in our old countryside who developed special powers over wild animals are inevitably remembered with awe:

122

""There used to be an old half-bred vet in the village called 'Ratcatcher Brown'," recalls Gillman Game of Glemsford, "And he could somehow 'draw rats'. One time he happened to say to a farmer in this village, 'Master you've got some rats about here – perhaps I can be 'of service'." "No," the old farmer replied, "There's nothing to worry about. I don't need you about here." Well because he'd 'crossed him', that farm was overrun with rats within a week!

"Another time at Blacklands Hall in Cavendish there were so many rats that the farmer asked Brown to come and help. Anyway Brown went to the farm. But then he told everyone to clear off – so they shouldn't see what he was doing! When he was alone, he went to the barn, got some straw and mixed it up with 'something else'. Then next day they put some wire round this straw and all the farm men got sticks – and they killed scores of rats there!"

Thus to the ancient woodlands of our Suffolk-Essex border. For the author, they are like our parish churches or ancient buildings. Once 'inside them', one feels humbled by the history they have seen, and the continuity they represent. Yet, unlike the reverence induced by some peaceful, white-walled parish church, the woods inspire an even stronger urge of wonderment and awe. They are quite şimply, an eternal linking with our Mother Earth; a visible manifestation of nature's benign providence.

Some of our woodlands may have been managed, through coppicing, since Roman, if not Iron Age times. (By charcoal burners, iron workers, brickmakers, hurdle-makers, thatchers, potters, carpenters, etc.). And thus it continued for centuries to follow. In 1603 for example, Thomas Appleton bequeathed, "Ten loads of wood to the poor of Little Waldingfield to be continued for ever." On August 9th, 1678, the Rector of Earls Colne, Ralph Josselin, noted in his diary:

"Cleared Chalkney Wood of my share of poles, faggots and long-wood, without any considerable hurt to beast and waggon . . ."

Just over a century later our woodlands were given the following values by Mr. Vancouver (circa 1790).

	Undergrowth at what stage cut (Years)	Value at stubs shillings/acre
Bulmer	12	95s
Ashen	12	120s
Belchamp St. Paul	12	120s
Great Maplestead	14	120s
Little Yeldham	14	140s
Braintree	15	160s
Gosfield	12	170s
Ridgewell	16	180s
Sturmer	14	200s
Birdbrook	15	270s

Yet a great change was already taking place. In 1791 Arthur Young had observed:

"Woods in this part of Essex are grubbing up (sic) and converted to tillage, which pays much better even when the growth of timber is taken into account."*

In about 1805 he recorded that the grubbing had particularly occurred, 'in the vicinity of Halstead,' and mentioned that Mr. Sewell of Little Maplestead had removed sixty acres of woodland and Mr. Saville at Bocking, forty. Additionally, an old workman had informed the latter that, "Five hundred acres of woodland have, within living memory, been grubbed in this immediate vicinity."† (Locally two thirds of the thirty acre Goldingham Hall Wood, Bulmer, where Joseph Andrews found several specimens were removed at about this time).

Whilst the first crops of cereals after woodland, reported Young, 'answered well', Lewis Majendie identified a consequent problem:

"Wood is now a dear article," he wrote to Young on 24th March, 1795, "and becoming more so yearly from the great quantities stubbed up. It is, I believe, generally agreed, now cheaper to burn coal than wood."**

*Young 1791: from *Annals of Agriculture*, Vol. 17.
†From *General View of Agriculture of Essex*, circa 1807.
**Annals of Agriculture*, Vol. 24.

Although wood continued to be, "the common fuel of the poor," wrote Young in 1805, the great traditions, skills and crafts of coppice and woodland were already being abandoned. In a headlong drive for new forms of technology they were almost forgotten. Thankfully the principles of woodland management have not only been saved and rekindled but are now receiving positive encouragement.

For the ancient woodlands of our Suffolk-Essex border are not merely visually beautiful and aesthetically pleasing. They are something more. Quite simply, the oldest, most elemental living product of our local Mother Earth.

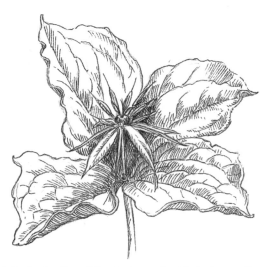

Herb Paris. Another of the specimens Joseph Andrews collected from Goldingham Hall Wood, Bulmer.

COLLECTING WOOD ASH FOR POTASH MAKING

One potash maker from Bures, states the Victoria County History of Essex, reputedly travelled through large areas of North Essex with a drove of eight or more donkeys purchasing ash from cottages and farmhouses.

After collecting ash from wood, straw, peas and bean haulm, the potash was obtained by a process involving repeated wetting and heating. Potash itself was used in dying, soap making and washing clothes. However, in areas of hard water the housewives often refused to sell their ashes, preferring to use them to 'soften' their own water for the weekly washing.

Potash making continued until the early nineteenth century. The industry is, however, still commemorated in 78 field or place names from 64 Essex parishes. Locally, these include 'Potash Fields' in Bocking, Felstead, Gosfield, Sible Hedingham, Pebmarsh, Toppesfield, Ridgewell and Wethersfield. Similarly in South Suffolk there was a 'Potash Pasture' at Newton, a ten acre 'Potash Field' at Groton, a nine acre 'Potash Meadow' at Lavenham and 'Potash Farms' at Polstead, Brettenham and Great Bricett. (Largely extracted from the Victoria County History of Essex Vol II, Essex Field Names by W. C. Waller, and the tithe awards from individual Suffolk parishes.)

PART TWO

MIGRATIONS:

– PEOPLE ON THE MOVE AND RURAL REBELLION –

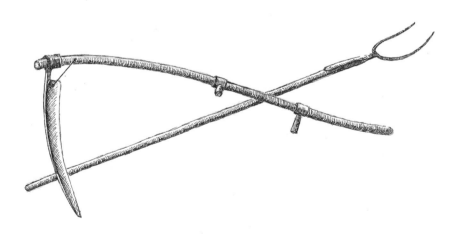

Chapter Nine

THE DIARIES OF A LONG MELFORD FARMER

"Between 1880 and 1940 there were two severe depressions in East Anglian agriculture. Every aspect of rural life was affected . . . the 1890's witnessed some of the worst years in the first cycle."

John Row farmed at Long Melford and Foxearth. His farm diaries from 1888 to 1898 have recently been discovered – and kindly lent to the author.

When the diaries commence Row was the tenant of a forty acre holding known as Kings Prentices. In September 1889 he also hired the fifty seven acre Highlanders Farm from Sir William Hyde-Parker. (Kings Prentices lies between Melford's main street and the new by-pass, whilst Highlanders adjoins Mills Lane and is between the by-pass and Newman's Green, Acton).

In 1895 Row also took on Lower Hall, Foxearth, before releasing Highlanders Farm the following year. Lower Hall's total acreage is not revealed but included some sixty-six acres of 'cropped land' in addition to possible grass leys and meadows, etc.

The diaries are a very special source of research and I must express my sincere gratitude to Mr. Geoffrey Jackson of Cavendish for allowing me to use them. I am especially indebted since they superbly illustrate local agriculture in those years.

Row had begun his career as the Station Master of Long Melford Railway Station, where he was also the passengers' insurance agent. (Insurance was then taken out for train journeys). In 1867 this developed into the fully fledged insurance business which still continues

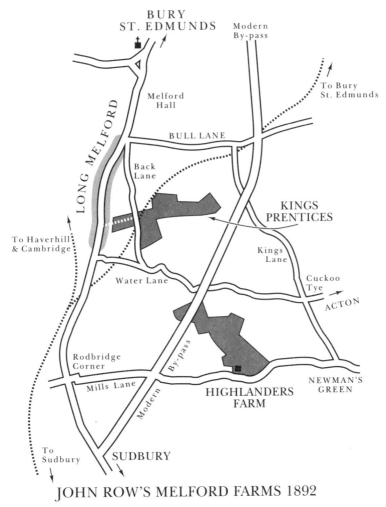

BURY
ST. EDMUNDS

Modern
By-pass

To Bury
St. Edmunds

Melford
Hall

BULL LANE

LONG MELFORD

Back
Lane

KINGS
PRENTICES

To Haverhill
& Cambridge

Kings
Lane

Cuckoo
Tye

ACTON

Water Lane

By-pass

Rodbridge
Corner

Mills Lane

Modern

NEWMAN'S
GREEN

HIGHLANDERS
FARM

To
Sudbury

SUDBURY

JOHN ROW'S MELFORD FARMS 1892

as C.J.N. Row & Sons Ltd. at the original offices in Hall Street, Long Melford. Later he also began farming and dealing in hay and straw. At some point however a small tower was added to the house which adjoins the Office, prompting locals to grumble, "He only had it built so he could see if his men were working properly on his farms!" (An impossibility I think as regards Highlanders Farm and Lower Hall, Foxearth. However, the tower may have been of some genuine benefit in noting railway movements for his forage business, whilst he could certainly have seen his fields at Kings Prentices).

John Row's Insurance Office in Hall Street, Long Melford. Note the tower on adjoining house.

Either way, the comments in his 'farm diaries' contain all the human emotions, whilst continually revealing similarities between the problems he faced – with those which confront us today. As the harvest of 1898 approached, for example, he soberly notes:

"July has been a fair month, but too cold and variable. Not at all like summer weather . . ."

One suspects it was a difficult season, for on Friday, August 7th he wrote tersely:

"Windy day. Commenced Harvest upon 'White Wheat' on Field no. 6 at King's Prentices. Exactly one week later than in 1897." (Row at the time was farming King's Prentices and Lower Hall, Foxearth).

But the day was particularly symbolic. For it was the first occasion – I believe – that Row had ever used a binder. It was not a happy introduction.

130

"Tried a second hand Hornsby 'Self-Binder'," he records. "Cut about 1¼ acres only. When I went home at 6 o'clock the whippletree had JUST BROKEN!" (i.e. the cross bar which enabled the horses to pull the binder).

His entries for the following ten days have some of the glum frustration that so many of us experience in a difficult harvest.

"Saturday 6th. Cut about ¼ acre in half an hour. Then commenced raining and rained all day long."

On Sunday 7th, he declares in dramatic red ink:

"RAINED ALL DAY LONG. *Heavily too,* from 6.0 a.m. to 6.0 p.m.!"

Of the 8th, 9th, 10th, 11th, he observes with sour impatience:

"No work possible: wet and windy."

On the 12th, he reports:

"Finally finished cutting wheat on Field No. 6. Sent machine to Foxearth . . . Very heavy crop of wheat, but 'down' (i.e. 'laid') in many places, had to use Hornsby's reaper as the binder *could not touch it.*"

In The Long Furrow, *the late Cyril Philp explains that as a crop became more 'laid', the farmer had to revert to more elementary systems of harvesting. In this instance Row has simply replaced the 'self-binder', (which cut and tied the corn into sheaves), with a 'reaper' which merely cut it.*

In the worst seasons however, 'laid' areas would still be cut by scythes or even sickles. (In addition to the headlands which were always cut by scythe – to 'open the field up').

It was becoming a wet and bedraggled harvest. Whole fields were 'laid'. Chickweed, cleavers and bellbine entangled the crop. Wheat was beginning to 'shale out'. The farmer was becoming anxious. But the situation worsened. On the 17th August he despairingly wrote:

"Broke part of Hornsby reaper."

131

Harvest had been halted again! Row was desperate. The time for decisive action had come. He brusquely continues:

"Wired Nicholls that I should go to Bury in afternoon. Requested him to meet me."

Underlined in the red ink that emphasises the momentous – and doubtless difficult decision taken, he declares:

"Bought a new Massey Harris Binder. It was at Thetford, but got it home on Thursday at 4 o'clock. Set to work at 12 o'clock on Friday. Did its work cutting barley on Melford Home Field *wonderfully* well."

How thrilled the writer was! How relieved he would have been. Goodwill would have radiated from his face . . . But can life ever be this straight-forward? On the next day he scrawled:

"Saturday: Only wanted 10 bouts to finish the field when the horses – by a sudden jerk, smashed three castings and rendered the ACCURSED MACHINE USELESS!"

Spare parts were not available locally. On Monday 22nd, our diarist:

"Went to Massey Harris's London depot, at 54 Burnhill Road. Obtained duplicate castings which were sent to Melford by 11.45 a.m. train. Machine was in working order, (by Bulmer Jim), at 5.0 p.m. . . ."

What would happen next in that harvest of 1898 we wonder: Would the weather hold? Would the castings survive? And what about that field of 'laid' wheat which had just been battered by a full week's rain?

It is this 'daily detail' which makes the manuscript so fascinating. Indeed I was soon sitting up – night after night – deciphering the diary and thinking of those far off seasons and problems.

Moreover as I go about my own routine – of 'top-dressing', spraying, harvesting and cultivating on the undulating fields of Bulmer and Gestingthorpe, I often think to myself, "I wonder what Row was doing <u>exactly</u> *a hundred and ten years ago today?"*

The 'sincere gratitude' proffered to Geoffrey Jackson at the beginning of the chapter – and also to his nephew David – who today farms at Red House Farm, Foxearth, is not a mere 'author's acknowledgement'. It is a most genuine and heartfelt expression of appreciation for so enriching this phase of my research.

We return to August 1898:

"Tuesday 23rd: Started carting barley off Home Field . . . only six loads left in the field when a sharp shower stopped us at 6.30 p.m."

"August 26th: Took machine to Foxearth and cut all the barley there with it. The crop was dreadfully laid and very unsatisfactory."

The pessimism continued:

"Sunday 28th: Rained in the afternoon."

"Monday 29th: Rained at 4.45 p.m. but got six loads of barley on to the stack. Of course, he adds dismally, ". . . in bad condition."

On the following day the weather improved:

"Tuesday 30th: Glorious day. Started at 2.05 p.m. on Bearlams, and by 7.22 p.m. got out 24 loads of barley off just 8 acres. A heavy crop. A record!" (The precise timings are Row's.)

The tide had turned. For a few days the entries are brief and optimistic. On August 31st he wrote just one word: "Glorious" . . . The brevity continues.

"September 1st: Glorious. 2nd: Glorious! 3rd: Glorious!!"

At last harvest was going to plan. No problems are recorded. The weather was blissfully settled. The following day was a Sunday. The horses and stock would have been fed but no land work would have been undertaken. The binder would be silent; the farmer would

133

probably have attended Long Melford Church. Possibly he strolled round his acres before dinner, but Row no longer felt a sense of frustration. Once again his entry declared:

"Sunday September 4th: GLORIOUS!!!"
(The exclamation marks *are* Row's).

Victory was in sight. A whole year's investment had almost been garnered. On Monday 5th, he ecstatically exclaims:

"<u>HAPPY AND GLORIOUS</u>! Only 4 loads of barley and 3 loads of wheat and rakings to cart."

The 6th, 7th and 8th of September were devoted to carting the rakings; then Row changes his pen. In the bold red ink that he reserves for his most ebullient observations, he exclaims:

"FINISHED HARVEST on 9th at 6.30 p.m. Settled up on 10th and men took the day for a holiday."

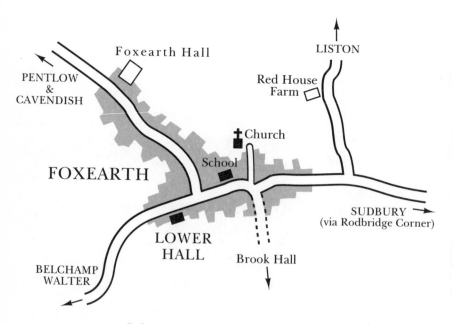

LOWER HALL, FOXEARTH

An Indian summer followed. In the first weeks after harvest we see Row "clearing out ponds," (so crucial for livestock), "thatching stacks," and "threshing 163 quarters of corn at Melford." Yet as the weeks went by and the dry weather continued the farmer again became anxious.

On September 13th he complacently wrote, "Fine weather continues." On 17th however he bluntly observes that Bearlams Field was, "too hard to plough." Seven days later the week's summary is compressed into just one despondent line:

"No rain all week."

On October 2nd he frustratedly notes:

"A dull week. But still no rain."

But the following seven days were no better and on October 9th, Row's pent up exasperation finally explodes:

"NO RAIN!" he scrawls. "SEVEN WEEKS DROUGHT. No water in ponds. Carting water every day. Have been ploughing wheat stubbles since Harvest. Have broken TWO ploughs and used up several dozens of shares!"

How we can share his frustration. Is there a farmer or gardener who hasn't experienced something similar?

On October 15th the weather finally broke and henceforth he describes the normal processes of autumn work.

"October 19th: 'Ploughed in' the Winter Beans on 'Common Field' [Foxearth]. Put one ton of Superphosphate fertiliser on about 6 acres. Getting mangolds carted."

"November 5th: Ploughing on 'Great Field' [Foxearth]. Getting ten acres of clover land ready for wheat. Put on ten loads of Farm Yard Manure per acre."

On November 7th the first wheat was sown (on 'Great Field', as above). "It went in well," recorded Row optimistically.

135

The sowing of wheat continued for the following fortnight and was completed on November 26th. Thereafter the entry for December is contained in just eleven words:

"December 1st to 31st.   Usual winter work. Ploughing, threshing, hedging etc."

For the farmer himself however, the misty weeks before Christmas provided – just as today – a good opportunity to catch up with the mindless drudgery of office work. The diarist continues:

"Balanced up year's accounts."

And dare I print the final sentence from John Row's diary of 1898? Will I not be banished from the N.F.U. forever? Will John Brand or David Jackson who farm at Foxearth today ever talk to me again? Can I not convince myself that the writing is indecipherably illegible? Must I really be a good historian and commit a heresy such as this?
Indeed the last line of Row's script is more convoluted than usual. Perhaps he too had to make the admission in an hieroglyphic that could defy his inner sense of treason. For there – as if penned with a painful and excruciating reluctance – he has scribbled:

"Am well pleased at profit realised."

*   *   *

To be able to see Row's actual figures – for the light they shed on his various farm enterprises – is especially interesting. (At the time he was farming Kings Prentices and Lower Hall, Foxearth and therefore had approximately 102 acres of 'cropped land').

1898

Receipts	£	s	d
Hay, Straw and Chaff	250.	2.	0
Milk, Butter and Eggs	45.	0.	0
Stock	255.	19.	8
Corn	752.	5.	1
TOTAL:	1303.	6.	9

Expenditure	£	s	d
(Labourers) Wages	230.	9.	10
Manures and Cake	44.	10.	0
Repairs; Wear and Tear	31.	10.	11
Corn, Hay, Straw	209.	2.	10
Stock Bought	189.	3.	2
Coal and Labour for Threshing	75.	9.	9
Tithe, Rent, Rates and Taxes	198.	7.	2
Veterinary, Harness and Blacksmith	9.	11.	11
TOTAL:	988.	5.	7

After allowing for his annual 'stock-taking valuation', Row made a profit for the year of £265.3.7d. As we shall later discover however, this was his second highest profit of the decade.

II

"To Be More Serious"

Although I have taken a light-hearted approach to Row's diary for the autumn of 1898, it would be misleading to leave the matter there.
To complete the chapter we will investigate his fortunes during the previous decade. Let us start then, with a glimpse at Row's ledger nine years earlier in 1889.

August 29th: Sold to Squirrel ... 29 coomb of wheat @ 17/9 per 'coomb' (£7.88p/ton).

November 7th: Sold to Branwhite ... 142 coomb of barley @ 17/6d .... (£8.65p/ton).

At these prices, the total return from wheat was £6-15s to £9-0-0 an acre. (Assuming a 'good average' yield of 16 to 23 cwt. an acre i.e. seven to ten 'coomb').

137

Yet at the same time he was paid £4-0-0 for a calf by Messrs. Ruse. (In other words the calf was worth half as much as an acre of really good wheat.) Similarly the two bullocks which sold for £18-6s each on February 4th below were worth well over double.

Figures can be made to prove (or disprove!) almost anything! Yet it is surely of interest that a century later the value of an acre of wheat – compared with that of a bullock or calf – is still in <u>roughly</u> the same proportion. Unfortunately however the fluctuating price of cattle since the B.S.E. crisis began makes exact comparisons particularly difficult.

In the following years other items include:

January 16th 1890:   Sold to Allen – 5 pigs................ £10   10s   3d

February 4th 1892:   Sold 2 bullocks to
                     Messrs Ruse............................. £36   12s   0d

January 20th 1890:   Sold to Cadge – straw..............   7s   6d

March 7th 1890:   Sold to Woodgate – faggots......   4s   0d

March 5th 1891:   Sold to Payne – 20 coomb of
                     wheat @ 19/- (£8-44 a ton)....... £19   0s   0d*

The crucial prices are those for wheat. It is here that we need to be more serious. For Row's price of 19/- a sack, (or £8.44 a ton), was barely *two thirds* of what it had been forty years before. Before the trickle of wheat from the American prairies had become a veritable flood. Before the price had steadily fallen for four decades.

LOCAL NAMES
*A hundred years later the RUSE family are still butchers in Long Melford, the SQUIRRELS grain merchants in Bildeston and the BRANWHITES, who have already been noted, farm at Belchamp Otten. Meanwhile the CADGE family are still represented in Long Melford and the PAYNES still farm at Belchamp Otten. In 1891 when they also owned Borley Water Mill, Row actually sold them a fair proportion of his wheat. As one contributor explained: "In those days they almost had sufficient land to justify owning the mill – and additionally did a little merchanting as well."

The 'coomb sack' above, contained four 'bushels' of corn. As such a sack or 'coomb' of wheat weighed 21/4 cwt. (18 stone or 114 kg). A sack of barley weighed 2 cwt (16 stone or 101 kg), and a sack of oats 12 stone or 76 kg.
By comparison a sack of beans weighed nineteen stone and clover twenty stone. Commenting to Cyril Philp that carrying clover sacks was exceptionally heavy work, he wryly commented, "Oh yes. It what you call used to 'press your socks down'!"
There are twenty 'hundredweight' (cwt.) in a ton.

The following is the *average* price per ton of wheat for each decade:

	£	s	d
1820	15	0	0
1840	14	11	7
1860	12	8	4
1880	10	6	7
1890	7	8	4

Depression had ensued. At Belchamp Walter an attempt to reduce farmworkers wages resulted in the strike of 1894.* Yet land was going out of production. During the altercation it was revealed that

*From *The Long Furrow,* Chapter Six. The prices of wheat come from *Agricultural Records,* by J. M. Stratton, published by John Baker 1978. Between 1875 and 1894, 124 MILLION acres of land were added to the cultivated area of the United States *alone.* By comparison the *total* acreage of England and Wales – including cities, mountains and road-ways – is just 37,336,960 acres. (Moreover Canada, Australia, South Africa and New Zealand were similarly increasing their cultivated area!)

two 'heavy land' farms in the Belchamps had already been abandoned, whilst *Bulmer: Then and Now* records, "that even the Auberies 'Home Farm' showed a deficit in some years."

Not surprisingly, Row's diary reveals a decline. By May 1893 he was selling wheat for 13s-3d a sack (or £5.88 ton.) After the harvest of 1893 he kept his wheat 'right round' to the following summer. Yet the price did not improve.

April 26th 1894: Sold to Squirrel......... 50 coomb of wheat @ 13/- (£5.77 ton).

July 21st 1894: Sold to Payne........... 40 coomb of wheat @ 12/6 (£5.55 ton)

The underlining is again Row's. How we can imagine him – irritated and frustrated as he returned each Thursday from Sudbury's Corn Exchange – with the price of his wheat still declining. But the following year was worse:

April 25th 1895: Sold to Clovers......... 30 coomb of wheat @ 11/- (£4.88 ton).

The depression had reached its nadir: land *was* going derelict: farms *were* being abandoned. In May 1896 the inevitable happened. Wheat temporarily rocketed to 26/- a coomb (£11.55 ton) – but probably because nobody had any left to sell! However when we leave the diaries in 1898 prices had become somewhat less volatile at around £6.46 to £8.00 per ton.

Row also meticulously lists his expenses. On October 7th, 1889 for example, he purchased half a dozen plough shares from King Downs of Gestingthorpe Iron Foundry. Their cost? Three shillings and sixpence. Other items include:

Jan 31st 1889	Goodchild: Seed wheat................£1	4s	9d.
Feb 26th	Dixey: re fine beer......................	6s	9d.
May 18th	Ward & Silver (of Melford):		
	Barley roll £6	0s	0d.
Aug 14th	Baldwin: White sow pig..............£1	4s	0d.

Sep 12th	Ransome & Co.: New plough......	£3	6s	0d.
Jan 9th 1890	Coe G.: Straw for thatching.........	£2	0s	0d.
Jul 1st	Sir Wm. Hyde Parker: rent.........£25		0s	0d.
Jul 20th	East Anglian: Advert...................		3s	6d.
Mar 2nd 1891	Orbell Threshing......................£29		9s	2d.

Seven years later there were still plenty of local names:

Jul 28th 1898	Francis: hire of sacks...................		9s	0d.
Sep 23rd	Boardman: 1 cow.......................£13		5s	0d.
Oct 12th	Chapman: 2 foals......................£35		10s	0d.
Jan 19th 1899	Spilling: harness........................	£1	8s	5d.
Jul 27th	Woods: Mending binder wheel ...		4s	0d.
Aug 16th	Kings: Mangold seed..................	£1	5s	0d.
Sep 21st	*Chinnery: for thatching stacks ..		18s	6d.

So how keenly did Row – on his slightly kinder soils – feel the depression that was so affecting his heavy land neighbours?

We are especially privileged to have his books, for 1898 was an exception. Indeed in the early eighteen nineties farmers who were paying a large rent, had no capital reserve, or were struggling with difficult soils, faced very severe pressure. Row at the time was a tenant and in 1890 paying a seemingly high rent of £2/acre.

In the very worst years then, when harvests were bad, or when wheat was only worth five to six pounds a ton – this rent must have seemed crippingly high. (Especially remembering that a ton an acre was a good crop). Indeed in 1891 our diarist notes that at Kings Prentices Farm – where he was paying £2 an acre plus tithe – the landlord would henceforth become

LOCAL NAMES

*DIXEY is a long-established name in Bulmer, Pebmarsh and Halstead; the COE'S were threshing contractors from Gestingthorpe and Bulmer, one also being involved in a footpath dispute in 1559 – see *Heart of our History*, p.15). There are still ORBELLS in Cavendish and Clare. FRANCIS was a Sudbury corn merchant with premises between the 'Bus Station' and Station Road; BOARDMAN was possibly a member of the Sudbury, Clare and Haverhill auctioneering family. Examples of SPILLINGS and CHINNERY still exist in the area; Joe Spillings of Gestingthorpe appears in *'Heart of our History'*, whilst Michael Chinnery of Pentlow today sells ploughs. Finally, KINGS the seed merchants of Coggeshall also continue – and have recently celebrated their bi-centenary.

141

responsible for the latter. At Highlanders Farm, the original rent of £105 on 51 acres was reduced to £71-5s-0d. However rents in the locality would continue to decline and, on heavy soil, landlords eventually offered vacant farms "RENT FREE," rather than have no tenant.

Nine years later in 1900, Mr. Goodchild of Clare told Rider Haggard that, "If he desired, he could hire 10,000 acres within a radius of ten miles at an average rent of seven shillings an acre." On the Marquis of Bristol's estates in Suffolk, (principally around Ickworth near Bury St. Edmunds), rental income actually halved – from £19,319 in 1880 to £9,590 in 1905.*

To have Row's actual figures is a real bonus for we learn that in:

		£	s	d
1888 he made a profit of............	266	5	4
1889 " " " profit of............	151	4	3
1890 " " " LOSS of	32	7	6
1891 " " " profit of............	122	17	4
1892 " " " LOSS of	402	18	0
1893 " " " profit!!! of	7	16	11
1894 " " " profit of............	106	19	5
1895 " " " profit of............	14	13	0

(The exclamation marks are again Row's).

Yet Row's accounts have allowed *nothing* for his own income – or any return on his capital invested. Indeed if we allow him a salary of just thirteen shillings a week, (i.e. that of a head horseman or junior bailiff), and deduct the resultant £28.50 a year from the farm accounts the final balance for the years 1888 – 1895 becomes:

Surplus accumulated in profit years................ £669

LESS losses accrued (£435) together
with personal wage for 8 years £663

After eight years work and investment, there was just £6 'return on capital'.†

Row was barely holding his own. Dejection was inevitable. On August 6th 1894 wrote glumly:

---

*West Suffolk Record Office.
†From 1896 to 1899 – when the diary ends – Row made a healthier profit of £217 per annum – or £189 after 'basic wage'.

142

"Raining slightly. No harvest work."

Then there is a space. The following twelve months were summed up in just two lines:

"Such a miserable wet time at the harvest – proved so disastrous to the whole district that I gave up memorandum."

It was two years before he resumed it.

Perhaps – in a human sense – this disillusionment by a once 'keen man', sums up the state of farming in the mid 1890's more perfectly than limitless figures or statistics.

Yet the crisis was to be nationally acknowledged. On June 2nd 1894, the *Essex and Suffolk Free Press* records that the Chancellor of the Exchequer had been questioned in Parliament. The subject was a Royal Commission on Agriculture. Astonishingly it revealed some '60 MILES OF DERELICT FARMS in the county of Essex.'

In the following year it was similarly stated:

"Suffolk could be GIVEN AWAY to anybody who will take it." (British Parliamentary Paper XVI pp 392, 365.)

So severe was agriculture's dilemma that a famous author, Rider Haggard, travelled the country investigating farming's predicament. In 1901–2 his findings were published in a book entitled *Rural England*. (Haggard, who was also a Norfolk landowner, is actually more famous for writing *King Solomon's Mines*.) Of local interest he reports:

"At Newton Green I was told by a Mr. Gardiner that: 'a nearby farm which had sold for £70 an acre had recently changed hands for £7-10s/an acre'. At Henny Ryes, Colonel Barnardistan gave "no cheerful account of agriculture in that locality," whilst at Melford Hall, Sir William Hyde Parker declared that, "tenants were scarce except for the best land. FOR THE HEAVY LAND THEY WERE NOT FORTHCOMING."

At Cavendish, Mr. Ambrose "could see no hope for the future of Suffolk agriculture," whilst a Mr. Ray of Clare pointed out:

"Grain can be shipped from New York to London for 1s-4d a

bushel. However from Clare to London, which is only fifty-six miles distant the cost is 9d to 1/-. The only salvation for the wasting countryside was Protection."*

On this, all were agreed. Indeed, Mr. Gardiner cryptically described the much vaunted 'Free Trade in Food' as simply being "PROTECTION OF OTHER NATION'S CORN!"

Yet for the actual farmworkers who worked the land, impoverishment was nothing new. For them it had existed throughout most of the nineteenth century.

MORE LOCAL NAMES
*The GARDINER family also farmed at Borley Lodge and Jenkins Farm, Bulmer. The Mr. Gardiner quoted here is the great-grandfather of contemporary Little Yeldham farmer John Gardiner, and was associated with the parish's Manorial Court, (see 'Heart of our History', p.16). The family were also highly active in the Tithe War (See Chapter Twelve). Both the BARNARDISTONS and HYDE-PARKERS are 'old gentry' – the latter's descendants still occupying Long Melford Hall. Mr. RAY of Clare is a probable ancestor of John Wayman who today farms in Cavendish, whilst Mr. AMBROSE, "who saw no hope," is the grandfather of Basil Ambrose who pioneeringly established the 'Cavendish Manor Vineyard' in the 1970's.

Possibly the most memorable moment in Far From the Madding Crowd: As Sergeant Troy indulges in a drunken harvest horkey the beautiful Bathsheba assists dedicated farm foreman Gabriel Oak to thatch the stacks as a monumental thunderstorm approaches.

When published in 1874 Hardy ascribes a value of £750 to the eight stacks that Oak is struggling to save. Yet if he had written the book exactly twenty years later, when John Row was farming at Melford, they would only have been worth £338-10s-0d.

Yet even Oak himself – the archetypal British yeoman, was to consider emigration.

"Leaving England", said Bathsheba in surprise and genuine disappointment, "Why Gabriel, what are you going to do that for?"
"Well I've thought it best", Oak stammered out.
"California is the spot I've had in my mind to try".

(Several of Hardy's other characters including Angel Clare in Tess of the d'Urbevilles, Donald Farfrae in The Mayor of Casterbridge and Arabella in Jude the Obscure also consider emigrating.)

145

Chapter Ten

EMIGRATIONS

"The Countryside Abandoned!"

"My brother (Abram) is uncomfortable about the state of things in Suffolk. They are as bad as Ireland – 'never a night without seeing fires near or at a distance'."

(John Constable writing to his friend Fisher in 1822.
From *John Constable's Correspondence*)

In 1835 an incidence of arson occurred on a Toppesfield farm. It was almost certainly a protest. A protest against chronic rural poverty; the introduction of threshing machines and the New Poor Law of 1834. The culprit was apprehended – and hanged. Even in those hardened times the case provoked debate and the *Colchester Gazette* despatched a correspondent to the village.

"It was a Monday in May; a time of the year when many kinds of farm work can be carried out to an advantage, yet in four adjoining parishes NO LESS THAN 200 ABLE BODIED MEN WERE WITHOUT EMPLOY.
"The unemployed labourers had been reminded of the facilities of emigration, but alas their answer to this was a ready one. Here they at least had sufficient to maintain existence, but feared that if they went abroad they might be left to die of hunger."*

*From the Colchester Gazette of May 18th, 1835. In the same year, one George Cranfield was also hanged for arson at Bures.

146

Yet emigration would increase, provoked by the harshness of rural life, the population explosion of the nineteenth century and the depression in agriculture from about 1880. It was compounded by the demise of cottage spinning in the late eighteenth century, and again by the sudden decline of straw plaiting between 1879-81. In just two years, the plaiting industry – which had so benefitted north-east Essex – was effectively destroyed. The farmworkers income had again been cut. And so, year after year, as the grinding struggle continued, the attraction of leaving one's birthplace increased. Initially work was sought in other parts of England.

"Before I was born," explains the late Bill Yeldham, (b.1908) of Little Yeldham, "men from round here would *walk* to the marshes near London to cut the hay. They carried their own scythes and a 'rub' and would return with about five pounds."

Another to go went from the village of Elmsett near Hadleigh.

"His name was Flasky Cousins," records local historian Janet Cooper, "but apparently when he and the other Suffolk men crossed into Essex – on the Cattawade Bridge near Manningtree – they always used to shout out, 'Good Bye to Old England!'"

To the author's surprise the 'marsh-work migration' continued into the twentieth century.

"Oh yes!" declares Tom Rowe of Bulmer (b.1903), "For several years my wife's uncle, Fred Theobald, went hay-making along the Thames at Foulness. In fact I almost went with him one year!"

There were other destinations for the unemployed farmworkers of Suffolk and Essex. For 'Northern Labour Agents' were sent round to recruit them. Some at the turn of the century joined the Liverpool Police Force. Others went to the maltings at Burton on Trent. Indeed George Ewart Evans estimates that during the 1890's, "As many as four hundred East Anglian workers were going to Burton each year."* (As the northern malting season lasted from September to June, the men hoped to find harvest work on local farms on their return to Suffolk.)

*From 'Where Beards Wag All', published by Faber and Faber.

Although the majority were recruited from north Suffolk, a few went from Bury St. Edmunds – with a smattering from other villages. (For instance Alfred Hiskey went from Elmsett, and in 1890 a Philip Meade went from Belchamp Otten.) However there are other local examples:

"Until the First World War time," recalls Boxford farmer's son, Claude Alleston (b.1912), "a number of men still went from Hadleigh to Burton-on-Trent each year. And when they came home – at the end of the season, they used to bring back tea pots from the potteries – as gifts for their mothers and girlfriends."

Another destination was Yorkshire.

"In fact three of the 'day-men' who worked for my father at Red House Farm went to Yorkshire," continues Claude, "there were two Martens and one of the Pattels. Then there was 'Conger' Marten – who went from Elmsett. They actually went two or three years running – although I'm not certain if they stayed for a whole year or not."

Interestingly, Oliver Prentice of Cavendish Way, Sudbury and retired farmer Bill Yeldham spontaneously provided other examples of local men working in Yorkshire. So too did Tom Rowe:

"Archibald Barrell? Oh yes! He came from Lower Houses, Bulmer. But before the First World War he'd go up to Yorkshire and work on the land 'for a year at a time'. I believe the idea was that they'd lodge in the farmhouse to be on hand for the livestock and milking. But to get work they first had to go to the local market. I suppose it was a bit like a 'hiring fair'."

(One wonders if the native Yorkshiremen had found more lucrative employment in the mills and mines? Rider Haggard certainly reported that agricultural wages were higher in Yorkshire than in Suffolk).

"The point is this," states Oliver Prentice (b.1913), "In my younger days, Suffolk was as hard up as anywhere – if not worse. Oh no! People would go *anywhere* for work.
"When I was a child," he continues, "we lived at Bildeston. But I

often walked with my Mother to Stoke by Nayland, and even as far as Coggeshall and Witham for the pea-picking. At Stoke Park we worked for Geoff Wier. We used to sleep underneath an old seed huller and get water from the stream. It was a tough way of life for all of us – especially my poor mother."

Other men – and women – made more permanent moves. Bulmer's John Dixey, whose ancestors have lived in the area since at least the sixteenth century, is typical of many in recounting:

"About 1850 one of my great aunts went to London to get work 'in service'. But from the next generation no less than FIVE members of the family – including my grandfather left the village to work there. It's extraordinary really – but so too did my other grandfather who was born in Twinstead!"

Astonishingly, by 1851 no less than THIRTY TWO THOUSAND Suffolk born people were already resident in the capital.*

"There were so many lads from Castle Hedingham," states Adrian Corder-Birch, "that by the end of the century they had actually formed their own club!"

In December 1898, the Gestingthorpe Parish magazine provided, "The address of a London Church, that helps rural lads find accommodation." At Wickham St. Paul, The Girls' Friendly Society recorded five 'service' positions being found in the capital between 1912 and the early twenties. One of them was for farmworker's daughter Ida Bird (1895-1993), the remarkable – and inspiring – nonagenarian whose reminiscences we included in both *Heart of our History*, and in the Prelude to this book.

Simultaneously, local newspapers carried advertisements to emigrate to the Dominions. On June 2nd, 1894 the High Commissioner for Canada informed readers of the *Essex and Suffolk Free Press*:

"160 acre farms are being GIVEN AWAY . . . The country offers free schools and good wages."

*From *Chartism in Essex and Suffolk* by Arthur Brown. Published by Essex Record Office.

In the same issue the Agent General for New Zealand invited readers, "to write for particulars of the reduced fares available to intending settlers." In the *Halstead Times* of October 9th, 1909, the Australian Emigration Officer announced:

"100 FARM HANDS are URGENTLY wanted; Good posts guaranteed to each; Part of the fare will be paid."

Similar advertisements appeared week after week . . . year after year. The inevitable occurred. Village populations began to decline. Among the best "human" sources are School Log Books. From Gestingthorpe's of 1875 we learn:

"Several children bade us farewell, their fathers having had employment offered them in Lancashire."

Eleven years later, the teacher reports:

"The children have generously decided to give a weekly dinner to thirteen of their school fellows whose fathers are unemployed."

At Wickham St. Paul, the schoolchildren sang, '*The Emigrant Ship*' to the School's Inspector in 1874. At Bulmer the headmistress obtained thirty copies of *The Visit of Tenant Farmer Delegates to Canada in 1890* – as reading material.* At Alphamstone, Amelia Wells charts a steady diminution of pupils. In November 1908 she dejectedly wrote:

"Two children have left during the month and gone to London . . . Today only fifteen children on register . . . meeting of committee to discuss closing of school . . ."

The following year the school she had served for thirty one years shut its doors for the final time. (It is now the Village Hall.)
At nearby Twinstead the school was closed in 1905. At Middleton

*For these references I am again grateful to Arthur Brown and the late Basil Slaughter. The quotations are extracted respectively from their *Notes on Gestingthorpe 1693 to 1903* and *Bulmer: Then and Now*. (Both Bulmer W.E.A.)

it lingered on until 1916. At Gestingthorpe the number of pupils fell drastically. (From an average of 98 in 1898 – to just 33 in 1918).

On the land itself the area under cultivation in England and Wales actually dropped by over TWO MILLION acres between 1866 and 1893. In the single decade 1871 – 1881 the number of farmworkers diminished by 111,000.

Not surprisingly there was real concern lest smaller villages should die entirely. (As happened to Culford Heath north of Bury St. Edmunds); and that whole areas of Eastern England would revert to wilderness. We recall the pessimistic depositions at the Hedingham to Long Melford Railway Enquiry where Gestingthorpe's rector protested:

"Half a dozen lads have recently left the parish unable to get work" In December 1897 he similarly wrote, "There is a very grave question in all rural districts – caused by the steady exodus of young men from the country to the large towns. In our own case the population has fallen by OVER A HUNDRED since the census of 1891."

It was a preoccupying theme. For Gestingthorpe's population was then about 520. But the most grim statistic comes from Dr. Arthur Brown. Lecturing at Bulmer W.E.A., he pointed out:

"When agriculture reached its lowest point in 1894 .... there were more unemployed than employed in this area."

In strictly local terms the population of most villages fell by approximately 25 to 30% between their numerical peak, (usually around 1851-1871), and the census of 1901. In the worst affected parishes such as Alphamstone, Great Henny and Toppesfield, all with difficult soil types, the population almost halved. In Little Maplestead it did actually drop by over 50% between 1841-1901. By 1891, one house in seven was unoccupied.*

*From the excellent *The Maplesteads: Then and Now*. Published by Maplestead W.E.A.

Corroborating our comments on soils, Arthur Young says of Toppesfield, "It is a parish with NOT a single acre of turnip land." (The latter was the best, most productive and easily worked soil – especially in the 'horse era').

East Anglia had become a derelict backwater. Like today's 'inner cities' it was comparatively deprived, lacked amenities and provided poor job opportunities for young people.

But the isolation continued until the Second World War.

"When I was a boy, in the 1920's," declared Alf Weavers of Henny, "everyone tried to get away from the countryside and into the towns! The villages hadn't got any facilities. No electricity, no mains water, no gas, no proper sewerage and not much work! What's more, if you did stay 'on the land' you were looked down upon. You were regarded as an 'old clodhopper'. A country bumpkin!"

During these austere times some villages at least had the brickyards, rural foundries, corn mills or 'Big Houses' that generated some degree of employment. (Foxearth for example had 'Ward's' brewery, Glemsford the silk and mat factories, Middleton a brickyard and maltings, whilst Gestingthorpe had brickyards, a pottery and iron foundry.) Other parishes however seemed unduly deprived. As farmworker Jute Chatters (b.1910) sadly observes:

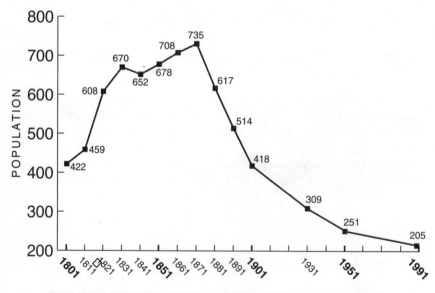

BELCHAMP WALTER'S POPULATION 1801–1991.

152

"Belchamp St. Paul and Belchamp Otten were very poor places. Just tumbledown cottages, everyone hard up and half the bloomin' farms gone derelict. Well there wasn't anything else was there? No brickyards. No industry. Nothing. What ever little business did exist, was a one-man affair – like Henry Cornell at the windmill. What's more, there was nobody of any real consequence living about here. That didn't help either. I mean a 'Big House' made no end of work for gardeners, game-keepers, cooks and parlour maids. But I honestly believe that Walter Belchamp was even poorer than we were."

(Corroborating Jute's comments, Belchamp Walter's population declined from 735 in 1871 to 309 in 1931. Its present population is less than half that of 1801.)

PARISHES WITH EXCEPTIONAL POPULATION DECLINES

North Essex	1801	1851	1901	1931	1951	1991
Alphamstone	237	324	170	153	184.	181
Belchamp Walter	422	678	413	309	251	205
Bulmer	421	807	645	561	559	568
Finchingfield	1606	2594	1333	1129	1109	1714
Gestingthorpe	544	819	475	434	403	397
Great Henny approx*	300	427	216	160	163	126
Little Maplestead	298	367	193	209	209	299
Pebmarsh	423	683	422	382	447	434
Pentlow	275	380	274	197	191	131
Ridgewell	483	808	518	357	448	458
Toppesfield	685	1051	652	483	520	497
Wickham St. Paul	316	425	253	225	229	296

*In 1801 Great and Little Henny's combined population was 357. In 1811 Great Henny was listed separately with 314 inhabitants, whilst Little Henny had a population of 51.

Both the rate of population increase – and decline – appears to have been slightly less pronounced on the Suffolk side of the border:

Indeed the Hinkford Hundred which comprises 49 parishes in North East Essex and includes Braintree and Halstead, saw a rise of **50%** in its population berween 1801–1851 followed by a decline of **18.4%** by 1901.

By compartison in the Babergh Hundred (being the Borough of Sudbury and 32 surrounding parishes), a population increase of **35%** between 1801–1851 was followed by a drop of only **7.5%** by 1901.

Nevertheless, the figures from the following *rural* parishes are still of interest.

Suffolk	*1801*	*1851*	*1901*	*1931*	*1951*	*1991*
Alpheton	204	370	244	189	219	243
Assington	471	776	560	429	381	361
Brent Eleigh	243	269	182	195	190	165
Cavendish	1042	1394	902	716	638	973
Chelsworth	234	255	199	165	174	133
Lt. Cornard	279	380	282	268	246	294
Hartest	646	832	537	440	373	440
Kersey	513	714	482	360	401	317
Newton	354	499	334	278	341	444
Gt. Waldingfield	564	659	462	348	564	1354
Poslingford	253	371	285	248	220	197
Hundon	824	1218	741	592	579	1457

Especially relevant are comparisons made with the 1801 census – before the population explosion of the following half century. For with the single exception of Bulmer, all of the parishes in the table above had higher populations in 1801 than in 1931, whilst over half had a higher population in 1801 than 1991.

Consistently isolation and remoteness from a market town exacerbated the late Victorian decline. (Note for example Pentlow, Wickham St. Paul, Pebmarsh, Gestingthorpe, Kersey, Alpheton, and Hartest).

By comparison, Bulmer, Clare and Bures, which had marginally larger populations in 1901 than a century before, had the benefit of either 'small town' status – or in Bulmer's case – proximity to Sudbury.

The decline fuelled a vicious circle. The fewer the inhabitants, the less cobblers, bakers and shopkeepers were required to supply them. The less land there was 'in production' the fewer blacksmiths, wheelwrights and harness makers were needed to support it. The whole of rural life was affected. At Belchamp Otten, the windmill dropped in value from £350 in 1845 to just £70 in 1892. Possibly because things were more stable in 1911 it then fetched £200.

Maybe we are revealing the unexpected in our local history. For we tend to think of our villages as being quintessentially stable, solid and enduring from generation unto generation.

Yet it was an era – as was shown in *The Khyber Connection* – when the interest in foreign news was insatiable. When week after week the *local*, (and often only) newspaper, carried strident reports of imperial expansion, geographical discoveries and hardy pioneers pushing the frontiers forward.

Rural mentality at the time contained an almost bizarre dichotomy. Every farmworking family had its uncle who had served with the army in India or Africa; its brothers who wrote twice a year from Auckland or Ontario and its daughters who were parlour maids in London. And yet conversely, at a time when "there was no such thing as a holiday," there were still others, "who had never slept outside the parish of their birth."

Many of those who did emigrate would not have seen the sea before they sailed. Few would have been to London.

There was an additional – more stirring impetus towards emigration. It was the National Agricultural Labourers' Union. The latter was formed in 1872. It was led by the great champion of Victorian rural workers – Joseph Arch. And its impact was immediately felt along the Suffolk-Essex border.

155

Arch himself visited nearly all the villages of our area. Initially he was assisted by one Charles Jay, a sympathiser, of Codham Hall, Wethersfield.

In May 1872 a meeting was held at Crouch Green, Castle Hedingham. Six hundred people attended. Here, Jay not only identified surplus labour as a cause of low pay, but passionately urged migration to factories in the north of England, the Liverpool Police, the Newcastle Locomotive Works and to Gateshead farms – where better remuneration awaited.

"Almost at once," reveals Arthur Brown in his fascinating book, *Meagre Harvest,* "scores of men, some with their families, went north, including 108 who left Braintree station for Newcastle."

The following year, the farmers of our area attempted to 'lock out' men who had joined the union.

"The N.A.L.U. immediately supported the dismissed men," continues Arthur, "providing not only 'lock out' pay, but additional opportunities for work in the North of England. Parties of 19, 25 and 58 – mostly young men – moved to Carlisle to work on a railway expansion scheme. 21 left Little Maplestead and 50 left the Belchamps *on a single day.*" (Again from *Meagre Harvest.*)

Yet the crowning achievement of the Union's policy occurred in 1874. For an entire ship, the '*Saint James*', was chartered by their officials and filled with three hundred men, women and children of farmworking stock from Suffolk and Essex. On April 14th that year, they sailed from Tilbury, Essex, as emigrants to New South Wales, Australia.

(We wonder if the strength of the Union in North Essex accounts for the more rapid depopulation of villages there, when compared with South Suffolk? Little Maplestead for example – whose population decline was extreme – had a particularly vigorous branch).

Yet even when the Union went into partial decline the departures continued. For despite being prompted by the exigencies of low pay and unemployment, emigration had also caught the 'spirit of the age'.

Indeed for many, emigration to the dominions was not merely an opportunity to gain full employment. It offered something more. The possibility that, 'on some wide tract of virgin territory' a man might eventually become his own master . . . and even the owner of land!

This chapter in fact was inspired by my surprise at *how many* of our farmworker contributors had relatives overseas.

Farmworker's daughter Ida Bird (b.1895) of Wickham St. Paul provides one example:

"I had six brothers and two sisters and my brothers all worked 'on the land'. Anyway, the oldest three brothers went off to Australia in 1910 and the others went in 1922, 1923 and 1933. One of my sisters went out to Africa and another went to Clacton, so out of the entire family, I am the only one to have remained in Wickham!"

"Why did your brothers choose Australia?"

"Because Reverend Shuttleworth, who was our vicar, had been a missionary out there and often spoke about it. [7] But originally one of my brothers was actually very keen to go to America."

"Why was that?"

"Because we had FOUR uncles there! They were all farmworkers by the name of Butcher and came from Gestingthorpe. But it's interesting you know, because one of their sisters went to look after them. And then she stayed as well! She actually got married out there – to a man called Ives. And he came from Foxearth!"

In our modern age of mobile telephones, E-mails and budget flights around the world, it is difficult to remember, or imagine, the finality of separation years ago. But how did Ida's mother actually feel as she bade farewell to her three eldest sons in 1910 – knowing that unless they truly prospered she would never see them, or hear their voices again? And what emotions did she then experience as her other sons and daughters later made their own departures?

Gestingthorpe's History Recorder Dorrie Pannell – whose ancestors have been wheelwrights and brickmakers in the parish for generations past – recounds a similar tale:

"In 1902 a seventeen-year-old lad who had worked as a page

157

boy for Mrs. Oates at Gestingthorpe Hall, went out to the Canadian prairies. However, he had already become friendly with my great aunt Edith, and during his absence they kept up a steady correspondence. Six years later, in 1908 he sailed back to England – and asked her to marry him. She did! They returned to Canada as true pioneers and 'homesteaders'. And although conditions were very hard, had twelve children! But she wasn't the only one to emigrate. Because my father's uncle went to New Zealand. It's extraordinary really because Cecil and I are the only Pannells left in Gestingthorpe – but we've got nearly a hundred relatives abroad!"

It wasn't only the young who were part of the movement. Blacksmith's wife the late Daisy Nice (b.1900) of Gestingthorpe continues:

"My grandfather was a shepherd in Suffolk – latterly at Newton Hall – but at the age of SEVENTY SIX he actually emigrated to America where nine of his twelve children had settled."

Another septuagenarian emigrant was the author's 'pot-making' hero, Edward Bingham of Castle Hedingham. Also aged 76, he too left his village about 1905-6 to join two of his sons in the United States.
Some village lads led extraordinary lives.

"Bertie Hasler," wrote his son Douglas, "was born at Toppesfield in 1881. His father was a thatcher but at eighteen he joined the army as the Boer War was on. He served in South Africa, Transvaal, Orange Free State and Cape Colony. Eventually he returned home, resumed thatching and got married – besides taking the 'Rising Sun' pub in Castle Hedingham.
"In early 1914, however, he went to Australia to join the Gold Rush. He left my mother with three small girls and enough money to last until the family could join him. But before he could get established the war started, so he returned to England and joined the Army, seeing service in Egypt. Finally he settled down in Gestingthorpe."

Bertie Hasler was not alone in leading such an adventurous life. Retired Maplestead farmworker Cecil Cook, spoke of his own grandfather, John Layzell, who was *also* born in Toppesfield (in 1863) – and later became the landlord of the Little Maplestead *'Cock'*.

"But he didn't always keep a pub," explained Cecil, with a twinkle in his eye.

"What else did he do?" I asked politely.

"Well, he was a shepherd boy to start with." Then Cecil paused. Before quietly announcing, "But then he ran away to sea . . . and sailed around the world in windjammers!"

Fortunately, the *Halstead Gazette* printed a graphic account of the shepherd boy's years aboard the 'stately square rigged ships' of the South Pacific and of stormy Cape Horn; of being away for nine to twelve months at a time, and of shortening the sails on a swaying mast – maybe a hundred feet above deck. (Layzell was interviewed shortly after his ninetieth birthday in 1953):

"After thirteen years at sea," the article continued, "Layzell returned to Toppesfield. But could still not find regular employment. Despite now being married, he had to leave his wife behind, to again seek work. Eventually he found it at a saw mill near Vancouver, in Canada.

"When – eighteen months later – he again returned to East Anglia, there was still no work. Fortunately Mr. Adams the brewer, gave him the opportunity to take one of his houses – *'The Victory'* at Wickham St. Paul. Ten months later he moved to *'The Cock'* at Little Maplestead."

But what of that most jarring revelation of all? Of John Layzell having to leave his wife and return to Canada in an effort to support her?

The emotional strain of waiting for letters from a husband thousands of miles – and a FOUR MONTH journey from home – can hardly be imagined.

And yet these feelings *have* been vividly described. In a most stirring account of rural life – slightly to the north of our area – at Ashdon, Helions Bumpstead, and Glemsford. The book – *Reuben's Corner* – is the childhood autobiography of Spike Mays (b.1907). First published in 1969, it was hailed as a classic and has been reprinted many times.

In 1911 however Mays's own father also went to Canada in a similar attempt to support his family. But the Canadian work schemes had been exaggerated. Mays's father could not even find continuous work. He was not alone in being disillusioned. One November afternoon shortly before his death, Gestingthorpe farmworker Bert Surridge (b.1907), quipped – without any prompting:

"If they'd built a bridge to Canada when I was young, you wouldn't have been able to cross it – for all of them who were trying to get back!"

Yet in 1913, relates Cecil Cook, thirteen members of the Binks family left Little Maplestead and emigrated to the same destination. Local history can sometimes be confusing!*

Yet even if some of the rural emigrants were disillusioned with what they found – what were agricultural conditions like in the far off dominions? What were the differences that the shy Suffolk farm boy actually discovered when he finally arrived in Canada or Australia? Although we move forward by twenty years the answers are directly relevant to our understanding of the decline of East Anglian farming – and the depopulation of our local villages. As such we are especially fortunate to have the memories of two existing contributors, the late Bob Pinhey who spent eleven years in Canada and Philip Lawson who was six and a half years in Australia. It should be emphasised that both were farmer's sons and neither had families to support. Yet both did leave East Anglia to improve their prospects in the nineteen twenties. Partly from their accumulated savings they were eventually able to start farming in their home counties.

Bob Pinhey was born in 1903. Robust and strong, he later farmed at Weston Hall, Liston near Melford. When I visited him at his retirement bungalow at Cavendish – in his eighty-third year – he vividly explained:

*Not all emigration was voluntary. Glemsford historian the late Richard Deeks , explains that transportation lasted from 1787 to 1868. Interestingly, there was a Suffolk man on both the first and last boats. In 1855 one Bulmer resident, Mary Hurrell received Four Pounds in poor relief, because her husband had been transported.
By complete contrast, a farm 'to train young men in the agricultural skills necessary to become colonists' was established at Hollesley Bay, near Ipswich.

Building Gestingthorpe Church Tower

It is early summer in the mid 1520's, (date approximate), and the red brick tower of Gestingthorpe Church is nearing completion. As the parson, architect and gentry converse in the foreground, mortar is being mixed and bricks unloaded near the tower. Almost certainly the chalk, sand and clay which were used – together with the flints in other walls – were obtained from the parish's very own soil.
(See Chapters One and Two).

i

John Morley of Halstead handing a Vervain root to a young girl to cure her of a
Scrophulous Disease, about 1770.

John Morley of Halstead's Herbal Remedies

In the illustration below we can see a Vervain root (his principal recommendation), which had to be:

> "worn at the pit of the stomach and held with a yard of white satin ribbon, half an inch wide around the neck of men and women of ordinary stature...but no other coloured ribbon must be used because the dye may be prejudicial" (He is holding the white satin ribbon in his left hand in the illustration opposite).

Vervain

Also surrounding the main picture are some of the other items used in his natural remedies. (Clockwise from the top) – Fig, Carrot, Hemlock, Groundsel, White Dead-nettle, Millipedes, Sow bugs, Damask Rose, Cabbage, Garden Snail, (with Parsley, and Ground Ivy), Sorrel, Vervain (with root), and Elder. Additionally, ground Antimony, Green Broom, Dock, Mallow and Lily were also used. Many of Morley's patients had forms of tuberculosis and were horrifyingly unwell with swellings, tumours, sores and ulcers. (For more on Morley's 'alternative cures' see *pages 114-120).*

Although found on highways, courtyards and uncultivated places in Morley's time, Vervain is now quite rare in our area.

* An earlier John Morley of Halstead had risen from being a butcher to a wealthy Halstead citizen. Together with one Samuel Fiske he paid for the market place to be paved in 1705. We wonder if the two John Morleys were related? (From *Discover Halstead* by Percy A. L. Bamberger. Published by Halstead and District Local History Society, 1982.)

Wild Flower Enthusiasts, 1738

Sudbury apothecary Joseph Andrews shows Braintree doctor, Samuel
Dale (standing), a rare Military Orchid somewhere close to Hilly
Field, Bulmer, on 13th May 1738. *See pages 108-113.* (We have imagined the scene as being close to the Gestingthorpe end of the field
near 'Chalk Pit Hill', with the Belchamp valley in the background.)
    Also illustrated are other orchids which Andrews recorded on
botanical forays around Sudbury. (From left to right, opposite page):
    Lesser Butterfly Orchid found at Link Hills, Maplestead on
        27th May, 1746;
    Fly Orchid discovered at Acton Lane, Sudbury on 25th May, 1744;
    Fragrant Orchid, again from Link Hills, Maplestead, (but on 14th
        June 1744);
    Green Winged Orchid;
    Military Orchid which is in the centre of the group;
    Early Spider Orchid noted on 3rd May 1745 at Gallow Hill Gravel
        Pit, (presumably near Sudbury's Waldingfield Road);

iv

Pyramid Orchid, recorded at 'Bulmer Limekiln' on 16th June 1746; *Bee Orchid* found at 'Middleton Hall Brickyard' on 17th June 1745; *Marsh Helleborine* observed at 'Woodhall between Acton Lane and the Hall' (Sudbury) on 7th July 1746.

"Of the twenty three orchid species in Andrews' Herbarium," writes Sarah Thomas, "seven are still reasonably common, nine are rare and seven are locally extinct. The Lesser Butterfly Orchid for example is now unknown in either Essex or Suffolk; Fragrant Orchid is rare in Suffolk and bears only one contemporary record in Essex; whilst Early Spider Orchid has not been recorded in Essex or Suffolk for the past two hundred years."

From *Orchids from the 18th Century Herbarium of Joseph Andrews (1688-1764),* by Sarah Thomas, published in the *Botanical Society of British Isles News,* September 1997, No. 76.

Andrews incidentally was almost certainly a relative of the Robert Andrews featured in Gainsborough's famous picture.*

* The Andrews family tree reveals several Josephs. One moreover was actually Robert's elder step-brother. Even more significantly, that Joseph Andrews was born – and also died – in the same years as those attributed to Joseph Andrews the apothecary and botanist. It is likely therefore – but not yet proven by this author – that the two were step brothers. (With thanks to Andrews's descendant, Lavender Hawkins of Milden for use of the Andrews family tree, and to Edith Freeman of Sudbury for further assitance.)

Gainsborough's Puzzling Farming Painting

Thomas Gainsborough's painting of Mr and Mrs Robert Andrews, is one of Britain's most famous pictures. Executed about 1750, it depicts the young squire, (b.1726), and his wife Frances, (nee Carter, b.1732), who was just sixteen when she married. They are seen in the grounds of Bulmer's premier estate, *The Auberies*, which is not far from Ballingdon Hill, and overlooks the valley towards Sudbury.

Frances originated from Ballingdon, and had been married at All Saints Church, Sudbury on 10th November, 1748. The couple were to have nine children and are both buried at Bulmer Church. However, the story is not entirely felicitous for the latter died in 1780, aged just forty eight.

Yet the picture contains an agricultural mystery. It is this. How were the rows of corn actually planted in straight lines?

The initial 'convenient' answer to our question is that a 'seed drill' was used. Indeed, many articles on Gainsborough make this assumption – since in 1701 Jethro Tull had developed such a machine and in 1733 published his seminal book, *The New Horse-Hoeing Husbandry*.

In Gainsborough's picture moreover, Mr and Mrs Andrews are on one side – enabling the viewer to look right down the rows of corn and see how free of weeds they are! Apart from one poppy near the front sheaf there is hardly a weed in sight just as if the field might have been ' horse-hoed'.

There is then a *possibility* that the seed was deposited by an early drill and that Andrews as a keen agriculturalist wished to permanently record his progressive husbandry in the picture.

However, other techniques also existed which enabled crops to emerge in rows. In 1784 for example, Arthur Young recorded that Kent farmers used special ploughs consisting of "one, two or three shares which formed *little furrows*". The corn was then broadcast by hand – but after harrowing emerged in crude lines enabling them to, "hoe the crops more than once".

Indeed, a similar observation was made within LIVING MEMORY!

"In the 1920's," recalls the author's father, "Bobby Bryce at Hintlesham (near Hadleigh) sowed some fields by hand over ploughed land. But do you know, they were so well ploughed, and the ridges so regular, that when the wheat came up, it was in rows – almost as if he had used a seed drill!"

Equally pertinent was the practice of 'spraining', (or dribbling the seed into the *furrows by hand*). Indeed 'spraining' was specifically described in Essex by a writer named Fitzherbert in 1532. Two hundred and fifty years later, Arthur Young actually noted that the practice *still continued* in the county and explained, "In some counties they sow 'under the furrow' in the spraining method: a seedsman to every furrow."*

(These seeds would also almost certainly emerge in rows – like winter beans which are still 'ploughed in' today.) Finally the crop may have been 'dibbled in' and the seeds individually deposited in straight lines. Yet although 'dibbling' was recorded in 1660, Young implies that it was a comparatively recent introduction to Suffolk in 1784.

What though of the near absence of weeds in the rows? Could this imply that Andrews was following Tull's drilling and horse-hoeing system? Not necessarily. For many traditionally sown crops of corn were also kept 'clean' by hand hoeing, observed Arthur Young.

In fact in 1785 – over THREE DECADES after the picture was

---

* From *The Farmer's Kalender*, published 1805.

painted – he categorically states that Andrews was "sowing his wheat", presumably by broadcasting or 'spraining', but actually drilling his peas. (Probably using a crude implement known as a 'drill-plough'.) Moreover if Andrews had been planting his wheat with a seed drill, Young – who had an infinite enthusiasm for recording every aspect of a landowner's farming technique – would definitely have mentioned it.

Indeed, it is another local estate owner, Lewis Majendie of Hedingham Castle, who provides our next glimpse into the use of a genuine seed drill. For writing to Young on 6th March, 1792, he declares;

> "When I first commenced the practice of drilling my crops in October 1786, the country around me were *strangers to the idea...*"

How then was the crop sown 'in straight lines' in the famous picture? Had Andrews possibly tried an early 'seed drill' in his youth – when Tull's ideas were still quite fashionable – but later abandoned it for sowing wheat because the early drills were too unreliable?

The answer – quite simply – is that we do not know. The mystery however continues – and readers must draw their own conclusions!

What else do we know about Robert Andrews's farming practices? Undoubtedly his husbandry was highly respected. "Mr. Andrews of *The Auberies* whose cultivation does such honour to this country..." declared Rev. Onley of Stisted Hall in a letter to *The Annals* dated 10th August, 1785. Young similarly described Andrews, as "a very able cultivator", and on 28th June 1784, additionally wrote;

> "I left Bradfield [Combust] and entered Essex by the beautiful grounds of Bulmer, the seat of Robert Andrews Esq. which gives a very agreeable specimen of that fine country."

Yet what was so exciting, as the dusty and sometimes dilapidated volumes arrived in Sudbury Library, was to discover four contributions from Andrews himself!

Three of Andrews's letters were published in Volume Four of *The Annals* in 1785. One not only reveals his rotation and yields but also includes his financial returns. His article is actually entitled, *'On the Profit of Farming'*.

"I have practised farming," he explains, "for above thirty years and kept very exact accounts." Initially the farm was 'inconsiderable', but

Cause of the Great Debate!

How were the rows of corn actually planred in straight lines? Researching the answer involved Sudbury Library obtaining the first thirty five volumes of the eighteenth century farmer's, companion, *The Annals of Agriculture* and Arthur Young's *Six Week Tour* of 1767. However, as the first of *The Annals* was not published until 1784, our conclusions are only tentative. Nevertheless, the author is not yet convinced that a 'seed drill' was necessarily used.

from 1762-1778 it consisted of 350 acres. During this time he made a profit every year; the highest being some £543 in 1775, the lowest just £83 four years earlier. After accounting for "rent, tythes, rates, labour, wear and tear", his average annual profit was £208 or twelve shillings an acre.

The acreage he farmed fluctuated curiously. Between 1779-1781 he farmed some 580 acres and maintained his average profit of twelve shillings an acre. After the harvest of 1781 however he reduced his acreage to just 220 acres, which then produced a profit of £1. 10s an acre. His rotation on land, "not dry enough for turnips to be fed off by sheep" was then:

1. Peas drilled in February or March
2. Barley, sowed as early as February, if possible
3. Clover, trefoil, or tares
4. Wheat.

Andrews then provides his yields. Between 1773-1783 his wheat averaged 16$\frac{1}{3}$cwt. an acre and barley 19$\frac{1}{2}$cwt. an acre, whilst peas which were grown from 1780-1784 were averaging 14cwt an acre. (By comparison, one might today hope to average three to four tons an acre of wheat; 50-65cwt. of barley and 35cwt. of peas. Andrews's pea yields, however, almost certainly soon began to decline – as they are being grown too close to another legume, clover).

Tim Scott calibrates a modern 'seed drill', close to the Bulmer parish boundary where Robert Andrews 'beat the bounds' on four occasions.

But what makes Andrews so remarkable is that he is the only contributor to the first thirty five volumes of The Annals, (from 1784-1800), to reveal both his yields and accounts in such detail. It is this that makes him – and his picture so interesting.

On a human level moreover Andrews was certainly a responsible, dedicated squire, presenting the vicar to the living in 1757, and leading four perambulations of Bulmer's boundaries between 1762 and 1804. On the last occasion moreover he still walked the "eleven miles and eighteen rods" – despite now being seventy eight years old. Firstly, however, he gave the, "seven men and six boys a breakfast at my house", before setting out at eight o'clock, and finishing at half past one. (When most of the walkers had a dinner at the *Plough Inn* on Tye Green).

Like many other local gentry he was also a J.P., attending the Petty Sessions and inspecting repairs to Ballingdon Bridge. The impression of a self-assured young squire, concerned solely with his own pleasure, that Gainsborough's picture perhaps suggests, is revoked by the testimony of Arthur Young: by the diligent – almost serious – application he applied to his role of farmer and village squire and by his apparent financial parsimony. Moreover, the monument erected to his memory in Bulmer Church says something of his personality – even allowing for the normal licence of eulogy.

Robert Andrews,
late of Auberies in this parish
sincere and ardent in his Christian faith.
It uniformly influenced his conduct
through a long and useful life
which he resigned in Peace
May 20th, 1806, aged 80.

Finally, it is pleasing to record that Andrews's erstwhile estate at *The Auberies* continues to be farmed to the highest standard. That new crops – such as Winter Linseed – are being investigated on the same fields where he once walked, that the Burke family who have resided there for over a century and a half continue to cherish and improve the landscape, and that the oak tree that Gainsborough portrayed is still alive and lovingly cared for.

Benjamin
Perkins 1998

Thomas Gainsborough...and Harvest Mysteries!

It is c.1750, and the young Thomas Gainsborough, with sketch book in hand, is planning Mr and Mrs Andrews's projected portrait. With them is Mrs Andrews's mother arranging the famous blue dress – which is also believed to appear in other paintings by Gainsborough at the time!

Now we return to the crop of wheat and ask, '*How was it actually harvested?*' Researching the answer to this question stimulated almost as much thought as the unresolved issue of how it was sown! Indeed many writers assume that scythes were used. They are almost certainly wrong. For the scythe was not widely used for cutting wheat until the mid-nineteenth century – almost a hundred years after the

painting. However, there is still a dilemma. For wheat reaped by sickle was usually cut, "at about ten to twelve inches high"*, (and sometimes higher). A secondary operation known as 'haulming' then occurred, during which the stubble was, "Raked together in heaps and removed."†

* Farmers' Kalender.
† There are numerous references to haulming. In 1775 Young details the cost at 1s 6d an acre and says it was 'universal practice'. If the haulming occurred, "before a little frost," wrote Messrs. Raynbird in 1848, it was regarded as being, "man's work, as the roots not having perished do not easily come up." The straw apparently made, "excellent walls for farmyards and lambing pens." In the sixteenth century however, Thomas Tusser described a slightly different technique:

The haulm is the straw of the wheat or the rye.
Which once being reaped they <u>mow</u> by and by.

xiii

But Andrews's crop appears to have already been cut quite low – either by sickle or another implement known as a 'bagging hook'. (The latter was larger than a sickle but had no serrated edge). Bagging hooks moreover were often used to cut low, where a farmer required more straw for thatching or livestock, or had a 'laid' crop.

Is there any chance however – that contrary to all normal practice – the crop had actually been mown by a scythe? The likelihood is exceptionally remote. In 1775 – over two decades after the portrait was executed – Arthur Young wrote,

> "Reaping, [i.e. with a sickle] is the common practice used since time immemorial. Mowing, [with a scythe] is a new method – invented to save labour. This is a subject that has been much discussed within a few years and with great warmth!
> "The advantages of mowing," he concluded, were mostly confined to situations like, "the neighbourhood of London, where straw sells from a guinea to two guineas a load."

Almost certainly then, Andrews's crop of wheat was 'reaped' by 'bagging hook' or sickle, although his barley would have been 'mown' with a scythe. (Our picture shows sickles being used.) In the foreground meanwhile two women are gathering the corn into sheaves, and tying them up with 'straw bands'.

However the author may himself have made a mistake when designing this part of the picture. For although women frequently helped in the harvest fields of most of the British Isles, they were less evident in Essex, (and some other parts of Eastern England).

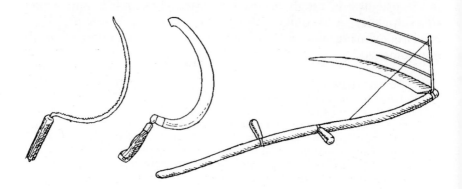

Sickle, bagging hook and scythe (not to scale)

Here gangs of men – who were FED and LODGED by the farmer during harvest, were more commonly employed to undertake the whole operation. (Although the men were often initially ill due to the surfeit of good food provided!)*

By the turn of the century, however, some other farmers in North East Essex, (especially within a 15 to 20 mile radius of Sturmer), were paying 'by the acre' and providing their men with 'hops and malt' instead. This system, wrote the Rev. Howlett of Dunmow in 1795,

"has long been adopted... principally amongst the larger, and more opulent farmers, whose wives and families do not chose the trouble, and fatigue, of boarding the men in the house.

"Many farmers," he continued, "very judiciously blend the two modes together. Older labourers work 'by the piece', with an allowance of beer per acre, and their wives and children are permitted to work with them. However men in the prime and vigour of life are taken into the house for the month of harvest, during which time they are fully and plentifully maintained" (abbreviated).

Whether forty years earlier in 1750, Robert Andrews's harvest gang had been provided with board and lodging and undertook the whole task, or were alternatively 'paid by the acre' – enabling wives and children to join them – we do not know. It is arguable however that women did not work on his harvest fields at the time.

Harvesting in Bulmer today

* *General View of the Agriculture of Essex,* published 1805.

A Famous Visitor Measures Trees at Bulmer

On 22nd July 1785, Arthur Young (b.1741) visited Robert Andrews at *The Auberies*, in Bulmer. Whilst there he measured the girth of some of Andrews's trees - to enable them to calculate their growth in subsequent years.

Realistically, we do not know whether <u>the</u> tree depicted by Gainsborough some thirty five years earlier was actually amongst those recorded. However it is 'convenient' to think so, since it enables us to capture Young – who was of such enormous agricultural significance – together with Andrews, surrounded by the farming system he described in *The Annals*.

In our artist's recreation the tree is being measured by Young whilst Andrews looks on. To the left we have included a small herd of bullocks. For in the same year Andrews also contributed, 'An Account of Grazing Twelve Steers' to Young's publication. Here his meticulous ledgers show a profit of only £2-3s-2d, following an expenditure of £117-17s-10d. Yet he still declares that the system is advantageous – because of the farmyard manure which was produced. "By keeping a good stock of cattle," Andrews prudently observes, "a farm is in heart and the corn crops large." Purchased on 1st December 1783, Andrews's bullocks cost an average of £3-0s-11½d each. Total expenses over the following eighteen months were as follows:

	£	s	d
12 steers as above	36	11	0
22 weeks straw @ 9d each	9	18	0
16 weeks May to August (1784) in roads and commons.			
Cost nothing but I charge 6s a week	4	16	0
Sept., Oct., Nov. 16 acres 'rouen'*	9	0	0
Bought a stack of hay	12	12	0
While at hay 25cwt. of barley	6	10	0
33½cwt of peas @ 30s	11	5	0
Grinding.	0	14	0
Eight acres turnips, with carting, @ £3.	24	0	0
Keeping last two beasts 12 weeks longer			
until July 7th	2	8	0
TOTAL EXPENDITURE:	117	14	0
TOTAL RECEIPTS:	£120	1	0

(at average price of £10. 0s.1d per bullock, between April and July 1785)

PROFIT: **£2**   **7**   **0**

* 'Rouen' says Young is a "provincial term for a second crop of hay." However Andrews later implies that other cattle were 'run with the steers' (on the rouen), suggesting it might be a ley which has had a second hay crop taken from it.

To the right of the tree – where Gainsborough had depicted the sheaves of wheat and rows of stubble – is a crop of peas. These, recorded Andrews, were ideally 'drilled in February or March' and then hoed twice. In our picture (above) the crop is being harvested when 'dry' by men using an implement known as a 'peas make'. Later the crop would have been carted back to the farmyard and built into stacks or stored in the barn, prior to being threshed by flail.

Behind the men is a large heap of farmyard manure. For the correct treatment of dung was yet another subject on which both Young and Andrews had strong feelings! Andrews in fact argued it should be mixed with lime. However, he adds an interesting caution, relevant to our study of burnt lime in *Chapter Two*:

"The dung must not be dry. If it is, IT WILL FIRE by being mixed with lime... Let it lie for three months and then stir it over again... Carry it on to a pea stubble as soon as harvest is over and plough it in for barley..." (my capitals).

Following Andrews's guidelines then, the 'dung heap' would have been spread onto the adjoining pea field as soon as the crop was removed. Later the field would have been ploughed and eventually sown with spring barley.

Arthur Young's extraordinary energy, eclectic interests and insatiable thirst for knowledge inspired this picture. His enthusiasm to measure the growth of trees is just one example of a constantly enquiring mind that examined everything from, "the influence of electricity on vegetation", to farming in the Crimea, the relief of the poor in Suffolk or carrot growing in Stisted.

The biggest tree measured at *The Auberies* incidentally – which in Young's own words was a "noble oak" – had a girth of 11 feet 1¼ inches. Nevertheless, even the remarkable Arthur Young was fallible. For when he published his article twelve months later, he openly confessed,

"There must have been some mistake in the measure. For Mr. Andrews measuring it again this year (1786), could make it no more than 10 feet 11½ inches!"*

Finally, we should not forget the men who actually did Andrews's work. Quite possibly they had names such as Dixey, Rowe, Humm or Bunn. For these also are the great names of Bulmer's past. It is they who ploughed and reaped the fields that Andrews wrote about; it is they who carted out the dung, tended the herd of steers or mowed the hay, and it is they – these other stalwarts of the parish – who lie in Bulmer Churchyard, not far from Andrews and his wife, and are recorded also in the parish registers.

Spreading artificial fertiliser today

Annals of Agriculture, Volume 6, 1786

The bailiff is summoned to Robert Andrews.

A Farming Blunder – 1786!

"About the 26th of June," declared Andrews in a letter to Young dated 5th August, 1786, "walking by the side of one of my fields of wheat, I observed a great number of ears of smut, or what we call 'burnt wheat'."

Andrews was very much surprised, "having taken every precaution to prevent it". He then perceived that the 'smutted ears' were only on the "last stetch of the field". Additionally, it was the last piece of wheat which had been sown the previous autumn.

'Had it been sown with untreated seed?' he wondered. Suspecting this to be the case he questioned his bailiff. The latter immediately confessed, "that, not having a sufficient quantity of dressed seed to finish the field, he took about a peck from the barn, as it came from

the flail and sowed it on the spot I have described".
Andrews then reveals his particular technique for treating corn
against such seed-borne disease. Although it involved using arsenic
he added the following proviso:

"Make a strong lye, by running water through wood ashes seven
times. Put it in a copper, with half a pound of arsenic; let it boil
about five minutes, which will so far take off the poisonous quality
of the arsenic as to prevent the destroying of fowls, or birds that
may pick up the uncovered seed."

(Later the wheat was put in the mixture, well stirred, and finally
assisted to dry by adding lime).

In our artist's impression of the event, we see Robert Andrews now
in his sixtieth year, holding some smutted ears of wheat and asking his
bailiff to explain the transgression. With him is his eldest son, also
christened Robert, (who Young implies may have farmed between
Witham and Maldon).

To the right of the 'famous tree' is a crop of barley, which as discussed in our previous illustration Andrews grew after peas and the
spreading of farmyard manure. His spring barley incidentally, "was
sown as early as February if possible", and occasionally gave yields in
excess of a ton an acre. At the time moreover good malting barley was
being exported from our area to the Netherlands and Germany, and
was worth about six pounds a ton.

What though of the crop of wheat which had produced the infect-
ed years? By 1786 it would have followed red clover. "In preparing his
clover leys for wheat," recorded Young on one visit to *The Auberies*, "he

Contemporary
'mobile seed
dresser'. To
increase quality a
gravity separator
is used.
In Andrews's day
a simi;ar effect
was gained as the
lightest grains
floated off the
water's surface.

Photograph courtesy of Steve Warner

generally goes over them with a spiked roller to prevent the seed coming up in the seams."

Andrews moreover declared that he started sowing his wheat, "on SEPTEMBER the THIRTEENTH – if the land is not too hard to plough". (My capitals!). Indeed his eighteenth century husbandry never fails to inspire this author – for with all the benefits of modern technology at hand, I have only ever succeeded in planting wheat before the thirteenth of September on just four occasions!

✣   ✣   ✣   ✣   ✣

Lewis Majendie's First 'Seed Drill'

One of Arthur Young's most interesting local contributors was Lewis Majendie who owned Hedingham Castle. The latter's first letter to *The Annals* dated 5th September 1789, advocates the almost revolutionary concept of sowing specific varieties of grass for livestock pastures. (Previously farmers used any seed which could be collected from the bottom of hay stacks and waggons – irrespective of the species or weed seeds included). Consequently Majendie sowed a small area of Meadow Fox Tail grass – on an experimental basis on "some old hop ground" in March 1787. (Although the trial eventually covered the seven acres of 'Little Castle Field'.*)

On 1st March 1793, he wrote of a new investigation – into another variety of grass – the now famous Meadow Fescue. Firstly however he had to procure the seed. Consequently he employed children to, "collect the panicles from the swarth." Next he arranged for the seed heads to be, "threshed upon a cloth." Yet Majendie also introduced Dutch White Clover into our area. He even made £40 by selling sixteen bushels of it for seed, whilst wondering why it was otherwise imported from Holland!

But Majendie was equally interested in arable farming. In the picture we see him proudly watching the performance of his first 'seed drill', in the company of a lady who is the SINGLE FEMALE

* The Meadow Fox Tail, reported Majendie, survived a severe winter better than Rough Stalked Meadow Grass, ripened earlier than Rye Grass, and "seemed to be more nutritious from the greater luxuriance of its foliage". Additionally he recorded, "The tons of hay carted from the field", together with the, "days and nights that nine large bullocks, five cows and four horses were able to feed off the pasture".

Lewis Majendie and Mrs.Clarke of Castle Hedingham watch the progress of Majendie's first seed drill in October 1786. (On the left of the picture is Meadow Fox Tail grass with Meadow Fescue adjoining. In the lower right hand corner is an example of White Clover, whilst the hops above testify to the Hedinghams' great reputation with the crop.)

CONTRIBUTOR to the first thirty five volumes of *The Annals*. Her name was Mrs Clarke. And she lived at Lawrence's Farm, Castle Hedingham – which is about a mile north east of the Castle. (Her letter which was published in 1785, actually recorded her own experiments on sowing wheat).

As noted our picture is dated October 1786. For in that month Majendie commenced the "drilling system", using a machine designed by the Rev. James Cooke of Heaton Norris, Lancashire. (A description of Cooke's machine had been published earlier that year in *The Annals*, together with an illustration from which artist Benjamin Perkins has made an exact copy). In a letter dated 6th March, 1792, Majendie enthuses:

"The drill husbandry is likely to prove successful in a very eminent degree... I seldom sow less than forty acres (of wheat)... and have occasionally sown barley, beans, and turnips... The sample of wheat," he states, "is better from a drilled crop. The weight per bushel is higher, the grains more even and there is less 'tail corn' –

which produces a more marketable commodity." (To fellow farmers this sounds remarkably contemporary!)

But the situation is clouded. On 1st July 1792, Young visited Majendie. Somewhat prejudiced against drilling he smugly wrote,

"Though a most careful and attentive farmer, Mr Majendie has given (it) up for barley, turnips, oats and tares, all of which he sows broadcast... as a consequence of experience."

The following year however one J. W. Allen of Whepstead exulted in the appearance of Majendie's fine crops of drilled wheat. By comparison when Young returned in 1794, Mr Majendie,

"Shaked his head and candidly owned that drilling declined so much in his opinion, that it would probably appear no more on his farm, except it might be for some very particular purpose."

Yet the use of the seed drill was not long restrained. Ten years later even the sceptical Young observed that in many parts of Suffolk and Essex, "drilling had become universal". Locally Mr Coker of Borley was using it for almost all his crops whilst, "Mr Burrell of Birdbrook has drilled wheat and barley on nine inch rows for four years".

What else then can we say about Majendie? By 1805 he was farming 450 acres, had, "twelve horses, three or four cows, 80 Wiltshire ewes and 100 'wethers'". Additionally he was purchasing 15-20 bullocks of Scotch or Welsh origin each autumn at Braintree or Woolpit Fair for £7 to £9 each, and selling them within twelve months. His cropping programme during that year of Trafalgar consisted of, "Fallow 28 acres, oats 14, barley 34, wheat 77, white clover seed 13, red clover seed 14, turnips 34, Swedes 4, potatoes 4 and cabbages 4".

Majendie was obviously a committed 'agricultural improver'. He contributed articles on tree planting and land drainage together with a design for, 'sheltering wheat ricks', to the *General View of the Agriculture of Essex*. And he also displayed a well-intentioned, but practical, concern for the plight of the poor, especially during the severe scarcity of 1795-96.

"In the parish where I live," he wrote on 24th March, 1795, "a sum of money has been raised with which flour is purchased and retailed to every poor family... Our fund which has now lasted nine

Majendie's drill. The basic components have changed little in the subsequent two centuries.

weeks will probably carry us to the month of June, but may have to extend beyond next harvest... The labourer cannot support himself and a large family under the existing circumstances of scarcity." (Slightly abbreviated)

Hedingham Castle around which Majendie farmed is nationally known. However the small Church at Bradfield Combust – where Arthur Young is buried – receives somewhat less attention. (It is directly beside the main road from Sudbury to Bury St. Edmunds and almost adjoins *The Manger* Public House). Yet the tombstone of our greatest agricultural thinker, writer and philosopher, whose output achieved so much for the public good can still be seen in the graveyard near the Church's eastern wall.

There, on a slightly neglected, undistinguished monument – typical of so many in quiet country churchyards, are the following words:

'Let every real patriot shed a tear
For genius, talents worth, buried here...'

'In Agricultural and Political economy pre-eminent.
Distinguished for public virtue, private worth and the
strict performance of every moral duty...
His natural genius, cultivated talents and benevolent exertions
were disinterestedly and successfully devoted to the Promotion
of the Statistical, commercial, moral and religious interests
of his country...'
(much abbreviated).

As one contemporary similarly remarked:

"To the labour of Mr A. Young, the world is more indebted for the diffusion of agricultural knowledge than to any writer that has yet appeared."

Tombstone of Arthur Young (1741-1820)

'Mole Draining' at Little Maplestead
with Eighteen Horses!

John Sewell of Little Maplestead Hall watches his mole drainer in about 1800. The parish's round Church is depicted as it appears in an engraving of 1765, dilapidated and without dormer windows. However there was an extended timber framed western porch, which was sometimes used as a school.

As an 'agricultural improver' Sewell was keen to drain his land, and with Mr Vaizey of Halstead, and two others, built a 'mole plough' at an expense of thirty pounds. Their machine was then 'let out' at 2s. 6d. an acre, reported Arthur Young. Meanwhile another farmer in the neighbourhood contracted to find the horses and labour for £1 1s. an acre, with the drains at three yards apart.

(Their implement pulled an iron bullet or 'mole' at a depth of fourteen to eighteen inches through the clay subsoil to create a tunnel about two inches wide. In the right conditions these channels can last for many years. Mole draining still continues, at a

Mole draining Old Barn Field, Bulmer 1996

depth of about twenty four inches – but with several hundred horse power of tractor on the front!)

"The mole plough," continued Young, in 1805, "has been in common use for four or five years about Halstead, and with great success... (They) first draw a furrow with a common plough; and then apply the mole, drawn by eighteen horses. There is no doubt entertained here of the great benefit of it. The drains, after four years, run . . . as well as, and in some cases better, than at first."

Locally Mr Kemp at Hedingham had drained 250 acres with their machine, whilst Rev. Mr. Thurlow at Gosfield, "found it of excellent use". Volume Two of *The General View of the Agriculture of Essex* actually contains a diagram of Vaizey and Sewell's mole drainer – complete with exact measurements – on which we have based this picture. (Note also the furrows which have been ploughed in advance of the mole drainer as Young described.)

Apart from his use of a mole plough Sewell was growing 'rib grass' and carrots for seed and also hops, caraway, coriander and teasel (*see page 72*). He had not however tried a seed drill by 1792.

Together with Lewis Majendie, Robert Andrews, Rev. Mr. Thurlow of Gosfield, Rev. Mr. Onley of Stisted and Mr Coker of Borley, an inspiring picture emerges, of keen, dedicated agriculturalists, enthusiastically examining their husbandry and attempting to push the boundaries of food production and local farming forwards, some two hundred years ago.

✛ ✛ ✛ ✛ ✛

Straw plaiting in north-east Essex circa 1860.

The Straw Plaiters

George Washington Brownlow's painting, *'The Straw Plaiters School'*, inspired the above picture. (Brownlow's masterpiece depicts a group of children being taught the craft in a Belchamp Walter dwelling in 1864.) For more on 'straw plaiting' see *Chapter Six*.

Bulmer Street in the Late Nineteen Twenties

As the young Jack and Evelyn Cornell (b.1918 and 1922) watch their father go past on his Ransomes traction engine, Emily Cornell emerges from the *Cock & Blackbirds* with Evelyn's coat. John and Emily were landlords for about fourteen years although it was always necessary for John to earn a second living as a threshing contractor. Also depicted is carrier Bill Humm with his flowing beard and donkey cart. In the background is the Rev. Mr Pannell's car, whilst following the threshing drum is possibly Tom Rowe. (Threshing and steam cultivation is further discussed in *Chapters Fourteen & Nineteen*).

Bulmer Street today.

With special thanks to Curtis Lane & Co., Sudbury, in providing copy transparencies of the original illustrations.

Tithe War Scene at Woodlands Farm, Ringshall near Stowmarket in 1934.

The Tithe War

The sheaves had been impounded for non-payment of tithe. The policeman standing outside the tent, recalls John Waspe (b.1914), is PC. Briggs of Bildeston, with Sgt. Bonner of Lavenham behind him. They were also assisted by another policeman, PC. Searle from Hadleigh and the bailiff. One curious aspect recalls John is that due to the field's location, there were West Suffolk policemen on the road, but East Suffolk policemen in the field!
(For more on the Tithe War, see *Chapter Twelve*.)

"Although my father farmed at Lamarsh, there wasn't any future here, so in 1922, when I was nineteen I went to Canada. My first job was on a 2000 acre farm at Hughton in Saskatchewan. Canada was unbelievable after North Essex. At home we had six or seven men on 200 acres. One year in Canada I was on a farm of a thousand acres with only the two brothers who owned it – and me – to work the entire place with only one extra man at harvest!"

"It must have been a big difference."

"Difference! There wasn't any comparison. In England three horses pulled a binder and then a gang of men came along 'shocking', 'pitching', 'loading', and 'stack building'. But in Canada! I drove an Olton tractor that pulled SIX BINDERS at once! Everything was so mechanised. These binders just left the sheaves in a long row to be picked up with a *mechanical* 'sheaf loader' – which elevated them into a trailer."

"So how did they build the stacks?"

"THEY DIDN'T! They simply pulled a threshing tackle out into the middle of the field and threshed it there and then – straight off the trailer! No messing about building stacks and so forth! But combines were rapidly taking over – and when I came home in 1933 they were fairly common."

As I talked to Bob Pinhey of those epic early years, his pioneering spirit constantly emerged. Yet ultimately it was his photographs – so well preserved from the nineteen twenties, that intrigued me most. Of the embryonic towns of Sovereign, Zelandia, and Hughton (all in Saskatchewan), with their 'General Stores' and saloon along a single street: of the towering grain silos beside the railway line, of the Olton tractor pulling *six* trailer loads of wheat, and of a trailer being pulled on *skis* – in snowy weather.

But there were more. Of the horsedrawn 'bunk house' which, "was pulled across the prairie to wherever we were working at harvest." Of Bob on a tractor pulling THREE corn drills and covering 30 to 40 feet in *one bout,* "on a stubble that had only been disced once or twice before sowing." (Remember! This is the 1920's!). And then there was the final photograph. Of the twelve horses breaking up virgin soil – that had never before been ploughed – on a massive treeless

161

prairie, where, "you could easily see seven or eight miles to the nearest town."

Overwhelmingly, there emerged one thing. The sheer – devastating – efficiency of Canadian agriculture in those lean and frugal years. For it was this 'prairie culture', which our predecessors of *The Long Furrow* were forced to compete with – by the 'free market' politicians of the nineteen twenties and thirties. No wonder so many of the patchwork farms of mid-Anglia, with their tiny fields and entrenched traditions went vacant and places like Fowes Farm at Belchamp Otten were abandoned for nearly 20 years.

During the winter Bob went lumberjacking in British Columbia. Here he lived in a log cabin with twenty other men. As a new arrival however he initially wondered, "Why the devil are all the trees cut off about four feet high?" . . . Later when the snow came he understood – it was then ground level!

The other farmer whom I interviewed was the late Philip Lawson of Bridge Farm, Ixworth (1901-1987). Although born at Hall Farm, Bradfield St. George he worked in Western Australia from 1923 to 1930.

"I was on a FOUR THOUSAND ACRE outfit at a place called Yangedine. It grew wheat and oats, had a flock of 1200 sheep and twenty three horses. As for the land? It was worth about two and six an acre!" [12½p]

Understandably young Philip was also staggered by the scale of what he found. On the entire unit there were only four employees whilst in England 4000 acres would have needed a small army. A single field was over 550 acres in size. One of his first jobs was to use six horses on a *FIVE FURROW PLOUGH!!*

Yet from Philip's photographs and memories, there emerged not just the awesome differences between Suffolk and Australian agriculture but something else beside. Something that is poetic in its simplicity and which brings to mind the stirring outback balladry of Banjo Patterson, and Dorothea Mackellar, who described her love of:

"... a sunburnt country
a land of sweeping plains;
of rugged mountain ranges
of droughts and flooding rains."

Sixty years later, Philip still evocatively described the gum trees, the shearing season and the drought times. Of which he joked, "it was cheaper to purchase a new shirt than buy the water to wash it in!" But he spoke too of the isolated homestead with its forge and carpenter's shop, its granary and bunkhouse and of the dusty droving of the season's sheep to Beverley market, "which was about a day's work, and 12 miles in distance." Yet as he continued to reminisce – sitting in his wheelchair and crippled with arthritis – a dreamy and faraway look came into his eyes as he spoke of the sunrise, the sunsets and seasons; of the camp fires in the evening at the offhand 'humpy'; of the enchanting smell of the eucalyptus trees, and of laying in his bunk at night – with a lantern beside him – as he read the *Bury Free Press* that his mother mailed him week by week.

Wherever they were in the world, and whatever type of agriculture they experienced, the memories of both Philip and Bob, were quite truly 'Of the Furrow Born'.

Chapter Eleven

IMMIGRANT FARMERS 1890-1940

'A Scottish, Cornish and Cheshire invasion!'

"In the 1930's we kept getting brochures of farms down in Suffolk which were 'RENT FREE for Twelve Months'. But what was the good of going down there when everything had been neglected for years on end and gone wild like a bloomin' rabbit warren!?"

Percy Darlington (1901-1990)
Cheshire farmer.

We have seen how emigration depopulated our East Anglian countryside. Yet there were also immigrants to it. They were farmers. They came to almost every parish. And eventually became an influx of hundreds. Often the newcomers arrived after a bad East Anglian harvest – when yet more land became available. For the great majority it was an opportunity to increase acreage, begin farming on one's own and maybe, ultimately, even purchase a farm. Nearly all came as tenants. A few – a very few – bought farms immediately. Doubtless they speculated that good times would return. Excepting the First World War, many had to wait for half a lifetime.

Yet although 'financial opportunism' was the overriding, compelling objective, there was another attraction of farming in an area 'where tenants were sought after'.
It was freedom of conscience.

"Unless the prospective tenant attended the Church of England,

164

[as opposed to the non-Conformist Chapel], and was willing to help the County Yeomanry", recalls the late Percy Darlington, "it was impossible to hire a farm up here in Cheshire – even at the beginning of the twentieth century!"

In Norfolk conditions were also restrictive.

"My grandfather," recalls retired Halstead vet Jim Waters, "lost the tenancy of a brickyard near Great Yarmouth because of his support for Joseph Arch and the National Agricultural Labourers Union. That was in 1880. But grandfather was a strong-minded man and also a Methodist lay preacher. And he always expressed his beliefs! So ten years later he lost another tenancy – this time of a farm – again because of his politically radical views!"

Another to describe similar experiences was the late Cyril Philp (1899-1992), of Kirby Hall, Castle Hedingham – who despite living in north Essex for eight decades was actually born in Cornwall. Interested, contemplative and kindly – and with a wry turn of phrase – one could almost imagine that he had grown out of the very clay of his picturesque farm. His understanding of local agriculture was exceptional. In addition to lending his Father's farm diaries for *The Long Furrow,* he has been one of this book's most valuable contributors. Within the area he was an acknowledged authority on 'steam power' and traction engines. And it was Cyril who on a grey February afternoon, in the sunset of his life, recalled again those bygone strictures:

"My grandfather farmed on the Boccouen Estate in Cornwall. Well, the owner let it be known that he expected him to attend the Church. But my grandfather was a staunch Wesleyan and of course the inevitable happened – HE GOT THROWN OUT!"

(In those days landowners could get possession by giving just one year's notice).

Cyril later explained that although the family found another farm to hire – near the coast at Polperro, it was very drought-prone so they then moved to a farm at Looe. However this also had problems:

"It was infested with rabbits! But as tenants we weren't allowed to do anything in the woods that might upset the landlord's game. So our place was swarming with bloomin' rabbits! They grazed *everything off*. It was just as though you'd had a flock of sheep on it!"

In time another Cornish farm was hired. So why I wondered did Cyril's Father then jeopardise everything by moving to Essex in 1909?

"I think the prospects for 'getting on' *appeared to be* rather better in these parts. The landlords here were more desperate for tenants and didn't hinder you so much. Besides, most of the farms down there were only 40-50 acres. When father hired Priestfields here it was 285 acres. We more than doubled our acreage overnight."

"Did he make a reconnaissance of the area first?"

"Oh yes. He visited an uncle, Jobus Scantlebury, who blazed the trail in the early 1890's."

"It must have been a very major decision."

"It was! It was like going to Canada or Australia except that the distance was shorter. It was a case of going from one type of farming to a totally different one."

"Did you bring any of your stock or equipment with you from Cornwall?"

"Only two horses and a pony. But they weren't 'sized'. They hadn't got the strength for the stiff land around here. It was nice to keep them and so on but they couldn't cope. They had to go on 'light duties' and we had to get some more that could stand the pain of heavy land."

"But why," I was bursting to know, "didn't the Essex farmers seize the opportunity of hiring extra land themselves?"

"What I think was this. Most of them had been used to a way of living which couldn't be sustained; quite a lot of them didn't adjust."

Cyril smiled, as if delivering a prophetic utterance for contemporary times.

"They didn't bring their ways of 'going on' down to their circumstances... That's about the size of it! In those days it was the exception to find an Essex farmer who would take a tool and go to work. That wasn't on. But we newcomers were different. We were more used to hard work and getting on and doing things ourselves."

Later, during that memorable February afternoon as we sat in the dark, wood-panelled parlour at Kirby Hall, my notepad become so full that I had to write along the margins and sides. Two C90 tapes had been recorded, and yet still, as evening drew on, I could not resist enquiring,

"What was the most impressive difference of all?"

"Oh the amount of steam tackle! The ploughing engines were monster things! They were right out of this world as far as I was concerned..."

And those who remember Cyril, and watched his own steam engines ploughing, will have no difficulty at all in guessing what we talked about for the following hour and a half!

Before I left this remarkable man however, he gave me a list of other Cornish farming immigrants. It is by no means definitive but well illustrates a point.

LOCAL DETAIL

J. Scantlebury (Cyril's uncle) – To Epping and then Rickling Hall. Came in the early 1890's.

R. Richards – To Nightingale Hall Farm, Earls Colne (1901) then to Shimpling.

J. Tinney – Descendants are now very big potato farmers.

A. Jasper – To Langenhoe Hall, Colchester.

Sam Gilbard – Between Newton Green and Boxford.

? Couch – To Ware, in Hertfordshire.

J. Lanyon – To Raine Hall.

C. Blewett – Came in 1910 and took Hyde Farm, Little Yeldham
before moving to 'Whitleys', Cornish Hall End

Robert and William Crago – Two brothers who arrived about
1911-12; Robert Crago went to Old Hall, Steeple Bumpstead;
William took Tagley Farm, Stambourne.

J. Burrow – When we arrived he was farming St. Mary's Hall,
Belchamp Walter but it was sold in 1914 and he came out of it.

? Tamblyn – A 'late arrival' in the early thirties. Came to Great
Dorkins Farm, Steeple Bumpstead.

Williams – Two brothers who came up before we did. One farmed
at Bubbards Farm, Shalford, whilst Wilfred's father took Little
Coldham Hall. Later he moved to Chelmshoe House Farm,
Great Maplestead during World War One.

Joseph Heywood – From Kilkhampton near Bude. Came to
Roxwell in 1910 (family now at Dunmow and elsewhere).

William Trembath "came to Essex in 1901 from Penrhyn near
Falmouth. Hired railway carriages to bring some of his goods."

"As you can imagine," says Cyril, "there was general communi-
cation between the fraternity to compare notes. But the great
majority moved up before we did. They came in the 1890's."

Whilst the Philps, Tinneys and Blewetts originated in Cornwall, a
less populous migration came from Devon.
One was called Pinhey. He was Bob Pinhey's grandfather and originally came to the Gosfield Hall estate near Halstead.

"But once he was here," recalls Joe Blomfield of Little
Maplestead Hall, "he created quite an impact! He was especially
known for sowing with both hands at once!"

However as Bob later explained:

"There was nothing that unusual about 'two handed sowing'.
No. The real surprise in those days was to actually see an Essex
farmer doing the job himself."

Yet the immigrant farmers came from all over Great Britain.

(Other notable contingents derived from Somerset, Cheshire, Lancashire, Northumberland, Lincolnshire, and especially Scotland.)

At Alphamstone, farmer Wally Twinn typically exclaimed:

"In the 1930's I was almost surrounded by immigrants! At Clees Hall there was a Mr. Ellrington from Darlington, at Newmans Farm, Lamarsh, there was a Yorkshireman by the name of Fowler, whilst at Le Mote, Pebmarsh there was a tall young Scot 'with two or three dogs', whilst another, Watson Steele, came to Colne Engaine."

From all over England came others – lured by the prospect of low rents or larger farms. Many have descendants still farming in the area. One example is the Gardiner family who still farm at Little Yeldham and whose ancestors played such a prominent role in the Tithe War – but who originally came from Radlett in Hertfordshire.

Another family to come from Hertfordshire today farm in Foxearth. They are Bob Jackson and his son David (b.1952). However Bob's father, George, was also part of our 'great migration'. Consequently one January afternoon in 1983, shortly after the publication of *The Long Furrow*, I was invited to meet grandfather George Jackson – then *ninety-nine* years old – in his daughter Peggy's home in Cavendish.

As we sat beside a warm fire Peggy offered us cups of tea, scones and cakes. George meanwhile explained that he had been born on a farm at Sandon in Hertfordshire, before his parents moved to Home Farm, Wyddial near Buntingford. But then, on 11th October 1903, the family had moved again – this time to Bridge Street Farm, Long Melford. Now, eighty years later, George vividly described the events of that day, when he was a lad, aged just nineteen.

"It was a very long day. We had to get up at about three o'clock! That was to milk the cows before driving them down to Royston Station and putting them on the train for Melford. My father and mother also travelled by train. But I came with our 'Hertfordshire' corn waggon and four of our horses. It was well over forty miles. A very long way for horses. They had to have a really good rest after that. Of course we stopped along the way. There were ponds beside the road where the horses could drink, and we would give them a nose-bag."

(Wyddial is about six miles south of Royston. The route he probably took would have been from Wyddial to either Saffron Walden or Newport, and then to Radwinter–Steeple Bumpstead–Birdbrook–Stoke by Clare–Cavendish–Long Melford.) Today, moreover, we can still imagine young George passing along the muddy unmetalled roads, through strange villages to a new and different countryside. And he observed it all 'at the pace of a horse'. Yet despite being an unforgettable adventure there was also one problem.

"It was the weather! It rained all day long – the whole way! When I got to Baythorne End the water was knee deep for the horses! In fact it didn't begin to ease off until I reached the top of Windmill Hill, coming into Melford. It was actually just getting dusk and a policeman told me to 'light up' the lamps on the waggon!"

But the wet weather had begun during harvest, as George explains:

"I saw one field of barley that hadn't even been cut! There were still sheaves in several fields! And the 'out-going' tenant at Bridge Street Farm, Mr. Abbot, had a very poor dispersal sale – because it had been such a poor harvest and no one had any money. His best horse only made twenty four pounds. And when he cleared the sheaves from his last field of beans they were so damp that water ran out of the back of the waggon!"

"Do you remember the names of the horses you came with?" I wondered.

"Yes!" George exclaimed with bright, twinkling eyes. "They were Beauty, Daisy, Punch and Johnny! But don't forget the cows! They had a long day of it as well. When they arrived at Melford Station they had to be driven right through the village to Bridge Street Farm. Several boys from near the station gave us a hand – to earn a penny or two. But those cattle were glad to stop and have a little feed from the grass on Melford Green – and a good drink from the pond there as well!"

And yet – soberingly – there were also less pleasant memories:

"We were shocked by the poverty. It was really distressing to see

170

how badly off the working people were here. In Melford some people were almost starving. One of the very first things I saw, was a woman with three children walking to the workhouse."

Another contributor also came from Hertfordshire. Harry Gilbert (1897-1986) of Colne Engaine. (Yes! Harry, our 'wildlife oracle' in *Heart of our History*, and fount of village memories of Colne Engaine – was actually born at London Colney near St. Albans). However in 1902, his uncle hired Overhall Farm, Colne Engaine. And Harry's Father moved with him to be farm foreman. The two brothers travelled to Essex by pony and trap. Harry however, with his Mother, brothers and sisters came by train. Consequently, on the evening of Boxing Day, 1902 the little boy – aged five – arrived at Earls Colne Railway Station.

"Then we had to walk to Colne Engaine. But my word! It was a bitterly cold, dark night – and there were only a few old cottages with little lights. And then we went through all these woods and little lanes and we all wondered, 'Where on earth are we going?' "*

Yet if the numbers of English farmers who migrated to East Anglia were surprisingly numerous, they probably amount to less than half the total. There was another group who came. The Scots.

"And they were EVERYWHERE!" exclaimed Alphamstone's Wally Twinn. "Every time you went to Sudbury Corn Exchange you would meet another one! Oh yes. You'd hear of a farm gone behind somewhere; someone gone bankrupt or just given up, and then a few months later there'd be a McTurk or McBride or a 'Mc-something-or-other' in there lean and hungry, and never stop working - and probably never employ anyone either!"

In 1900 Rider Haggard declared of the area around Billericay:

---

*For many years Harry's name was almost synonymous with Colne Engaine. His memories of the village were both encyclopaedic and vivid. See especially, Colne Engaine, The Story of an Essex Village, published by Colne Engaine History Society.

"Hundreds, or rather thousands of acres of strong corn lands that have tumbled down to grass . . . are in the hands of Scotsmen who take it at a small price."

More recently I asked Halstead farmer Bill Waters if he knew any Scottish farmers.

"Did I! In my youth NINETY PER CENT of all the land in the Tendring Hundred was farmed by Scotsmen. In fact people said there were only two original English farmers there!"

For Bill however there was one consolation . . . He married a Scottish farmer's daughter!

EAST ANGLIA INVADED! 1890–1940

Although the great majority of Scots migrated down between 1890-1910, I was still fortunate to meet one of those from 'the first wave' who could recall both the journey South and the subsequent struggle to get established in Essex. His name is Willie Brown. He lived at Little Horkesley near Nayland. But he was born in Ayrshire, in 1898.

Consequently one June afternoon, I took the road from Sudbury to Nayland and once across the meandering river, branched off along a narrow, cow-mumbled lane, wondering if I had correctly followed the directions.

I need not have worried. For turning a corner, I saw the most enormous barn and on its roof a flag – St. Andrews flag – the banner of Scotland! A few hundred yards away was Willie's retirement bungalow. Although ninety-eight years old he enthusiastically recalled:

"When I was three years old, my father hired Beacon Hill Farm, Ongar, and with two other farmers who were also moving south, *hired a train* from Kilmarnock on which we put the nucleus of our stock. Although I was only young at the time, I do remember that at Leicester the cows – all Ayrshires – were taken off to be watered, fed and milked. But what a time it was for my poor mother! There were six of us children and we all had whooping cough! The old doctor said about my sister, 'You'll never get this wean (child) to England alive'...but she survived."

"But how did the local farmers react to all you Scotsmen?" I wondered.

"Oh, there was a certain feeling of resentment. I mean, we took our jackets off and got on with the job! They used to call us 'cow keepers' and looked down on us for letting the women do the milking – while we got on with the 'land work'.
"If I'm honest, Scots women did have very tough lives. But the thing was this. Although our neighbours had wives like ladies, we were the ones who survived! They had to give up their tenancies! But in those days you could pick and choose farms as you liked and slowly get a better one as you became more established. People actually said that Scottish farmers always moved three times – climbing the ladder as they went."

"So your father moved farms as well?"

"Oh yes. In fact I remember when he had just taken one very wet, badly-drained farm – which had actually been empty for two years. Anyway his new neighbour, who was rather jealous, 'came across the hedge' and grunted;

'You taken this farm?'

'Yes,' said father.

'Well,' came the reply, 'you've got plenty of damned water to drown yourself in then!' "

"It's extraordinary to hear you say that a farm had 'been empty' for a couple of years."

"Well, it was nothing unusual! On one occasion a landlord in Essex was so desperate to find tenants that he paid for NINE Scottish farmers to come down by train and inspect all this unfarmed land. And when they took the train back to Scotland, seven of them had hired farms!

"On Lord Petre's estate at Ingatestone Hall, *three quarters of the farmers* were Scottish. A lot of Ayrshire men – like us – hired cattle farms because that was what they were experienced in doing."

"So they put the farms down to grass?" I asked.

"No! THAT'S WHAT YOUR GENERATION DON'T UNDERSTAND! These farms weren't 'put down to grass', they had simply reverted to grass, because they had gone out of production!"

As Willie Brown continued he revealed more. Of the *Kilmarnock Standard* being posted to his parents week by week; of an Ayrshire tailor who travelled to Essex to visit Scottish farmers once every year; and of his relatives – the McMillans, who followed them down to Stisted near Braintree and of his own indebtedness, 'to the original trailblazers'. Legendary men like John Nesbitt, who went to Stock in Essex and James Alston who led the way in Suffolk.

From other sources I was told of the Scotsmen's enormous appetite for hard work.

"At Nettlestead, near Ipswich," relates Janet Cooper, "a farmer named John Alexander Cullen, came down from Stirling and took High Hall Farm in 1910. He was a cousin of the Brices who had

174

moved to Hintlesham. But my goodness! How that man could work. He drained the whole of that farm *himself*. BY HAND! He wouldn't stop! His children had to bring porridge out to him in the fields. It's hardly credible really but when he arrived he hadn't got any machinery at all! He had to borrow it all from my Uncle – Orlando Jackson. There wasn't even a house with the land – so he had to set about building one. He might have been in Alaska really!"

At Alphamstone, near Bures, the late Wally Twinn (b.1902) explained:

"The incoming Scotsmen would hire farms on which there had been seven or eight men. But they would just run it with the labour of their own families and two or three dogs. They could keep every farthing they took – because they'd got no wages to pay!"

The need to do likewise soon became crucial.

"When I first came to Alphamstone in 1921, wheat was 35 shillings a sack; within two years it was down to eighteen. By 1934 it was only worth ten. It was unbelievable. You'd go to farm sales and see 'almost new' binders, which had cost a hundred pounds, selling for seven or eight pounds only. Around here there were acres and acres of derelict land growing nothing but ragwort*"

Happily, there were some light hearted moments. Muriel Pickering – and many others – humorously recall going to market in the nineteen twenties when:

". . . all the old Scotsmen would suddenly start jabbering away in their broadest accents and no-one else would have a clue what they were talking about!"

Not surprisingly, 'Caledonian' societies were soon formed. Those at Colchester and Halstead are still in existence.

---

*Corn prices crashed in 1922 following the repeal of the Corn Production Act. The Act had been passed in 1917 to guarantee minimum prices for wheat and oats.

175

Spear Thistle. If land had gone derelict, it was difficult for the visiting Scotsmen to assess the farms they were inspecting. "However," declares Willie Brown, "they used to say that if there was a thistle big enough to tie a horse to, then it was good land – and worth farming!"

Intriguingly, a few Scots descendants believe that their ancestors came down to East Anglia in the early to mid nineteenth century – and drove cattle with them as they came. As the late Jack Wallace of Lavenham recounts;

"Although it is a long time ago, there was a family tradition that my grandfather's father had actually walked down with 300 bullocks."

(As Jack was born in 1894 this might roughly date the event between 1820-1840). Indeed corroboration that Scottish drovers brought cattle to eastern England comes from a Northamptonshire poet. His name was John Clare, and his masterpiece, *The Shepherd's Year,* was written about 1823-24.

SUMMER

'Along the roads in passing crowds,
Followed by dust like smoking clouds,
Scots droves of beast, a little breed
In sweltered, weary mood proceed,
A patient race from Scottish hills
To fatten by our pasture rills.'

Clare explains that they camped on fields and commons before wryly describing;

'. . . men so oddly clad
In petticoats of banded plaid
Wi' blankets o'er their shoulders slung
To come at night the fields among . . .'

Just before going to print a fascinating article on the subject appeared in the *Proceedings of the Suffolk Institute of Archaeology & History 1996.* Here Cynthia Brown reveals that until the coming of the railways, cattle had been driven from Scotland down to Norfolk, Suffolk and Essex for at least two hundred years.

The cattle, she explains, were shod for the journey and a drove would consist of at least 200 – but often many more cattle. There was usually one drover to about every sixty cattle and they normally averaged a steady twelve to fifteen miles a day. But it was arduous, challenging work. On the journey South there were bad roads, snowstorms and floods to contend with. Whilst the drovers walked with the cattle their 'topsman' would ride ahead to locate overnight grazing and possible accommodation for his men. As the journey proceeded he would need to plan his arrival in East Anglia – to coincide with the local cattle fairs, or his own advertised sales*

*Proceedings of the Suffolk Institute of Archaeology and History, Vol XXXVII, Part 4, 1996, pages 428-441.

(We recall that Lewis Majendie of Hedingham Castle purchased Scotch and Welsh bullocks at Braintree market and Woolpit Fair. (Page xxiii). After being fattened up by East Anglian farmers, the cattle were eventually driven to Smithfield Market in London. One droving route to the capital passed through Sudbury and Braintree).

✝ ✝ ✝ ✝ ✝

We have deviated a long way from our enquiry into the farming immigrants of East Anglia – although the above does give credence to Jack Wallace's contention of a distant ancestor, 'walking down with 300 bullocks'.

Yet whatever the year of migration from Scotland there was one single compelling force.

"In Scotland," said Tom Black of Bacton, "everyone had large families but small farms. Quite simply they had to 'get out' to 'get on'. The Scots went everywhere."

Maybe we can draw some conclusions. Most pertinent is that in those years of crisis it was the best farms – those with the deep loamy soils – which were the least affected. But for the past fifty years of 'protected' farming, the 'heavy land farms' have been equally profitable. Today, with cereal prices declining and straw burning banned, heavy land may again become marginal.

We observed too, that whilst there was a steady stream of immigrants in the first depression from 1890-1912, there were some – but considerably fewer, who came during the second phase from 1922-38. What we may have omitted is that even during the first influx, there were some who in Tom Black's words,

". . . had 'taken' a heavy land farm and then suffered a terrible wet time in their first year. Well, they might not be able to carry on – and had to go back to Scotland again!"

One interesting example of a Scot who was unable to survive and become insolvent occurred at Belchamp St. Paul. In its issue of 19th March, 1938, the *Halstead Gazette* reported that the bankrupt farmer,

John Mason, had hired Butlers Farm. The latter had previously been derelict for THIRTY-THREE YEARS. Not surprisingly a rent was only to be paid in the event of Mason making a profit. Upon learning this, the Official Receiver commented:

"It was the type of agreement that would appeal to you as a Scotsman?"
"It would appeal to an Englishman too!' came the quick-witted reply." (Mason in fact, had never been asked for any rent).

Indeed, in 1934, when the price of wheat was less than at any time since *1687* many other immigrants must have sorely questioned their wisdom in moving.

And what can we say of the immigrants themselves? Simply that they invested our great 'Long Furrow' with new energy and unfettered perspectives: that they took on farms which were largely abandoned and brought with them rigorous vitality and drive.

Their spirit was typified by John Brooks of Ashbocking, who came to Suffolk from Cheshire in 1908,

". . . and lived on rabbits and pigeons throughout his first winter, until," recalls his daughter Mary, "my poor mother was heartily sick of them!"

Their determination and calibre is equally exemplified by the late John Glass of Rattlesden. The latter was a Northumberland coal miner until becoming unemployed in the great depression of the 1930's.

Today his grandson Chris – who is a past Chairman of Stanningfield Agricultural Club – continues the story:

"After losing his job he went to America – and found work in a coal mine. From there he sent money back to his wife and three children whom he had had to leave behind. After about 1½ to 2 years however, he had actually saved enough, not only to return to

*Other unemployed Northerners came to the 'Land Settlement' holdings created in the area during the mid nineteen thirties, (e.g. at Great and Little Yeldham). Each had a small plot of land for pigs, poultry and vegetables which were initially cooperatively marketed.

England, but to move South and buy Red House Farm, Rattlesden which was about 70 to 80 acres. This was a dairy farm. Today people can still remember him with his milk cart, churn and ladle, as he went round the village on his milk round!"*

Many newcomers have had an inspiring influence on our local agriculture. Indeed there can be no better, or more popular examples of commitment to 'farming perfection' than the late Tommy Hogsbjerg, once of Denmark, but since 1946 of Belchamp Walter; or of Stephen Wise of Cavendish who for over forty years has been the inspiration behind the South Suffolk Crop Judging Competition and whose family came to England in 1938.

And finally, there is a twist to this chapter. It concerns a Long Melford inn, *The Black Lion*, and the fourth of October 1906.

That afternoon a lad of seventeen approached the hostelry with a waggon and two horses. He had been travelling south for ten days. On September 25th he had left the bleak, wind-swept hills of Macclesfield, Cheshire. Journeying some twenty five miles a day he had subsequently stayed in coaching inns at Waterhouses, Derby, Leicester, Kettering and Cambridge.

The Black Lion was to be his last. His destination was near Hadleigh in Suffolk. It was a small village called Elmsett. At Long Melford noone had ever heard of it. But an ostler noticed the 'seals' on the horse's collar;

"Nothing like the usual Suffolk 'seals'," he said.
"Comes from the 'sheers', I reckon 'but," muttered a horseman.
"Be about it. One of they from the 'sheers'." (i.e. shires – but colloquially almost anywhere outside East Anglia).

Years later – and now advanced to old age – the erstwhile lad described his departure from Cheshire for the benefit of a little boy.

"The first day's journey," he recalled, "became quite difficult. The horses," he explained, "didn't want to keep going forward during the afternoon – because they thought they would have to walk home again the same day!"

He told too, that as he travelled past the looming hills of

Wildboarclough and Wincle, he had passed the graves of his own forefathers. Those who had farmed there and struggled against cattle plague and the elements, for generations before him. He remembered also that as he left Ashbourne, a 'trace horse' was hired to help his team up the infamous hill. And that later, at Derby, the axles of his new wooden waggon became so hot that he put some of the load onto the train instead.

And what is the relevance of this? Simply that the seventeen year old lad was the author's grandfather. Percy Cooper (1889-1961), was also a part of the 'great migration'*.

*See Appendix for a list of some of the other farming immigrants to the area.

THE COUNTRYSIDE ABANDONED

"My Father was apprenticed to a shoemaker. But he had a bit of 'go' about him and in 1910 he hired about fifty acres at Dullingham. Then a little later on he somehow bought a Marshall steam engine and thresh-ing tackle – so he went out threshing. But when the hard times came, some of these ol' farmers got months – and sometimes years – behind with paying their bills. Around Wickham Market there was no end of good land for sale at FIVE POUNDS an acre. But eventually one of these people who owed us money simply could not pay – so he offered us his farm instead – just for the price of a threshing debt and a little bit of cash on top!"

DENNIS HOLLAND (b.1910)
Park Farm, Lavenham

"Sir Joshua Rowley's old gamekeeper told me that in the depths of the depression he could, 'walk-up' partridges all the way from Nayland to Assington and even beyond, on nothing more than derelict farmland and waste grassland .... He said you could go the whole way – there were miles of it."

DAVID TAYLOR-BALLS,
Nayland

"Wilsons of Hadleigh would grind your corn – for your livestock – without you paying for it, and then when harvest came they would say: 'Right. How much wheat have you got to sell?' And you'd pay for it like that. There was no end of grinding done on that basis in the hard times before the War."

The late CLAUDE ALLESTON 1912 – 1994,
Boxford

182

"When the Scotsmen first came to Essex in the 1890's, they said that you could walk all the way from Colchester to Harwich on land that had gone derelect. You might have to meander about a bit – but they reckoned it was possible."

DUNCAN BROWN, Little Horkesley

"It was real depressing to see stacks of wheat two or three years old with no buyers and rat runs all through them and half the wheat 'shaled' out. And in the barn there were sacks of wheat, one on top of the other, all eaten up with rat's holes .... and no one wanted it."

DENNIS HOLLAND
– recalling Suffolk agriculture
in the nineteen thirties.

183

Chapter Twelve

REBELLION: THE TITHE WAR

'Gestingthorpe; Stoke by Nayland; Elmsett and Ringshall'

"The rector of a parish", said Mr. Collins, "has much to do.
In the first place he must make such an arrangement for tithes
as may be beneficial to himself and not offensive to his patron."

From *Pride and Prejudice, Jane Austen*

The village of Elmsett is approximately four miles from Hadleigh
and eight from Ipswich. In 1931 its population was 282. The parish
church is dedicated to St. Peter. The latter stands on a gentle incline
overlooking open fields, a gentle stream and nearby Hall Farm.

But opposite the church is something unexpected. A grey concrete
memorial. It reads:

> "To commemerate (sic)
> the seizure of Tithe
> at Elmsett Hall.
> Of Furniture including
> Baby's Bed and Blankets,
> Herd of Dairy Cows,
> Eight Corn and Seed Stacks,
> valued at £1200 for
> Tithe valued at £385."

Tithe itself, explains the *Encyclopaedia Britannica*, stretches back to
the ancient world. To the civilisations of Persia, Egypt, Classical

184

Greece and Rome. It possibly existed in China. It certainly did in Israel.

"Thou shalt surely tithe all the increase of thy seed, that the field bringeth forth year by year"
Deuteronomy, Chapter 14, vs 22

In Anglo Saxon England 'tithe', (or one tenth), became the recognised means of 'supporting' the Church. But payment can seldom have been popular. At King Edmunds synod in 974 non-payment was actually made an offence punishable by excommunication. Six hundred years later, during the Reformation, Henry VIII seized the monasteries lucrative 'tithe rights' and gave – or sold them – to new colleges, schools or his personal friends. (In other words the rights to the tithes in some parishes were now owned by ordinary 'lay' people.) One good example comes from Bulmer where in 1785, the squire Robert Andrews informed Arthur Young:

"I have the advantage of also gathering the tithe of three capital farms in the parish. This gives me 40 to 50 acres of corn every year MORE THAN GROWS on my own FARM." (Slightly abbreviated, my capitals).

However we should not exaggerate. For the majority of tithes were still 'ecclesiastical' and continued to be paid to the parish clergyman whose remuneration was – ironically – genuinely 'Of the Furrow Born'
Originally, tithe was extracted from many forms of produce such as corn, hay, wood, colts, lambs, eggs, fish and mills. At Foxearth for example:

"The payment of tythe milk was made in the Church porch at six o'clock in the morning, and six o'clock at night every *tenth* day in May, June and July."*

Earls Colne's seventeenth century rector and diarist – Ralph Josselin – mentions his tithes of poles and faggots from Chalkney

*Rephrased from An Essex Pie which attributed the information to 18th century manuscripts among the deeds of local historian C.D.F. Sperling.

Wood. In 1425 the vicar of Bulmer – as we know – received the tithes of one lime kiln. Additionally he also enjoyed, "the tithes of doves, wool animals, white meat, fruits, herbs and hay etc. not otherwise retained by his patron, the Abbey of Bruisyard," (who before the Reformation had the 'Great Tithes' of corn, etc.). At Borley the Tithe Barn stood not far from the Church. In about 1679, Long Melford's rector, Dr. Bisbie typically complained that, although he has received two pounds for 'tythe pigs' – he has also "been defrauded of many." In 1803 Arthur Young recorded an average figure of £1-1-0d as the tithe on an acre of hops in Stowmarket, but just 1s-6d on an acre of cabbages in Bradfield, whilst in 1801 Great Waldingfield's windmill paid, "by custom, five shillings tythe yearly."*

Not surprisingly, disputes over tithe had existed for centuries. As early as 1178, in the reign of Henry II, one such controversy between the churches of Bulmer and Brundon was finally settled by the Bishop of London. Five centuries later in 1705, the Rector of Belchamp Otten anxiously noted in a folio, now preserved in the Essex Record Office:

"A parcel of the glebe lands of Allbrights shall tithe one sheaf to Otten and the other to Allbrights."

(Belchamp St. Allbrights is a 'lost' village not far from Belchamp St. Pauls. Following ecclesiastical reorganisation, its tithes were divided between Belchamp Otten and Ovington).

But possibly the most extraordinary controversy of all occurred at Wickham St. Pauls during the reign of George III in 1768. Here, the protagonists were the Rector (Mr. Erskine), and two farmers, Jeffrey Ruffle of Hall Farm, and John Brewster of Butlers Hall, Bulmer, (who also farmed forty-two acres in Wickham).

So high did feelings run that the defendants, (Ruffle and Brewster), spent a staggering FOUR HUNDRED and FORTY POUNDS in counsels' fees, published a pamphlet of their grievances, requested voluntary donations to meet their advocates' bills and also, pertinently observed that:

*Extracted respectively from, *Dr. Bisbie as Accountant* published in Long Melford Historical and Archaeological Society's Newsletter December 1995; *Great Waldingfield* by Louise Kenyon; and *A Guide to St. Andrew's Church, Bulmer* by Richard Slaughter.

"The Rector, Mr. Erskine was formerly of the law and knew well how to introduce prolixity and expense."

At stake was the 'means' of tithing. For the Rector insisted that, "*an entire field* of wheat should be cut and then 'shocked up' before *any* was removed." Yet the long-established custom in Essex and Suffolk was to leave the Rector every tenth sheaf as they were carted from the fields – irrespective of whether the entire field had been cut or not. For as the farmers pointed out, in a wet season, some sheaves might well be carted before the field had been completely cut. Their counsel expressed the following opinion:

"It would be exposing the farmers to great damages in bad weather. For in 'ticklish seasons' it is very common to cut and carry (the corn) directly."

Even more confrontationally, the Rector also demanded that barley and oats (described as 'soft corn'), together with peas, should no longer be cut in a swath and carted loose – with every tenth swath being left as tithe – but contrary to local practice – 'set up' in sheaves and shocks. Yet as the farmers argued, soft corn had been "tithed in the swath", since, "Time immemorial within the parish of Wickham St. Paul .... and in 'general' throughout the enclosed parts of Essex and Suffolk."

Here again – as with the shocks of wheat – the Rector was interfering not just with the tithes but the established system of farming itself. (In Chapter Eighteen several contributors recall, 'cutting barley in the swath and carting it loose' – during the *twentieth century*!).

Unwilling to comply with the Rector's impractical demands, the farmers subsequently, "set out the tithe as in previous years." Astonishingly the Rector refused to accept it:

"so that corn which had been set out for tithe was left in the fields to perish – except for what the poor fetched away."*

Two centuries later we can still imagine this rotting 'tithe' corn. For the fields of both Butlers and Wickham Hall actually lie beside the busy road

*Again with thanks to Wickham St. Paul's historian Marion Smith for obtaining a photocopy of Ruffle and Brewster's pamphlet from Reading University and so willingly making it available for this project.

187

". . . except for what the poor fetched away."

from Bulmer Brickyard to Wickham St. Paul's Church. How bizarre it must have seemed! What a talking point it must have been on neighbouring farms, at Sudbury market and in our public houses. Indeed we can picture boisterous farmers, squires like Robert Andrews, and weather-beaten ploughmen all shaking their heads in disbelief as autumn rainstorms slowly drenched the sprouting, worthless ears of corn. And how incensed too, Ruffle and Brewster must have felt as they confronted such an implacable adversary.

But tithe disputes were to continue. In a letter to artist John Constable, dated January 28th, 1821, his brother Abram wrote:

> "I notice what you say about Fisher's [tithe] lawsuit – they generally end in favour of the Clergy and throw heavy burdens on the already depressed agriculturalist. The Clergy get in their [tithe] sheaves and make memorandums and entries of money received . . ."*

*From *John Constable's Correspondence*, edited by R. B. Beckett, published 1962, by Suffolk Records Office.

Consequently, to reduce these altercations all tithes were commuted into monetary payments from 1836. (Hence the large number of 'Tithe maps' from this time). In some parishes however monetary payments had been made for many years. In 1803 Arthur Young recorded that for seventy-five years the tithes at Wickhambrook, north of Clare:

"have been invariably three shillings an acre for corn, when a fore [or first crop], two shillings the after crops and eleven pence an acre for hay."

(Young also notes that *at the time* calculations were, 'generally compounded at a very reasonable rate . . . and must be considered favourable to the occupier'.)

In 1794 a Mr. Vancouver published a Table of Tithes from some other local villages which had arranged their own computations.

Great and Small Tithes per acre

	s	d
Great Yeldham	5	0
Great Maplestead	4	0
Ashen	3	9
Belchamp Walter	3	6
Mount Bures	3	0
Belchamp St. Paul	2	6
Middleton	2	3

Yet disputes from these localised settlements continued to arise. In 1792 it was reported that forty-two farmers in Sible Hedingham had given notice, "to pay in kind", because they believed the financial payment was excessive. Similarly in Pebmarsh. Here the Rev. Grimston actually leased the tithes of the parish to ten leading landowners for, "£460 per annum, for a term of seven years", in 1814. However when the term expired in 1821, a typical controversy occurred. For following the conclusion of the Napoleonic Wars, grain prices had fallen – and the Pebmarsh landowners naturally sought to reduce their computation *.

From 1836 when tithe commutations became 'official', a degree of

*From *Pebmarsh Church, Essex*, by Rev. Bayley. Mr. Vancouver's table of tithes, etc. comes from the General View of the Agriculture of Essex.

flexibility was incorporated into the calculation – to reflect the price of the three previous grain crops. But farming was again buoyant and profitable. It was the Victorian 'golden era' which was to last until about 1879. Then came the beginning of the great agricultural depression. Inevitably resentment re-surfaced. On 15th January 1887, "a crowded meeting was held in Colchester Public Hall." Here, reported *The East Anglian Daily Times,* Mr. J. S. Gardiner of Borley, *and* a Churchwarden declared:

> "The farmer was now paying tithe out of his *capital* for the benefit of people who did not do much to earn their living. The struggle against this established confiscation began years ago . . . The Tithe War was breaking out again – because the farmers were determined not to submit to the injustice any longer." (Loud Cheers).

But farmers did continue to submit – however resentfully – until after the First World War. Then in 1925 a new Tithe Act *fixed* tithe at 105% of it original 1836 value. But the price of wheat was already falling. Within six years it was worth *only half* of its 1836 value.

Price of Wheat

	£	s	d
1840	14	11	7
1925	12	3	4
1928	10	0	0
1930	8	0	0
1932	5	18	4
1934	4	16	8

Consequently the disquiet which had been developing for the past half century began to coalesce. Increasingly farmers queried the justice of tithe – which their competitors on the American prairies did not have to pay. Others – particularly non-conformists – resented supporting a church which they did not even attend; all looked with envy at other businesses which had long since foregone the practice, whilst paying tithe to 'lay owners' was clearly an anachronism for which there could not be the *remotest* justification. (The latter could even be bought and sold like stocks and shares.) One London firm said that the average value of 'lay tithe' – if sold – was approximately 8 to 10 times the income it provided. By 1930 resistance was growing. On June 10th, *The East Anglian Daily Times* observed, "after only a few months the Colchester District Tithe Payers Association numbers nearly 1000 members and the Suffolk Association 500."

Amongst their number were some notable leaders: Lady Eve Balfour – who was later to gain prominence for her stance on organic farming; novelist and farmer's wife Doreen Wallace; farmer A. G. Mobbs; and the Rev. R. Kedward, a non-conformist minister and former M.P. – who was President of the *Central Tithe Payers Association.*

As the depression worsened, confrontations arose. Some clergymen it must be said were particularly kind and helpful. "How much can you spare towards the tithe this year?" would come the tactful question. (Often farmers would offer a proportion of the tithe – which might well be discreetly accepted). Others were equally insensitive. They demanded "All! . . . or Nothing!" (And doubtless then got the latter!). One rhyme of the time sums up a growing mood:

"God save us from these raiding priests
Who steal our crops and take our beasts.
Who cry, "Give us our daily bread."
Then take it from our mouths instead."

As arrears developed, the 'Lay Tithe owners' or Church Commissioners targeted selected farms. On 10th June, 1930 an attempt was made to 'auction' animals and equipment from Stonards Farm, Stoke by Clare. The farmer was J. M. 'Digger' Jones. He had bought the near derelict property some years previously – and still managed to pay over half his tithe. (In this instance he had actually offered £50 of the £105 still outstanding). The auction was a farce. All 'bids' were ludicrously low. The items were later returned to Mr. Jones. And just £5-11s was raised for the *lay* tithe owner.*

On November 9th, 1930 a similar auction was held at Red House Farm, Shelfanger, Diss, Norfolk. Again the farmers showed solidarity. Again a farthing was bid for a cow. Here the auctioneer refused less

*Some of the 'lay tithe owners' appear to have been even more avaricious and unsympathetic than the Church Commissioners. Other 'lay tithe' owners to initiate actions include King's College, Cambridge; Merton and New Colleges, Oxford; and Lord St. Audries, a Sussex tithe owner. (From *The Tithe War*, by Doreen Wallace, published by Victor Gollancz, 1934).f tithes, etc. comes from the General View of the Agriculture of Essex.

than a shilling. Finally he sold thirteen steers at two shillings each and 32 sheep for just three shillings. Again all was returned to Mr. Bailey, the farmer. Eventually the crowd began to disperse. But first they stood to attention. And sang the National Anthem.

Tithe owners had suffered two reversals. Now they attempted other measures. At Elmsett Hall on 2nd May, 1932 an attempt was made to remove eight corn stacks, (valued at £329), against a tithe debt of £132-6-4d.* The farmer was Mr. Charlie Westren. His accounts for the previous year showed a loss of £350. Yet he had still offered to pay £50. This had been refused.

At about 6.30 a.m. six lorries arrived at Elmsett Hall. News of the hauliers' arrival spread quickly. Within three hours some 300 farmers and farmworkers surrounded the hauliers. *The East Anglian Daily Times* takes up the story:

"Things began to quicken by the middle of the morning. Hitherto the haulage men had been hampered only by insistent requests to shift their lorries in order to allow farm vehicles to come through. On the face of it, the demands were reasonable if a bit frequent and awkward."

More 'routine farm work' was to follow:

"A trench had been dug in front of the gate that led into the farmyard and it was not possible for a lorry to enter until it was filled. The *ostensible* reason for digging the trench was to inspect the pipe which carries the ditch water underneath!"

If this brought a smile to the newspaper's readers, more was to come:

"Now a farm tractor was requisitioned to drag a large fowl house from its moorings and to plant it *just where the private lane* enters the highway. The wheels were taken off, and there it sat, squat and large and stubbornly obstructive."

Now 'other measures' were adopted:
"A small elm tree was sawn through. It was ready to crash across

*The figures on the Tithe memorial, quoted at the beginning of this chapter are presumably the compounded amount of the protracted quarrel.

the lane except that its branches were strongly entangled in those of a much larger elm . . ."

The reporter's 'tongue in cheek' account continues:

"So farm hands set to work to fell the big elm, using a large amount of zest and a somewhat inadequate two handed saw. They were probably relieved when, half an hour later, the contractors decided to withdraw their lorries . . . So exalted were three local farmers' wives that they rang the church bells in celebration."

Other action had also taken place: Joseph Pryke, one of Mr. Westren's employees was later charged with obstruction,

"for taking a 'two wheeled tumbril' onto the Somersham road. Here he took the horse out of the shafts and led it back to the farm – leaving the tumbril in the middle of the highway. This prevented a tithe lorry loaded with corn from getting by." (Westren doubtless paid the five pound fine).

Across Southern England other distraints and legal proceedings were taking place. So intense were farmers' feelings that 'Gift Auctions' were held to raise funds for the Tithe Payers pressure groups.
One of the most remarkable occurred at Ipswich on Tuesday, 5th April, 1933. Here, three auctioneers selling simultaneously, raised £800 of desperately needed finance, for solicitors fees, counsels' opinion, etc. As Doreen Wallace points out:

"At every 'gift sale', the carting contractors and auctioneers gave their services without remuneration."

In May attention focussed on Gestingthorpe. For at Delvyns Farm, (near today's *'Pheasant'* Public House), occurred an attempted seizure of goods. The farmer was a widow – Mrs. Marjorie Gardiner. Due to a 'technicality' however, the seizure was thought to be illegal. Consequently, some 100–150 farmers rapidly mustered to 'delay' the removal. A degree of 'unruliness' developed. Eventually the police were called. Thirty-six protesters were charged with 'unlawful assembly' – and compelled to attend Chelmsford Assize Court. Amongst those charged was Mrs. Gardiner herself. This raised an interesting point. For if Mrs. Gardiner could not 'assemble' on her own farm, then where on *earth* could she lawfully be? (For a fuller report on the Gestingthorpe case – including Cyril Philp's personal memories – see *The Long Furrow*, pages 174–180.)*

In July, Lady Eve Balfour's farm at Haughley was raided. Despite firing a red maroon to summon assistance, eight cows were successfully removed.

By now the Tithe War was regularly making news headlines. On August 4th, *The Daily Mail* carried a photograph of the 'GESTINGTHORPE THIRTY SIX' whilst beneath it another headline declared:

HARVESTERS GUARD.
– POLICE TO GUARD RINGSHALL CORNFIELD –

[details to follow].

On August 17th the *Daily Herald*'s headline revealed:

"RECTOR TALKS OF TITHE DISMISSAL"
"Full details of the astonishing tithe situation in the
Essex village of Gestingthorpe."

Here a farmworker, John Felton – whose son Chris today lives in Bulmer – was dismissed by his employer James Wilson of Hill Farm, to enable the latter to pay his tithe. (Despite Wilson first approaching the clergyman, Rev. Greening, to appraise him of his financial difficulties).

Questioned by the *Herald*, the Rector replied:

"The farmer's business affairs were no concern of mine. It was his business to pay as best he could . . . "

The following day, (August 18th) *The East Anglian Daily Times* revealed three more areas of dispute.

At Stansfield, (near Clare), the Congregational Chapel had been

---

*According to the *Daily Herald*, the tithe on Delvyns Farm was actually 'Lay Tithe', which Gestingthorpe's incumbent the Rev. Greening had purchased privately. Any corroboration of this point would be appreciated).

asked to pay tithe '*on their burial ground*'. At Walsham-le-Willows, a farmer and butcher named Granger had the rents of two cottages impounded by the bailiff in lieu of tithe. He promptly retorted,

"In that case I do not care if my tenants live rent free for a year. It is the principle of the thing. I am not going to pay tithe!"

And at Stoke by Clare a sheriff's officer seized the 700 acres of land belonging to J. M. 'Digger' Jones. Matters were getting out of hand.
On 5th February, 1934, a hundred and thirty four pigs and eighteen bullocks were distrained from Wortham Manor, (the home of novelist Doreen Wallace – alias Mrs. Nash). Later forty-five of her husband's farmworkers,

"marched to the Rectory to ask the Rector what right he had to demand tithe – at the expense of their livelihood."

And in August occurred another raid on a farm at Ringshall. The latter is a small village about eight miles from Hadleigh and five from Stowmarket.
I have treated Ringshall lightly thus far. And for a very special rea-

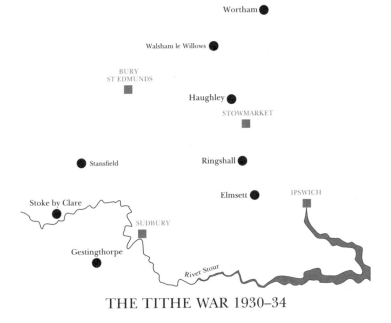

THE TITHE WAR 1930–34

195

son; it must be one of the very few 'tithe war' confrontations from which direct, 'first hand' memories of an actual victim still exist. For it was here, at Woodlands Farm that John Waspe, (b.1914) worked on his grandmother's land, together with his Father and uncles.

Today, John lives in the mid-Suffolk village of Whatfield – about three miles from Hadleigh. With a deeply imbued love of the countryside he radiates warmth and traditional, rural goodwill. In recent years moreover he has assembled a fine collection of old farm tools which he displays at summer fetes and charity events – where he also demonstrates the historic task of flailing corn by hand. His testimony then is not only a vivid account of the Tithe War. It additionally provides a penetrating insight into Suffolk's pre-war farming history – with its abundance of endearing, 50 to 100 acre 'mixed' family farms that have now so sadly disappeared. For the Waspes were genuine, traditional yeomen. They were struggling to earn a living – and to support their seventy year old mother on 116 acres of difficult mid-Suffolk clay. They were victims of an archaic, outdated law. Their 'tithe owner' was the splendidly wealthy Kings College Cambridge. (It was thus 'lay tithe'). And the £47 demanded – so uncompromisingly each year – was increasingly perceived as arrogant indifference to an impoverished and 'down at heel' industry.

In a rich, Suffolk accent John further explains:

"To pay our Tithe required a field of wheat of approximately ten acres . . . not forgetting the labour which had to be worked all year – and the cost of the seed.

"Well, by 1932 the tithe on Woodlands Farm was in arrears. So Father and uncle were summoned to appear at Stowmarket Court."

Their attendance provided the Waspe family with an initial victory. For their intrinsic Suffolk common-sense soon out-witted a rather 'too clever' London barrister.

"My uncle, Arthur Waspe, went into the witness box to be questioned. Now Arthur was a typical Suffolk countryman who always thought well before answering any question. The more educated the person he talked to, the more shrewd or cunning were his answers. He could – as we say – 'cut them down to size'."

(As it was a 'family farm' the commissioners wanted to establish who the owners were – and who was responsible for the tithe.)

"First uncle was asked his name. Well it took him quite a while to reply.". . . As a report of the time makes clear!

The Judge: Are you H. W. Waspe?
The Farmer: No, your Honour.
The Judge: Aren't you H. W. Waspe?
The Farmer: Not that I'm aware of, your Honour.
The Judge: Whose is this farm?
The Farmer: Mother's.
The Judge: What's her name?
The Farmer: We generally call her 'Mother'.
The Judge (patiently):   What do other people call her?
The Farmer: They generally call her "Mrs. Waspe."
The Judge (despairingly):   Hasn't she another name?
The Farmer: Hannah, your Honour.
The Judge (brightening):   Ah, we're getting warm.   Is she "H. W. Waspe", by any chance?
The Farmer: I don't know anything about the W.
The Judge: What about brothers? Have you a brother called H. W. Waspe?
The Farmer: I don' know that I have.   There's E. J. and Tom, and W. F. and G. M. –
The Judge: How many Waspes altogether on your place?
The Farmer (innocently):   Oh, thousands!
The Judge (nearly at the end of his tether):   I don't mean wasps, I mean Waspes . . ."*

Despite the temporary 'moral victory', the Judge ordered 'a sale by tender' – to raise sufficient funds to pay the Tithe.

"Some months later," continues John, "a bailiff – accompanied by police – came to distrain our farm implements.   They were assisted by five or six men from a mysterious company called 'General Dealers'.   This had been formed by the commissioners to seize goods for non-payment of tithe."
    "Despite the jeers and shouts of our neighbours they collected all

*From *The Tithe War* by Doreen Wallace.

197

the implements and impounded them in a large shed in a meadow. These included the seed drill, two or three sets of harrows, a horse-rake and a horse-hoe. They even came into the field where I and another horseman were ploughing, *unharnessed our horses and took our two ploughs away* – so we were denied the use of our tools."

"How were you able to carry on?"

"Everyone was all for us! We were like heroes! Kind neighbours lent us a plough and we borrowed a drill and harrows. We had to carry on work as it was springtime."

"What happened next?"

"It was intended that these implements would be taken by 'General Dealers' to some unknown destination for an auction to recover the debt."

"Did they succeed?"

"Ah. Not so fast! First of all the Waspes got to work! We weren't going to take this sitting down. One night four of us went to that shed – to make the tools unusable. One wheel was taken off the drill, one wheel off the horse-rake; and one off the horse-hoe. Then our two ploughs were stripped of all the removable parts – which were then taken to a *hiding place never to be found.*"
(Nor ever to be revealed – not even 60 year later!)

About a week later the remaining tools were 'officially removed'.

"The raid on the farm was at 4 a.m. – just as it was getting light. 'General Dealers' arrived with three lorries and a gang of men – all we believe from the East End of London – supported by about 25 police officers. Fortunately a neighbour raised the alarm and woke us all up. We rushed out – some of us not fully dressed and found them loading up our implements. Although there were only five or six or us we started to put up obstructions – anything we could lay our hands on. But the police soon bundled us away."
Not surprisingly quite a fracas ensued – and blows were

198

exchanged. But at that moment,

"Another brother came on the scene with a skip of bees! As soon as I saw him, I rushed forward, got hold of that skip of bees and hurled it amongst the raiders. It worked marvellous – they soon cleared away! But the lorries were already getting through. However they only just made it – because help was beginning to arrive. If we could have only held them up another five minutes they would never have escaped with our implements. Of course next day it was headline news. 'SUFFOLK FARM RAID AT 4 A.M. RAIDERS GET AWAY WITH FARM TOOLS!' "

It might be imagined that Kings College Cambridge would have been satisfied with the example it had made of the impoverished Waspe family and chosen a different target in the ensuing years. But it was not so! With bright eyes twinkling in his kindly, weatherworn face, John evocatively continues the story of those great events over six decades ago when he was still a teenager. With an almost Biblical sincerity, he explains:

"The next year – 1933 – it happened again! It was one morning. A large company of police arrived – with a bailiff – to impound some standing corn. But as we were expecting something like this I had had a great thought – a brainwave. So in every field I had put a notice saying: 'THIS CROP IS SOLD'. This caused considerable concern for the bailiff – as he dare not impound the crops in case they *had* been sold. Father and uncle were approached to establish who the crops were sold to. Well they immediately tried several merchants and millers but to no avail. Unfortunately no one would give a 'bill of purchase', as corn could only really be bought by the sample and not 'as standing'."

"Consequently the bailiff impounded a ten acre field of wheat and a seven acre field of barley. But then he pitched a tent *between these two fields of standing corn!* And three local police officers guarded them – day and night!"*

"Of course the Press were soon on the scene. Again it made headline news and crowds of people came to witness 'the POLICE TENT IN A WHEAT FIELD!' At times the roads were jammed by

*See painting on centre page xxxii.

199

crowds of farmers and farmworkers who came from a wide area. Townspeople even came too. Ringshall was certainly put on the map!"

"How long did this go on for?"

"About ten to fourteen days. But Kings College had taken on more than they could handle. To get the corn they would have had to do a couple of days work 'bindering' and then 'shocking up' before they could even think about loading and removing the corn."

Because of the great public opposition – and because the job was too complex for 'General Dealers', the Tithe Commissioners were forced to withdraw.

"However" I suggested, "I believe they might have found the binder work a little 'frustrating'?"

"Yes they would have done! Hidden in the field were all manner of 'obstacles'! I am certain their binder would have had a good many 'breakdowns' – if they had tried to cut that corn!"

Throughout the Tithe dispute, farmers usually managed – *just* – to keep within the law. Indeed as John is keen to point out:

"We actually got on very well with the bailiff and local policemen – who of course we'd known for years and understood our position well."

"So you weren't ever tempted to . . . 'distract their attention'?"

"Well I was involved in one little incident. One day a crate of beer arrived for the police and I 'watched' an opportunity. I grabbed a couple of bottles of beer! Course one or two of us soon drank that and then I went and filled these bottles up with water from the horse pond – which looked just like beer!
"Goodness knows what it tasted like! I bet they spat that out in a hurry! Needless to say from that day onwards the food and drink was given a proper escort!"
"So at least you had a couple of free pints of beer!"

200

"No! Father was right roilled. He actually made me pay for it. 'You can have a game with them' he said, 'But don't you ever dare steal again!'."

"Did you hear any more from the tithe commissioners?"

"Not that year – 1933. That ended the second round in our battle with Kings College.. . . So we cut our corn and carted it to the stackyard. And it was with great joy, and satisfaction that we 'gathered in, that which we had sown'."

By 1933 it was estimated that there were over a thousand warrants for distress on unpaid tithes in Essex and Suffolk. Again one might have thought that the quiet, conscientious Waspe family – deeply immersed in their rural non-conformist traditions – would be left to pursue their impecunious farming; and that the might and power of Kings College Cambridge would be focussed on a larger farmer; someone less likely to go bankrupt; someone with greater access to legal, even political advice. Someone more of the College's own size. If ever there was a case of a Suffolk 'David' being confronted by the 'Goliath' Tithe!

Moreover – to the best of the author's knowledge – no other farm *anywhere* in Britain was targeted for three *successive* years. It is this, that makes the story of John Waspe so remarkable. For although it may hint of 'school boy fun', (from our cosy, present day perspective), at the time, their very livelihood, and their farm was desperately under threat.

As I sat in John's cheery sitting room on a bitterly cold December afternoon and looked out across the open fields of Whatfield and Aldham – that for over a thousand years had themselves borne tithe – I couldn't help pondering that to record his memories was an almost unbelievable privilege.

"So that brings us to 1934", I resumed. "What happened then?"

"Well, General Dealers or Kings College Cambridge had obviously learnt one lesson that year. They left us alone until well into August – by which time all our corn had not only been cut – but was ready for carting. Then the bailiff and police once more descended on Woodlands Farm.

201

"Once again a tent was pitched in a ten acre field of wheat – to be guarded by a bailiff and the same three policemen. Again the reporters and photographers came in good numbers – as well as the public. And again we Waspes set about hindering the seizure of our corn."

"So what 'preventive measures' could you take?"

"First of all we blocked all the entrances to the farm – except one – with loads of farmyard manure or large branches. Then we arranged for a little sabotage to take place."

"What was that?"

"As we'd already cut the corn and 'shocked it up', we came up with a plan to cut the string that bound the sheaves together. But if we cut the string on the outside of the sheaves they would open up and be noticed. So we decided to cut the string on the inside of the sheaves instead. 'Course that's a lot more difficult!"

"One night round about midnight – and a damp and drizzly night it was too – three of the Waspes set to work. One took one row of shocks round the field. One took another and so on. They crept and crawled round this ten acre field until it was almost daybreak and every string that held the sheaves together was cut."

"'Course we could see a light in the tent and the movement of the police as they came out and occasionally looked round. But the worst thing was a searchlight – which was played across the field every half hour or so. Now this did cause us a little worry – as we had to freeze and lay still until it had passed."

"Were these cut strings ever noticed?"

"Yes they were! But three or four days went by first. But then it caused quite a panic for the police! They really had to go 'on the carpet'. We were being questioned too. Detectives – or whoever they were, came and questioned us, but nobody 'knew' anything. No one had missed us having a night's sleep – not even the women folk – who vouched that their men were safely in bed."

"They crept and crawled round this ten acre field."

But all the schemes and obstructions, (including several we have not mentioned), were eventually of no avail. On the morning of Monday 10th September, the inevitable finally happened.

"That morning between 75-100 police descended on Woodlands Farm to guard the robbers – General Dealers and their lorries. All the nearby roads were blocked off and transport was brought to a standstill. But some farmers and farmworkers still managed to come across the fields and congregate around the farm to jeer and shout at these men from General Dealers – as they went round collecting the corn. Of course, *every single sheaf* had to be tied up again – before it could be loaded on the lorry! And *that* took them nearly all morning!"

Despite all the 'lawful inconveniences', (and why shouldn't a muck heap be built in a gateway?), the sheer presence of so many police eventually enabled the road to be cleared. As John explains:

"The police prevented the public from getting to grips with the robbers. However just before they got to the road, my aunt flung

203

herself down in front of the leading lorry. She was roughly handled by the police and led away. A farmer tussled with the policeman and he too was treated roughly but after a few further minor incidents the lorries got to the road."

Although the lorries rumbled away with their loads of corn, it was a Phyrric victory. The great displays of public hostility; the unbounded *support of the Press* for the Farmers' Cause; the fine leadership of the Central Tithe Payers Association and the blunt fact that Tithe was not getting paid, instigated questions to be asked in the Houses of Parliament.

On Wednesday, June 25th 1936 the *East Anglian Daily Times* reported:

"A GREAT ANTI-TITHE BILL DEMONSTRATION IN LONDON."
"5000 MARCH IN PROCESSION."

Due to all efforts a restructuring of tithe took place. It was given a fixed duration. And was due to expire in 1996.

In the early nineteen seventies however it was found to be costing more to collect than the revenue repaid. In 1976 tithe was finally wound up.

LOCAL DETAIL

For some years prior to 1976 the purchasers of land were allowed – and sometimes compelled – to redeem the tithe in a single payment. When Goldingham Hall, Bulmer was advertised for sale in 1972 the 394 acres carried redeemable liability of some £500.

By comparison the annual tithe paid on the 460 acres of Kirby Hall, Castle Hedingham was £145. At Hill Farm, Gestingthorpe, the 220 acres were assessed at £84.24p a year. But tithe was not only paid by large landowners and farmers. Horseman Bert Surridge paid one shilling and fivepence on his half acre garden next to the Gestingthorpe *'Pheasant'* and when he "redeemed it", during the Second World War, it cost him £3 – or the equivalent of two weeks wages.

✠ ✠ ✠ ✠ ✠

In discussing the Tithe War it is sometimes difficult to disentangle

204

the myths and legends which have grown up around the principle events. 'Did you really do _____ at Elmsett?' I asked one contributor. "Well everyone talked about it so much that we might as well have done!" came one spontaneous reply.

Undoubtedly there was an element of boisterous resistance; high spirited practical joking and ebullient determination. Alternatively there was a stark gravity about the plight of many tithe payers.

In many ways the whole episode is one of contradictions; the bizarre spectacle of rural 'pillars of the establishment' – many of whom had been Church wardens, Overseers and Parish Councillors resorting to mob demonstrations and brushes with the law – in protest against a Church for whom they had read the Lesson and taken the collection week after week.

Indeed many *larger* farmers at the time still enjoyed prominent positions. They would have been the first to call for 'law and order' in other walks of life. Possibly this 'behavioural transformation' reveals the depths of agriculture's decline.*

Moreover the revolt was expanding. As one contributor put it, "at the beginning, a lot of the bigger farmers wouldn't be associated with us – because they could still afford to pay – and keep their social dignity. But as the economic situation worsened they realised that they were also in jeopardy."

And what of those farmers who had lead the resistance? They became folklore heroes. The Gardiners, Westrens and Waspes became – however briefly – unintentional celebrities. They were photographed, recognised, eulogised and most of all encouraged in their acts of defiance.

Yet although economic impoverishment ignited the conflagration,

*One interesting aspect of the Tithe War, was the presence in many troubled villages of small groups of Oswald Moseley's 'Blackshirts'. One independent Gestingthorpe observer comments: "They seemed to turn up, wherever there was the chance of getting some publicity. I don't think that the half dozen or so who camped at Delvyns Farm had been invited by the farmers or the Tithe Payers Association, but there was a certain feeling that the farmers were wrong for not sending them packing – straight off back to London again!"
In their defence one farmer crisply retorted:
"The blackshirts had only just been formed! No one really knew what they stood for or what they would later get up to. They were just out for themselves!"

the resistance was fuelled by a deeper drive for social justice; the modernisation of the Church of England; the quest for 'individuality in worship' and an end to the bizarre anomaly of 'Lay tithe owners'.

Today it can seem almost as inconceivable that in 1976 this author paid tithe – as it was that until 1918 women could not vote. Like the Suffragette movement, the Tithe War represented a deeper groundswell of feeling which was bringing the world into a new era – where the last links with its medieval past were finally being expunged.

Yet within the history of East Anglian farming, the Tithe War represents something else.

Together with the Barley March of 1939 it was the last major occasion when the entire agricultural industry – supported by the Press – rose up in defence of farming, against both Tithe, and agriculture's neglected straits.

Since that time – and since those boisterous memorable days, Suffolk agriculture has enjoyed almost sixty years of relative prosperity and protection.

As a sadder consequence, farms have progressively got larger. Today it would be almost impossible to muster a fraction of the number who turned out for the protests of the 1930's. Like its sister industries of fishing and coal mining the agricultural workforce – and its individual holdings – decline year by year. And with it too, those from Suffolk's days of truly yeoman farming – who like John Waspe and his relatives – were so genuinely, 'Of the Furrow Born'.

*   *   *

Thus I ended this chapter and prepared it for publication. And then, on 1st March, 1998, some 284,000 fellow countrymen congregated in central London to protest against another decline in the rural economy, and new threats to its 'way of life'. One of the younger marchers, seventeen year old Cornard Upper School pupil, Anna Partridge of Park Farm, Lavenham explained her reasons for attending:

"I felt it was really important to stand up for the traditional countryside, farming way of life . . . I love animals and am hoping to pursue a career caring for them; I also love rural pursuits and feel they are part of our heritage. I never want to see them end."

The last embers of the spirit that had burned so brightly in the Tithe War, sixty-five years before, were suddenly glowing again . . .

PART THREE

OF THE
FURROW BORN

"You were both talking of other things, of business, shows of cattle, or new drills –"

Emma by Jane Austen

✛ ✛ ✛ ✛ ✛

"Have you ever seen a reaping machine?"
"How do they work?" asked Dolly.
"Exactly like a pair of scissors. A plank and a lot of little scissors. Like this . . ."

Anna took a knife and fork in her beautiful white hands, sparkling with rings and began to demonstrate . . .

"What a pity it does not bind, too! I saw one at the Vienna exhibition that bound the sheaves with twine," said Sviazhsky.

(*from Anna Karenina* by Leo Tolstoy)

✛ ✛ ✛ ✛ ✛

"The reaping machine had left the fallen corn behind it in little heaps, each heap being of the quantity for a sheaf; and upon these the active binders in the rear laid their hands . . ."

Tess of the d'Urbevilles, by Thomas Hardy

Chapter Thirteen

HORSE PLOUGHS and REAPERS

'Local Inventors and Farmworkers' Memories'

"Mr. Hale of Goldingham Hall, Bulmer, uses a 'ridge and skim' [cultivator]. He had a summer fallow ploughed on two ridges on which thistles and other weeds got up. The cutting blade of the 'skim' carved a ridge at a time, leaving all the weeds to die . . . a stout lad and a pair of horses worked it."

Arthur Young describing a locally modified
farm implement circa 1800

The Suffolk Show provides a good opportunity to evaluate new machinery. In the current year, there were combine harvesters from Germany, Belgium and Denmark, ploughs from France, Sweden and Norway, and just one – a Dowdswell – from England. By comparison there were 'land rolls' from Norfolk and trailers from Ipswich and Framlingham.

Yet in 1850 the author could have equipped his entire farm with implements made in either Gestingthorpe or Sudbury . . . And some of them were not merely functional – but downright revolutionary.

For in 1852 a Ballingdon 'millwright and iron founder', one William Bear boldly declared:

"The want of a machine that will SUPERSEDE THE SICKLE OR THE SCYTHE, having long been felt, William Bear has now the pleasure to introduce one that will answer the purpose . . . The implement has been publicly tested in a field of wheat stubble on October 31st, 1851, upon the estate of C. Alexander of the

Auberies, Bulmer." (From the Sudbury edition of Moore's Almanac for 1852).

Some of those who attended the demonstration – on the same land that Robert Andrews had farmed a century before – are already part of our story. Others have descendants who farm in the area today. Indeed we can still imagine their Victorian forefathers, with their buskins, tweed jackets and whiskered sideburns – sceptically scrutinising the pioneering machine, as Sudbury nestled in the valley beneath them.

Amongst those present were:

Edmund Cook, Henny
G. Mumford, Cornard
John Orbell, Foxearth
George Coe, Hartest
Samuel Viall, Foxearth
Henry Meeking, Chilton
William Baker, Brundon Hall
R. Branwhite, Gestingthorpe
James Turner, Gestingthorpe
G. D. Badham, Jenkins Farm, Bulmer
Charles Underwood, Acton
John Hudson, Assington
Edward Tattersall, Newmarket
F. C. Fitch, Steeple Bumpstead
William Frisk
Ashurst Majendie, Castle Hedingham
John Turpin, Cambridgeshire

S. W. Raymond, Belchamp Hall
Henry Coker, Borley
Wm. Hassell, Henny
Thomas Taylor, Gt. Cornard
Wm. Goodchild, Lt. Yeldham
W. H. Garrett, Borley
Thomas Prat, Belchamp
Henry Smith, Henny
John Viall, Bulmer
John Firmin, Goldingham Hall, Bulmer
R. Weston, Ballingdon Hall
Daniel Mills, Melford
Richard Tattersall, Newmarket
E. Parson, Stoke
J.B. Ruggles-Brise, Finchingfield
F. C. Finch, Steeple Bumpstead
H. R. Wade, Lt. Waldingfield*

*LOCAL NAMES

We have met ORBELLS and COES – in the Diaries of John Row; a BRANWHITE was a signatory to the Hop Fair referred to in Chapter Four, whilst the family were also millers at Long Melford. A Mr. Coker from Borley provided information for Arthur Young (p. xxv); RAYMONDS and WADES still farm in Belchamp Walter and Newton respectively; whilst John GARRETT is well-known today for producing honey. The MAJENDIES have already been noted, as have the RUGGLES-BRISE family who have resided at Finchingfield since 1784, with a descendant, Sir John Ruggles-Brise being Lord Lieutenant of Essex from 1958-1978. TATTERSALL is a name still associated with Newmarket; whilst the GOODCHILDS were important farmers at Great Yeldham earlier in the twentieth century.

Bears reaper being demonstrated at the Auberies, October 1851. (Although the design of his machine is not known, we have based our illustration on Hussey's successful reaper.)

TECHNICAL DETAIL

Although the above may read like a standard advertisement of the time, it was actually a declaration of iconoclastic significance. For the MECHANICAL REAPER had reached our Suffolk-Essex border. After some four millennia of more manual, laborious methods the first embryonic attempt to mechanise the harvest of our great Long Furrow had occurred. It was a watershed in local agrarian history. Within thirty one years a 'self-binder' which both cut AND tied the corn would be demonstrated in the same village,* whilst a Combine Harvester, (which 'combined' the functions of both the mechanical reaper AND the threshing machine), would be commercially used at Stoke by Clare in the early 1930's (we believe), and at Elmsett near Hadleigh in 1936.

Yet the development of the mechanical reaper had long exercised men's minds. Experiments had even been conducted in Roman times, for both the Elder Pliny (A.D.23–79), and a later writer Palladius, describe a Gallic 'reaping cart' – or vallus – of which the former wrote:

*From Rowe family records: courtesy of Robin Rowe.

211

"On the vast estates in the provinces of Gaul, very large frames, fitted with teeth at the edge and carried on two wheels are driven through the corn by a team of oxen pushing from behind. The ears thus torn, fall into the frame."

(Pliny: On Natural History, Book XVIII, Loeb edition)

The above – to be realistic – sounds almost *too* simple to have effectively worked. Was it just a failed experiment? Or an exaggerated claim, 'greatly enlarged in the telling', between Gaul and Rome? Not unreasonably some archaeologists have subscribed to the latter view.

Until 1958. When a stone carving of one such 'vallus' or reaping cart was discovered at Buzenol in southern Belgium.*

Roman 'vallus' or reaper. Artist's reconstruction based on the incomplete monuments found at Buzenol in Luxembourg and Arlon in Belgium. (Fragments from the latter suggest that another man walked behind the draft animal – possibly to adjust the height of the machine.)

But how did it function? Could it have really worked? Clearly it would have required a level field and consistent crop height to have performed satisfactorily. But were there additional 'moving parts' to which Pliny does not allude and the sculpture does not show? Drive

*From *The Farmer's Tools and Farming Technique from Prehistoric to Modern Times* by G. E. Fussell E.R.Hist.S. (Mr. Fussell incidentally spent his later life in Sudbury).

shafts, 'cog wheels' and 'mechanical tensioners' were clearly understood by the Romans – as manifest in their water mills and ballistic
weapons. But even today, nobody really knows how – or if – the *vallus*
actually functioned.

Over fourteen hundred years later in 1785, the ancient Gallic reaping cart again aroused interest. And two Suffolk farmers were
responsible! For on the instigation of Arthur Young, one Capel Lofft
from Troston, (approximately six miles north of Bury St. Edmunds),
translated the passages from Pliny and Palladius into English. Young
then published them in Volume Four of *The Annals*, and lively interest ensued! Two years later a William Pitt of Stratford actually produced a design to illustrate how the 'vallus' might have worked, (with
some additional parts).* Although his prototype failed in practice,
the resultant discussion inspired a steady stream of further inventive
but unsuccessful designs. Then, between 1826 – 28 a Scottish enthusiast, Patrick Bell, produced a genuinely functional reaper with a
'shear-type knife' and 'reel'. His story is worthy of note.

Initially very secretive, he experimented in a barn at night, before
conducting his first-ever 'field trials' by moonlight. Yet his tenacious
determination bore fruit. In 1828 his machine cut seven acres. By
1832 ten of his reapers were working in Scotland, and in that year
harvested some 320 acres.†

But despite this genuine breakthrough, (and some were exported
to the U.S.A.), the problem of manufacturing reliable components
resulted in Bell's machine making little further headway.

Then came the 'Great Exhibition' of 1851 – held in London's
Crystal Palace. Two successful American reapers were exhibited.
One was produced by Hussey, the other by Cyrus Hall McCormick.
(Although both may have drawn on Bell's original design for the 'cutting knife'). Both were acclaimed and Bell's machine was resurrect-
ed. This was the turning point. Henceforth the reaper never looked
back – becoming increasingly reliable and cutting a larger acreage
each year.

But our *specific* interest is in the 'Ballingdon/Sudbury' reaper produced by Bear. Had the latter actually visited the Great Exhibition
and seen McCormick's and Hussey's reapers in this same exciting

---

*From *Annals of Agriculture*, Volumes Four and Eight.
†From *The Farmers Tools*, by G. E. Fussell.

year of 1851? Since it opened on May 1st, he would have had some months to produce his own imitative variation. The advertisement itself, makes no reference to either McCormick or Hussey. Indeed it loudly proclaims the implement to be, 'BEAR'S CORN REAPING MACHINE', (surely refuting the possibility that he was selling them 'under licence'), before persuasively adding:

".. . notwithstanding the very Low Price at which he is offering this valuable Implement, the best materials will be used, combined with sound workmanship, and every Machine will be fitted up, and completed, under his own inspection: **Price: £16-0s-0d"**

Moreover Bear was not only an, 'Agricultural implement manufacturer, and Iron and Brass Founder', but also a millwright of high local repute. In his latter capacity he had erected a large towermill at Buxhall, probably those at Preston and Stansfield and the enormous smock windmill at Highfield, (between Sudbury and Long Melford) which was almost SEVENTY feet tall! (From *Suffolk Windmills* by Brian Flint).

To such a man the opportunity to apply his mechanical expertise to producing a pioneering reaper – after the enthusiasm engendered by the Great Exhibition – might well have represented a tantalising challenge. (Other engineers were certainly inspired, and at the Royal Show in 1852, no less than ten British manufacturers exhibited 'their' reapers.) Moreover the sheer number of farmers who visited the Bulmer demonstration – from as far away as Finchingfield, Steeple Bumpstead, Cambridgeshire and Newmarket – testifies to the real excitement that both the Great Exhibition and Bear's 'reaping machine' had ignited.

Yet if a Gestingthorpe farmer had to journey to Ballingdon or Bulmer to view an early reaper, he could have purchased a plough that was actually forged and cast within the parish itself.

Today the village crossroads is shaded by chestnut trees and overlooks the nearby playing field, brick towered church and entrance to the one-time home of Captain Oates at Gestingthorpe Hall. Locally the junction is known as FOUNDRY CORNER. It is a remote, rural spot. But from near here, for some seventy to eighty years, (until about 1908), the Downs family not only produced their famous 'ESSEX A' and 'T.D.O.' Ploughs, but also:

Land rolls	Boot scrapers
Farm waggons	Sign posts
Flat irons	Iron railings
Pig troughs	Poultry troughs
Iron troughs for pigs and chickens	

Indeed so healthy was the demand for implements produced from the Downs's 'most rustic of foundries' that the eleven men employed there in 1851 had increased to "twenty seven men and four boys" in 1877, whilst at the turn of the century there was still a staff of between four and ten on the payroll.[5]

More excitingly the foundry's production could still be recalled, by our oldest contributors, as the book was being researched. For in the Old People's home at Nash Court, Halstead, erstwhile horseman Charlie Martin of Belchamp Walter, (b.1903) instantly exclaimed:

"Oh yes! I can remember ol' Downs all right. In fact I've bicycled up from Belchamp Walter to Downs' foundry dozens of times to get more shares. But something else they made were pig troughs. And wherever you went in my young time you'd see these pig troughs – and they'd all have DOWNS'S name on them!"

As noticed however, the firm's best known products were the 'Essex A' and 'T.D.O.' ploughs. So what did T.D.O. stand for?

"Officially it was 'Turn Dirt Over' – but all us Belchamp lads used to call them something else! – TURN THE DEVIL OVER ploughs!"

*From *Essex and the Industrial Revolution* by John Booker, Essex Record Office Publication No. 66.
Despite leaving Foundry Corner in about 1908 the family appear to have continued as retailers of their old stock for another ten to twelve years from Rectory Farm, Gestingthorpe. Both John Downs and his son King Downs are buried in Gestingthorpe churchyard, and their gravestones proudly record their profession as 'IRONFOUNDER'. A descendant of the Gestingthorpe 'Downs' family started 'Downs Garage' in Sudbury and manufactured the 'Cool as a Cucumber' radiator.

Interestingly one 'T.D.O.' plough was bought by the late Jack Wallace's father.

"It cost £2.10s," recalled Jack, "although that was only for the basic frame – the actual wearing parts cost another couple of quid or so. But I can tell you why he bought it. You see we'd just moved from Wethersfield to Poslingford – where the soil is much heavier – and our old light land ploughs weren't really suited to it."

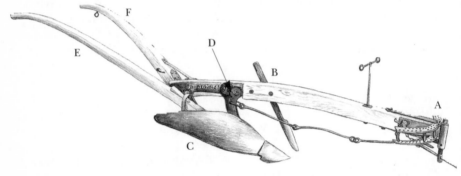

DOWNS T.D.O. PLOUGH

Originally made in Gestingthorpe, it was recently restored by carpenter Brian Ambrose using Ash from a Gestingthorpe tree.

The retaining pins in the semi-circular plate on the front (A) were adjusted to, "hold the plough into the furrow wall, to close up the furrows, and to adjust the furrow width." The horseman could additionally adjust the height of the coulter (B), the 'twist' of the mould-board (C), and the 'bite' of the share on the eccentric clamp mechanism (D). The Downs name was clearly embossed on the main casing. The 'Shaft' (E) was lighter than the main handle (F). Farmworker Les Downs of Bulmer recalls that if the 'shafts' got broken they were often replaced with a "good piece of wood cut out of the hedge."

Curiously, the foundry was actually positioned on both sides of the road to Little Yeldham. To connect the furnace with the steam engine, (which drove a fan to make the blast), a tunnel was built beneath the road.

"However I've heard say," relates retired Gestingthorpe crafts-man Les Smith (b.1921), "that water would sometimes get into the tunnel . . . 'Course that was a rare old trick to get someone to stand near the exit – when the blast started! Oh yes. That would have 'em! – But they only ever caught them once though!"

216

Occasionally however, hand bellows were used and a village boy would be paid to do the pumping. A hundred years later, Dorrie Pannell tells of one legendary exchange when the school register was being taken.

Teacher: "Where is _____"
Pupil: "Please Miss, he's blowing up the foundry!"

Finally there is a recurring local legend, about the origins of the Gestingthorpe foundry, that is not inappropriate in our present era of financial chicanery. Les Smith explains:

"They used to say – my Father's generation did – that when Down started his foundry he couldn't afford to pay for the raw iron to begin work with. So to 'create the right impression' he stuffed a lot of coppers and iron washers in a 'Long Melford', (a great big long purse), and thumped it down on a table in view of a Halstead ironfounder. Apparently the ruse worked; people thought it was full of sovereigns; the iron was released and the business began!"

Although it was unusual for a village to have an iron foundry, Gestingthorpe was by no means alone. In 1848 one Henry Golding was listed as iron founder in Ashen. In 1806 Greenstead Green had the second earliest foundry in Essex. In neighbouring Earls Colne, 'Hunts' began their major works later in the century, whilst at Long Melford, the firm of 'Ward and Silver' employed a labour force of EIGHTY men – of whom no less than twelve were blacksmiths. Here they remained for 110 years, (until 1953), producing:

Hand Threshers	Rakes	Tumbrils
Barn Threshers	Cultivators	Stand Elevators
Dressers	Waggons	Harrows
Iron crosses for gravestones		

Across East Anglia flourished the other 'great names' of farm mechanisation. Many like Ransomes of Ipswich and Bentalls of Heybridge, (near Maldon) – who both originally made ploughs – trace their origins to humble blacksmiths' shops. Similarly around

217

1770 another blacksmith, named John Brand, of Lawford, near Manningtree, manufactured the first plough to be almost entirely made of wrought iron – which was not only highly acclaimed, but used on George III's farm at Windsor.

What then of our *locally* produced ploughs from the horse era? What comments and preferences had been expressed about them in previous years?

Thankfully there are still those who used them – year after year – on the fields of our rolling countryside. They are the same men who ploughed their 'acre a day' in downpouring storms; who fed their horses in the cold darkness of winter mornings; who marked out the bouts and 'opened up the furrows'; and who more than anything else had lived at a time, when to be known as a 'good ploughman' was tantamount to gaining the respect and recognition of their fellow workers.

"Old _____ was telling me that iron framed ploughs, (e.g. Ransomes), ere far better than wooden ones," I commented to one contributor. (Irrespective of whether a plough was described as 'wooden' or 'iron', the share and mouldboard were made of iron.)

"Silly old fool," came the retort, "what the devil does he know about it! I couldn't stand an iron plough!"

Soon then I was re-visiting all of my old contributors – to solve another mystery of our great agrarian past! Initially I went to Bulmer Tye, where, in a red-brick cottage next to the erstwhile smithy lives one of our most knowledgeable authorities on bygone farming. His name is Horace Elsey. He worked at Jenkins Farm for many years, and I have often listened – enraptured – for hours on end as he revealed the techniques and procedures, the skills and the crafts of horse era agriculture. Indeed Horace, who first 'went to plough' when fourteen – has no reservations in declaring:

"I much preferred a wooden plough! You had a lever where you could alter it 'ranker' or 'fleeter' – and if that was set right it would just glide along! It did actually have a place to fix a wheel – but if you could plough properly you didn't need one!"

"But what was wrong with an iron plough?"
"An iron plough had two wheels – and when you 'opened' a fur-

218

row you had to adjust these wheels – but to me they never seemed to pull as easily as a wooden plough – they always seemed to want to be 'grabbing'. However I will say this, once they *were* 'set up', they'd pretty much go on their own . . ."

"Did you ever use a Downs plough – from Gestingthorpe?" I excitedly asked. (The Downs being a 'wooden plough').

"Yes! I have done. But I didn't like it as much as a Bentalls – even though the shares were easier to change. The Bentalls plough was handier – you had more leverage to alter them. The other wooden plough we had was a 'Cornish and Lloyds' from Bury. That was a little heavier than the Bentalls, and I reckon a little stronger because the 'counter', (or coulter – a vertical knife), was on the side – not in the middle of the beam."

From Bulmer I returned to Gestingthorpe where in his cottage next to the *'Pheasant'* public house, Bert Surridge, provided an almost identical reaction:

"I'd choose a wooden plough any day! You see a good plough-man didn't need wheels – and to use an iron plough you'd got to have them – because they are so rank" (aggressive).

Then I remembered a visit I had made to another horseman who had used a wooden plough – the late Frank Turner (1903-1992), of Twinstead. On a beautiful summer's afternoon we had sat in the garden of his retirement bungalow, as the surrounding fields of ripening wheat, and distant encircling woodlands, were bathed in bright warm sunshine.

"When I was a boy," he had recalled with a rich voice and happy smile, "I worked at the Mote Farm in Pebmarsh. Then one day – when I was about seventeen – the foreman asked me if I'd like to try my hand at ploughing. 'Course I jumped at it. But when I went to plough – it was at Garlands Farm – I said to the 'head man', "Can I put the wheel in?"
"No," he said, "Not till you've learnt to plough." That was a wooden plough you see. . . He say, "when you can plough you can put the wheel in – but you'll never learn if you put the wheel in first."

"Why was that?"

"Well they reckoned you'd never be able to 'feel' if it was running true or not."

"After you had learnt, did he let you use the wheel then?"

"No. I never needed to! I never used wheels!"

In part, the preference of Frank, Bert and Horace can possibly be attributed to the heavy soils of the farms on which they worked. As another retired horseman, Fred Chatters of Borley explains:

"A wooden plough had a straighter 'mouldboard'. So it stood the furrow 'up' better. That meant that the frost could get in – to help 'weather' the heavy land down. But an iron plough laid the soil flatter. It was a prettier piece of work. But I've actually used both – and I don't know that there's any great difference – but of course people didn't like to part with what they were used to."

Next I ventured to Alphamstone to see Eddie Tuffin and later Frank Billimore at Bulmer. Both had worked on 'light land' farms, (the latter at Flempton near Bury St. Edmund's). Both preferred iron ploughs. Indeed, Frank Billimore unhesitatingly declared:"On light land you couldn't beat a Ransomes Y.L. iron plough!.," whilst Eddie Tuffin makes an additional point:

"One of the problems of a wooden plough, was that you had to keep going back to the blacksmith to get the coulter sharpened up. That may not sound much. But we hadn't got a blacksmith in this village!"

Finally I wended my way around the numerous corners from Gestingthorpe to Belchamp Otten and then to Belchamp St. Paul's. Here I visited the late George 'Jute' Chatters, who effectively sums up:

"Each has got its own advantages. If you set an iron plough right, it would go by itself – in fact it would go right across the field – and you didn't need to hold it.
"But an iron plough didn't turn round so well," (because of the

220

wheels at the front). "So when 'in work', I used to take the 'small' wheel off and put a 'foot' on instead. That ran on the land, whilst the big wheel went in the furrow. But when I worked at the Fowes in Belchamp Otten – which is a real 'heavy land' farm – we had a couple of wooden Downs' and then Bentalls I.P.W. ploughs – and they flung the land up really well. They were better for heavy land."

+ + + + +

On Saturday 29th June, 1995, the dispersal sale occurred of one of the 'grand old men' of our local farming community – the late Cyril Philp, of Kirby Hall, Castle Hedingham.

Amongst the 1063 lots to be auctioned, was a range of vintage equipment from blacksmiths' tools and stationary engines to threshing machines and traction engines. Lot 820 however was rather special.

It was a Downs T.D.O. wooden beam plough.

The auctioneer and massed crowds surged around. The bidding began. Determinedly we responded. Later we triumphantly loaded it onto our Ford pick-up truck and exultantly brought it back to Gestingthorpe!

But that evening when we unloaded it in our old barn at Hill Farm, and again looked at the broken beam, with its rotting, wood-wormed handles and rusty flaking iron work, a sense of deflation inevitably occurred. Perhaps – after all – it was not much to get excited about.

But coincidentally – purely coincidentally – in the week following our drive up the long narrow lane to Kirby Hall to collect the ageing Downs plough, a brand new piece of tillage equipment also arrived at Hill Farm. (It was a modern 'state of the art' five furrow plough).

It was a made in a foreign country almost a thousand miles distant. And it was incomplete! Vital components were missing! Worse it didn't match the product specified. And the paint work was in abysmal condition . . . The 'phone lines became incandescent!

And then I looked at the Downs again. It had been made just a 'ten minute walk' from where I live, by local men who lie now in our parish Churchyard, from local timber, and from iron that was cast and worked in the centre of our village. And then it had been used on local fields. It was genuinely, 'Of our Furrow Born'.

Yet despite the differences of design, the art of good ploughing was often ultimately governed by human considerations. At Bulmer Tye, Horace Elsey recalls his days at Jenkins Farm beside the Bulmer to Hedingham road:

"You take ol' _____. Well he'd damn near kill the horses! He never got a plough to run level, it was always up and down. But ol' Bill Toatley – he was different. He was a rare good ploughman. I reckon I learnt a lot by watching him. I mean the old darvil wouldn't tell you nothing! You wouldn't get much out of these old boys!"

But even Horace concludes with a confession:

"When ol' Bill Toatley ploughed, he could lay his land like a piece of butter – the whole way up the field. Well it never mattered how much I altered my plough, I could never lay it like him. And I've even used his plough – and hell if I could get it like him. That was just something to do with the way he held the plough.

"You'd see his furrow and it would lay as clean and there wouldn't be a break in it. I could never lay it like he did . . ."

His skills were truly, 'Of the Furrow Born'.

Chapter Fourteen

STEAM CULTIVATION and EARLY TRACTORS
'A Remarkable Lady'

The quest for improved husbandry, which had been initiated in the eighteenth century, created a steady impetus for new or better implements. As we have seen it was often our enterprising local blacksmiths who attempted to satisfy this demand. However interest remained strong, and by the early twentieth century well over twenty firms were producing agricultural implements within a twenty five mile radius of Sudbury. Indeed the list which follows can surely be extended by other local historians. Many produced a far wider range of equipment than noted here.

Acrow Pygro, Saffron Walden:	Steerage hoe.
Bartons, Sudbury (later Bruntons):	Portable and stationery steam engines. (Made railings beside Friars Street Cricket pitch).
Bentalls, Heybridge	Founded 1808. Produced a plough, named the Goldhanger after village of his birth. Also chaff cutters, root pulpers, grass mowers, reapers etc. (latterly grain driers and handling equipment). Additionally produced a motor car, described as a 'costly failure'.
J. Bitten Pash, Chelmsford	Ploughs, water carts, etc.
Blyth & Pawsey, Saffron Walden	Ploughs, rootchoppers, etc.

Boby, Bury St. Edmund's	Established 1843, especially renowned for 'corndressers' (i.e. cleaners or winnowing machines), but also for butter churns, hay-making equipment, horse rakes, and malting equipment.
Brand, Bures	Sack lifters, etc.
Catchpole, Standen	Beet harvesters.
Christy & Norris, Chelmsford	Mills, etc.
Caulkett, Clare	Wheels
Coleman & Morton, Chelmsford	Horse-drawn 'clod crushers', culti-vators, water carts, elevators, stacking machines, milling and dressing machines. (Sold over 25,000 cultivators).
Cornish & Lloyds, Bury St. Edmund's	Ploughs, Rakes, rolls, Horse-hoes, hay sweeps etc.
Sidney Darby, Plessey	'Darby Digger'. (An innovative steam driven cultivator which worked on digging principle.)
Downs, Gestingthorpe	Ploughs, rolls, pig troughs etc. – as noted
E.C.F., Ipswich	Pea cutters.
Eddington, Chelmsford	Traction engines, stationary engines etc.
Hunts, Earls Colne	Land rolls, chaff cutters, corn and maize grinding mills, etc. Also steam engines.
Josselins, Colchester	Harrows, tillage equipment etc.
Maldon Iron Works	Ploughs, rolls, etc.

Ransomes, Sims & Jefferies, Ipswich	Vast range from threshing machines to ploughs. By mid-nineteenth century Ransomes were exporting to Europe, Russia, India and Argentina. Some orders were huge – 338 sets of threshing tackle for Russia, 50 sets to Turkey, 140 sets to the Argentine. Later made a motor car, the 'Napier Landaulet'.
John Salmon, Dunmow	Beet harvesters.
Taylor (later Partridge), Hadleigh	Scales, sack lifters, sackbarrows etc.
Thurlow, Stowmarket	Crombs (harrows), horse hoes etc.
Ward and Silver, Long Melford	Rakes, Waggons, Dressers etc., as noted.
Webb, Exning	Beet drills.
Whitlocks, Great Yeldham	Chaff cutters, cultivators, poultry huts, trailers, diggers etc.
Woodsbury, Sudbury	Cast iron ware.

Yet this is not a dry academic list. For these firms were of pivotal importance. Not only did they provide machinery for a progressively improving agriculture, but also crucial work for local people. At Earls Colne, for example, Hunts employed almost two hundred personnel in 1915, and additionally provided 120 new houses in the village. At Bury St. Edmund's, Boby employed upwards of 300 men at the same time, whilst at Great Yeldham, Whitlock's once had a workforce of nearly SIX HUNDRED.*

Other firms like Smyths of Peasenhall – also deserve mention. They were a family of wheelwrights, who about 1800 produced a genuinely effective seed drill – based on Rev. Cookes' machine. (See picture pxxiii).

*A History of Great Yeldham by Adrian Corder-Birch, F.Inst.L.Ex.MICM, published by Halstead and District Local History Society, 1994.

So successful was the Smyth however, that for several decades in the early nineteenth century Suffolk men went out 'contract drilling' with them – as far away as OXFORDSHIRE and WILTSHIRE. (Smyth's initially started contracting to demonstrate how effective the drill was. Farmers paid around 2s-6d an acre for the service).

Later Smyth drills are still clearly remembered by older contributors. Retired farmworker Frank Billimore provides one interesting memory:

"It was so gentle," he says, "that at Flempton [near Bury St. Edmund's], one farmer used it to sow barley – that he had actually got to 'chit' first!"

In the nineteenth century a similar, successful drill had been made by yet another blacksmith named Garrett of Leiston. And together with Smyths, they continued the trend set by Brand, Ransome and later Boby of Bury St. Edmund's – of putting Suffolk and North Essex into the very forefront of agricultural innovation and improved farming practice.

The pattern would continue with the development of steam power. (No less than fourteen steam engine builders were based in both Essex and Suffolk with forty one more in Norfolk). Agriculturally however, it was Burrell of Thetford, Garrett of Leiston and Ransomes of Ipswich who were the leading 'East Anglian Trinity'. And together with Fowler of Leeds and Marshalls of Gainsborough, they still conjure up an era of 'ploughing engines' and threshing machines.

Yet the role of steam was crucial to agricultural progress. As the late Cyril Philp of Castle Hedingham explained:

"Those 'ploughing engines' had the power! They could 'get into' this heavy land to a depth impossible with horses. They could 'bust it up deep' – to let the air in – and the water out. They could get the twitch out – 'on top' – and into the sun. But most of all they could 'mole drain' it. For the first time ever we had the ability to master this heavy clay land – and really farm it to its full potential!"

Farmworkers however, who had the subsequent job of 'rolling' the jagged, uneven clods which the steam cultivators created were less complimentary. Commenting to Horace Elsey that steam ploughing was like 'poetry in motion', he instantly retorted:

"B___ poetry in motion! You want to go 'rolling' or be on the water cart when those two engines were about!

"One year at Jenkins Farm, 'Baldocks' from Haverhill came and 'steam cultivated' Forty Acres Field. (At the back of Bulmer School). I had to be ready at five o'clock in the morning, to cart water for them. And those big engines needed a damn big water cart as well! Then just when you'd got up against the engine they'd blow this b___ ol' whistle, and the ol' horse would jump and start – and you'd be 'half an hour' quietening it down again! I mean those engines were monster big ol' things – and the horses wondered what the hell was happening!

"But a bloomin' ploughing engine would take nearly a whole load of water! And you had to take one to each engine and THEN they'd want coal. So you'd have to take the water cart off, and then hook the horse onto the tumbril and take them a load of coal – and then right away get more water again! And that wasn't easy either! You couldn't just go and turn a tap on! Oh no! We had to back into the pond, and then stand on the cart and 'bucket it in' with a pail! Good job the horse didn't jump forward then! The thing was this; you could just about keep two engines going – but you'd be 'flat out'. They'd work from early morning until nightfall – and so about mid-day, Bill Toatley would come and take over from me."

The undulations of the area also provide some pertinent recollections:

"When ol' Stennett had Armsey Farm, (beside Ballingdon Hill), he did 'hell and all' steam cultivating. And he'd make them do it about a foot deep as well! Well on those hilly fields the wire ropes sometimes had to go over the brow of the hills – and then they would slice in the ground anything up to EIGHTEEN INCHES DEEP!"

The arrival of steam contractors on a farm was always something of an event, and the firm of 'Baldock's who undertook it in our area have passed now into our rural folklore. (Several contributors actually remember seeing, "up to a dozen ploughing engines," in the firm's yard, on the outskirts of Haverhill beside the road to Cambridge). At Gestingthorpe, Bert Surridge continues:

"Most years at Parkgate Farm, Baldock's would come and do one

227

or two fields. It was usually the same gang who came – so after a while you'd get to know them. There were five of them in the gang, and whilst they were here, they lived in a little wooden hut, which they towed around with them. There was one man on each engine, two on the plough and one who did the cooking, made the tea, and then relieved the others. 'Course there were some real ol' characters amongst them! I remember one old man who drove a steam engine. He was one of them *who never got ill*. But he kept a root of White Bryony in his pocket. And every now and then he would just cut a bit off with his penknife and nibble it – and he reckoned that kept him right!

"But 'rolling' behind the bloomin' steam cultivators was a cruel ol' job! You'd bandage the horses legs up – but they'd still get grazed and gashed. And it was none too comfortable for your own ankles either – getting twisted and wrenched around as you hobbled behind them!"

Even when the first tractors became available to pull the rolls there were still problems.

"I actually used to keep a *crow-bar* on my first ol' Fordson tractor," recalls Castle Hedingham's Bunny Brown. "Then if I was 'rolling' behind the steam cultivator I could move the biggest clods away from the wheels. If not, it was so unlevel, I'd have kept on 'getting set'!"

The surge of development and experimentation undertaken by East Anglian firms continued into the twentieth century. In 1914 for example, the innovative Crawley Tractor, (or motor plough), was developed by two farming brothers from Hadstock, near Saffron Walden. Production continued for about ten years, for a while being linked with Garrett's of Leiston, (near Aldeburgh). However it was the latter firm, who in 1929-30 produced Britain's – and possibly the world's – VERY FIRST DIESEL TRACTOR.

The significance of this development could be easily overlooked. But at one stroke the problems of petrol/paraffin engines – where the operator, 'warmed up on petrol and then switched over to paraffin', were overcome. As one older farmer observes:

"Before tractors had diesel engines they had to have 'spark plugs', 'points' and 'distributor caps'. And they were ALWAYS GIVING TROUBLE! Usually only niggly problems such as spark plugs 'oiling up' or the distributor cap getting damp on a foggy day, but it was unusual to go two or three days without some sort of a problem. If you left them 'ticking over' for too long when it was cold, they'd 'oil up', so you'd have to go back and start them on petrol again. You really needed to be quite keen – and a bit of an engineer – to drive an old petrol/paraffin tractor."

But in 1930, at the World Tractor Trials, held at Wallingford in Berkshire, Garrett's pioneering diesel tractor foretold a new era to come. It ploughed for NINE HUNDRED and SEVENTY SEVEN hours – night and day – without stopping! It then 'stalled' once, was immediately re-started and continued for another SIX HUNDRED hours. (The previous record for 'continuous ploughing' had been a 'mere' 481 hours). Between 1929–35 the firm manufactured some twenty eight such tractors for agriculture and industry.

However there was a price to pay. At a time with the International 15/30 tractor – which ran on T.V.O. – cost £320, the Garrett was priced at between £500–£525. As Robert Whitehead comments in his definitive book, *Garrett Diesel Tractors*:

"They were far ahead of the major tractor manufacturers in the power units they were offering. Sadly however they were amongst the most expensive at a time when agriculture was in the midst of a world-wide depression . . ."

(The firm did however continue to produce specialist tractors for excavating peat until 1960.)*

Reciting the statistics of the Garrett's extraordinary, 'Fifteen hundred hour marathon' to a recent farmers' meeting at Stoke by Nayland, a contemporary farmer exploded:

*All drawn from *Garrett Diesel Tractors*, by Robert A. Whitehead, published by R.A. Whitehead and Partners. Mr. Whitehead further kindly explains: "The significance of the Garrett tractor was that it was 'full compression ignition', without recourse to vapourising coils, blow lamps, or similar devices. Lanz and others had marketed what they termed, 'semi-diesels'."

"Bugger me! I bought a new tractor this year (1998) with electronic 'this' and electronic 'that' on it – and its forever 'breaking down'!! I'd say – without exaggeration – that our tractors now develop faults every 150 hours – and its nearly always due to electronics. Bring back the Garrett!"

"Huh!" Came a neighbourly retort, "you wouldn't say that on a cold frosty morning without any cab and your ears getting frozen off!"

Either way, Suffolk's tradition of developing new farm implements has continued. In the 1930's-40's Catchpole of Stanton began to address the harvesting of sugar beet, (with the Cathchpole 'Cadet' passing into the country's 'agrarian folklore'). More recently Sherborne Reynolds of the same village pioneered and produced their revolutionary 'stripper header' for combine harvesters which is exported around the world. (The concept incidentally was inspired by the Roman vallus.) Meanwhile Wickhambrook farmer Geoff Claydon designed and developed a combine mounted weigher – for measuring the yields of fields and 'trial plots'.

Notwithstanding the above, both East Anglia – and Britain's – position as a producer of farm machinery has drastically declined in the past three decades. Today for example, the seven hundred acres of Hill Farm, Gestingthorpe are worked with a German combine, Norwegian plough, Italian and Dutch 'power harrows', German seed drill and Norwegian 'seed bed cultivator'.

Yet until the nineteen seventies *it was still possible to equip an arable farm COMPLETELY with products from Essex and Suffolk. For Ransomes of Ipswich alone made combines, beet harvesters, sprayers, ploughs, cultivators and grain driers, while tractors were produced at Dagenham and Basildon by Ford. (At Ulting, Ernest Doe & Sons actually harnessed two Fordson 'Major' tractors together, into a combination known as 'The Triple D', selling 289 units during the nineteen sixties. Two other models, the Doe 130 and Doe 150 were also produced.)*

AN EXTRAORDINARY LADY

Yet for fear that these chapters should be dominated by traditionally male professions, it is interesting to find exceptions. One of the most remarkable relates to Ann Rudd. In 1831 she was listed as liv-

ing in Sible Hedingham. And her profession? She was a blacksmith. Ninety years later another lady was doing something even more pioneering. Her name was Muriel Pickering (b.1900), and around nineteen twenty – when it was unusual for women to drive cars . . . young Muriel did something even more exceptional.
She taught sceptical farmworkers to drive tractors.

"How did it all come about?" I asked her one memorable June evening, as we sat in her cottage close to Gestingthorpe Church.

"Well, towards the end of the First World War I joined something very similar to the 'Land Army' and after a while was sent to Kirton, near Felixstowe where I did milking with six other girls. Anyway after I'd been there about two years, they purchased a Fordson tractor from Mann Egertons of Ipswich. Well, I volunteered to drive it, so they sent someone out and I was taught all about it."*

"Do you have any particular memories of the first days?"

"Yes! It was perishing cold down there! I've even sat on the tractor bonnet to keep warm! And of course the seagulls only needed the slightest hint that I was going to start and there would be flocks of them around! In fact I was the very first person to plough up some of the grassland down by the sea wall. But occasionally as you were going along it would 'all turn out again' – just like a snake going across the field, so I'd have to get off the tractor and stamp it all back!"

"What about the other farmworkers," I asked keenly. *"How did you start teaching them?"*

"Oh goodness!" she exclaimed. "Don't rush. It was almost seventy years ago you know!" After pouring out a cup of tea and passing me some cake, Muriel continued: "Once I had had plenty

*On Sir William Pauls Farm. Kirton is near Felixstowe. Some 6000 Fordson tractors, ordered by the British government in World War One, started to arrive from about 1917. (Amongst other places Muriel visited were farms at Brettenham, Leavenheath, Tannington Hall in north Suffolk, and the Allestons at Boxford).

of experience, Mann Egerton's agent, a Mr. Green, asked me to go and 'start off' other farmers who had just bought their first tractor. I enjoyed that enormously, because I would travel around and stay on a different farm for two or three weeks until everyone was happy."

"Did you meet any real hostility from 'doubting' old horsemen?"

"No. Not a lot, except for one old horseman at Hoo Hall Farm who absolutely hated the sight of tractors and kept saying what useless and awkward things they were. In the end, I said, 'Look, I bet I can plough a straighter furrow with my tractor than you can with your horses!" That shut him up for a while."

"What about the maintenance and repairs?"

"I did it all myself – and I loved it! There wasn't much I couldn't put right on my own. Of course, there were a number of little tricks which helped. For example, if I went to collect a new tractor from the railway station, I'd stand on the starting handle if the engine was a 'bit tight inside'. And on very cold mornings I'd light a little fire beneath the crankcase – to warm up the oil because it used to get so thick in the winter."

"Could the old horsemen always get these early tractors started?" *I wondered.*

"Well, they could whilst I was there! But I do remember one old man who did the threshing. You see, I emphasised to him that the 'coil' must be kept warm and dry. So what he did was this. Every night he unbolted the coil and took it home with him – which was quite sensible – but then he took it to bed! Goodness me! I've no idea what his wife thought. But she didn't half give me some funny looks!"

She was not the only one. For the early tractors only had iron wheels – and on roads made, "the dickens of a row!" (Bands were put round the wheels to prevent the lugs damaging the road).

"However," explains Muriel, "there were no 'spring washers' on the early models – so the nuts and bolts which held them on were forever coming loose!

"In fact one of the things I will never forget is clattering and clanking up Kersey Hill one night – and all those old women looking out of their windows to see what on earth was going on. It was probably the first tractor they'd ever seen – and certainly the first which was driven by a girl!"

"What did your Mother think?"

"Dear me! I've no idea. I'm sure she wanted me to do something much more ladylike! But the thing is this, I really cannot imagine what a woman's life would have been like without the First World War. But I am sure that I would never have been able to drive a tractor – and quite possibly not a car! It's strange really, because looking back, I suppose that I was a sort of pioneer, and yet I never thought of myself as one at the time."

POSTSCRIPT

Two or three years after Muriel Pickering died, I interviewed another of our most enthusiastic contributors, Boxford farmer's son and haulage contractor Claude Alleston (b.1912). Midway through our conversation I mentioned Muriel and his face beamed with delight:

"Yes! I do remember her! She was a remarkable woman. She actually stayed with us for a few weeks whilst she taught my Father how to drive an International 'Junior' tractor – in about 1920. But do you know, she always had a spade on the tractor – and if ever she 'scuffed up' the soil – when she turned on the headland – she'd get off and level it out again. And several of our neighbours like Fred Brown and Joe Young also bought International 'Junior' tractors. So she came back several years running to start them off as well . . . But my goodness she was tough! Out there in all the cold weather and sharp winds!"

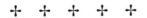

PRELUDE TO MILLS

Here watermen on barges passed,
Through verdant meadows lushly grassed,
And millers dusty heaved great sacks
On gnarled and knotted muscled backs.

As o'er the mill stream swallows glide,
Where cloth was fulled and weavers dyed.
And labourers sturdy, pitched the hay
Beside the river's wending way.

Thus solemn cattle graze by path,
Where old folks muse and youngsters laugh
-Til lovers, holding hands, are spied
On meads across this countryside!

This Countryside

"There used to be a windmill beside the road between Gestingthorpe and Wickham St. Pauls. And it was a damn nuisance! I mean, if you were carting corn and one of your horses was young and nervous, it would shy about and be as frightened as anything if the sails were turning as you went by!"

The late BERT SURRIDGE (1907 – 1997)

"Boxford had a mill up to the Second World War and a chap by the name of Happy Baker used to go around from one mill to another to dress the stones . . . But a lot of these country mills that had once done flour finished up only doing grinding for livestock".

CLAUDE ALLESTON of Boxford and Sudbury 1912-1994

"After Henny mill closed I used to go to Bures Mill with a horse and tumbril about once a week. I'd usually take about six sacks of oats for crushing or perhaps some barley for grinding. But that was such a big ol' mill, and the machinery made such a noise, that the poor old horse didn't like it! That was a job to keep it calm down there".

EDDIE TUFFIN, Alphamstone

"You know what my hands were don't you? Time I was working in the mill and handling all that ground up meal? They were the envy of all the girls around here! Your hands became as soft as baby's!"

JIMMY THEOBALD of Borley 1919-1995

Chapter Fifteen

WINDMILLS and WATERMILLS

'Borley and Belchamp Walter'

"One William Bridgeman of Weston Mill, Foxearth, has made a new water course, by reason whereof the common way for horses, carts and carriages is wholly flooded, worn away and very dangerous for about 4 perches".

(At the time Weston Mill was used for 'fulling' whilst the new course was to enable corn grinding. From *Essex Quarter Sessions*, 1612)

Historically, milling was done with quernstones. Watermills were developed by the Romans – who may well have introduced them to this area.

By the time of the *Domesday Book* in 1086 there were no less than 186 watermills in Suffolk. Locally these included, a 'winter only' mill at Edwardstone, together with one each in:

Assington	Lavenham	Kersey
Cornard	Milden	Clare

Similarly there were two in Bury St. Edmunds, Cavendish and Long Melford, whilst Hadleigh had four. In Essex three were recorded at Halstead, one at Great Yeldham and five in the Colnes. Equally interesting however, is that prior to the Norman conquest, there had also been a watermill at Nether Hall, Gestingthorpe.

Watching the languid trickle of the Belchamp Brook today, it is intriguing that such a gentle stream could ever have been harnessed. Was it a 'winter only' mill like Edwardstone, we wonder, or was there a much greater head of water?

Windmills arrived in Britain over the following hundred and fifty years – having been originally developed in Persia in the eighth and ninth centuries. An early windmill is recorded at Bury St. Edmunds in 1191, whilst by 1222 there were also examples at both Wickham and Belchamp St. Pauls.* Indeed by 1300 no less than forty nine windmills existed in Essex. Others in the locality – with their earliest date of reference include:

Toppesfield 1252	Bulmer (Smeetham Hall) 1265
Finchingfield 1254	Gosfield 1266
Hartest 1256	Belchamp Otten 1282
Little Yeldham 1263	Chelsworth 1286

For this, and much other information, I must record my debt to three superb books – which have so enhanced this portion of my 'journey'. They are:–

Essex Windmills, Millers & Millwrights by Ken Farries, (published by Charles Skillon Ltd. 1981)
Some Essex Watermills by Hervey Benham, (published by Essex County Newspapers, 1976).
Suffolk Windmills by Brian Flint, (published by Boydell Press 1979).

*   *   *

And now I must dedicate this chapter. To a local man, Jimmy Theobald (1919-1995), who worked at Borley watermill for many years. Sadly, Jimmy passed away before this book was published. But until that time he still loved to reminisce about the river and the millstones, the cog gears and the waterwheel, and of the creaking wooden mill where he spent his early life. It was Jimmy who inspired this chapter.

*When a survey was conducted of the manors belonging to St. Paul's Cathedral.

Let us return then to that era – his era – when our mills resounded to the clump of heavy horses, the rattle of the wooden waggons and the boisterous shouting of the miller who was standing in the 'lucam' – just beside the sack hoist.

For many old horsemen it is the steep climbs away from the watermills that are most vividly remembered.

"Think of Clovers Mill at Sudbury!" exclaimed Jimmy of today's *Mill Hotel*, "That really was a rum ol' place! Even with an *empty* waggon it was a sharp pull up that hill to Stour Street – and if you went the other way – by Walnuttree Hospital – you had that bloomin' corner to contend with! Then there was Clovers Mill at Halstead – right on that sharp corner! [Near today's Public Library]. That was a terrible place to get in and out of!"

Other old horsemen made similar comments. The late Ernie Lott of Bulmer described the road from Bakers Mill, Cornard as being, "Steeper than anyone would ever think for." Fred Chatters spoke of the 'tidy pull', up from Belchamp Walter watermill. Reg Rippingale of Gestingthorpe didn't merely mention the steep incline from Clovers Mill at Sudbury, to which he would take two waggon loads of

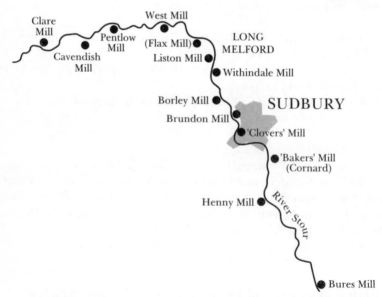

WATERMILLS ALONG THE RIVER STOUR *c.*1890

thirty 'coomb' sacks a day from Hill Farm, Gestingthorpe, but went on to explain:

"A lot of these farm horsemen would break the return journey at a pub like the Ballingdon *Kings Head*. Somewhere there was plenty of room for the waggon and horses to be left clear of the road. Of course", he continued, with a twinkle in his eye, "A lot of them reckoned that if you didn't stop – well – the horses might not like it!"

Another horseman, Alf Finch of Borley (1901-1996) – with whom I spent so many happy hours recording his memories of the village and its bygone farming – further clarifies the situation:

"What happened was this. You used to get 'journey money' for going out – so that was like a little bonus. I used to get threepence a load extra when I went to Clovers Mill in Sudbury. So on the way back I'd probably stop at the *Old Red Cow* in the Melford Road. I didn't have beer mind! I never ever drank – not in all of my life! Course I'd need an extra horse at Clovers – because of the steep rise. I'd need three – or even four horses to pull a 32 'coomb' load of wheat. But if I went to Brundon Mill I only needed two horses for a thirty coomb load."

"What else do you remember about Clovers Mill?"
"We always reckoned it was ever such a cold old place for some reason. And we had to take off the 'trace horses' – to let the traffic get past on the road. Then you'd either back your waggon close to the pit and shoot the corn out, or you'd pull under the sack 'hoist'. Most of these mills had 'hoists' which were driven by the waterwheel you see.
"What happened was this. A rope or chain would drop down. Then you'd slip the end through a 'ringle' and 'loop it over' the throat of the sack. But you had to watch out – because it has been known for the chain to come off the 'throat' – and the sack come crashing down!"

Jimmy Theobald elaborates:

"At Borley, father and I could unload SIXTY sacks in just three quarters of an hour! That was fairly going mind! What we did was

239

this. The horseman slipped the ringle over the sack; Dad stood in the 'lucam' and worked the rope and I was inside the mill – to take the sacks off and tip them out. But being as the sacks went through several trap-doors I'd always have to shake the chain – to let Father know I was ready. The other thing was this. Every single time father would call out to the horseman: 'FINGERS!' .... Because if they didn't look out they could easily get their knuckles grazed or even break their thumbs." (The 'lucam' is the projecting doorway at the top of the mill through which sacks entered.)

'The horseman slipped the ringle over the sack . . .'

TECHNICAL DETAIL

Borley Mill, where Jimmy worked, was owned by the Payne family who farmed extensively around the village. It continued to be powered by the river until 1947. Thereafter a stationary engine, a tractor engine and eventually electric power were utilised until the mill finally closed in 1969. As with many other country mills, it was latterly only a 'grist mill', cracking beans, rolling oats and grinding wheat and barley into meal for farmers' livestock. Flour production itself had ceased in 1916.

Most other rural mills were similarly unable to produce flour in later years. George 'Jute' Chatters (1910–1995), typically recalls that the mill at Knowle Green, Belchamp St. Paul had, "once been able to do flour," (as had Henny Watermill), whilst the late Wally Twinn (b.1902), explains, "Pentlow Mill could do flour when I was a boy. Eventually however it just became too expensive to replace the silk screens and it finished up as a 'grist' mill only."

One which certainly continued however, was at Elmsett, where in the 1930's, Ladbrooks had a 'three sack an hour' flour plant. In the main, however, it was the larger mills beside the rivers, (e.g. Bakers Mill at Cornard and Clovers at Sudbury), which continued producing flour into the 1930's and beyond. (Along the River Colne it was the same. Here Alderford Mill at Sible Hedingham, ground 'wholemeal flour' until the Second World War, whilst Hulls Mill at Great Maplestead produced flour for Hovis until the early 1950's.)

By comparison with the mighty mills beside the River Stour, (and even Borley Mill had three pairs of stones and storage bins for 500-600 sacks of corn), a surprising number of tributaries to the Stour and Colne were also harnessed. Courtauld's, for example – who later

Clovers Mill, Sudbury, (now the Mill Hotel), was capable of driving fifteen pairs of stones with the assistance of a steam engine. (See chimney in drawing). The actual waterwheel – which could work four pairs of millstones – weighs fifteen tons and is clearly visible from both the Bar and Restaurant. In 1900 there were some twenty to thirty working watermills on the River Stour. Today there are none.

241

evolved into the giant textile manufacturers – had their original mill in the uplands of Pebmarsh about 1800. Similarly, when farmworker Harry Gilbert, (1897-1986) of Colne Engaine was a lad, he took:

> "our grinding to Millbrooks on the River Peb. But several of these smaller mills had farms or something to help boost the income. At Langley Mill they farmed – as they did at Millbrooks."

However, for a really 'small' stream my thoughts inevitably turn to the Belchamp Brook and the pastoral water mill beneath the parish Church.

INTERLUDE AT BELCHAMP WALTER

Today, all that remains is a small building, about the size of a two-bedroomed house, in the midst of a wide, pony-grazed meadow. There is not even any sign of water. Yet for *at least* four hundred years a watermill operated amidst the idyllic surroundings.

The *location* however is still fondly remembered. As Gestingthorpe farmworker the late Dennis Rippingale explains:

> "On Sunday afternoons it was a regular thing for families or friends to walk from 'Gestup', through the meadows, down to the old watermill, and then come home round by *'The Eight Bells'*. It made a really nice route."

Similarly, Evelyn Reeve of Bulmer (b.1922) happily reminisced of "swimming in the mill-pools as children." Tom Rowe who had some-times done the 'haysel' work, instantly commented on, "the beautiful kingfishers darting over the 'causey'" (causeway), whilst horseman Charlie Martin of Belchamp Walter spoke of, "picking mushrooms off the surrounding meadows. Mind you, it was about four o'clock in the morning! Still it was really lovely down there."

Indeed it was these descriptions of the 'mill in the meadows', with its 'overshot wheel', millhouse and miller that motivated me – after obtaining permission – to visit the site one June afternoon in 1988. (The area is strictly private and the property has since been com-pletely renovated). However, it wasn't a solitary excursion. I took a companion. It was retired threshing contractor and countryman, the late Jack Cornell, whose wonderful reminisences – and love of the area – had largely inspired my first book, *The Long Furrow*.

Together we rummaged between tall nettles and over wire fences, along old trackways and through crumbling buildings, pausing only to make speculative reconstructions and listen to Jack's inevitable anecdotes.

"Well, that 'ere tree is more than seventy years old" he points out, "so that was here when the mill was a going concern."

Then we clamber into the loft and see the 'lucams' winding gear. Peering down we work out where the grinding stones were laid – and how they were raised for 'dressing'. Re-emerging into the daylight, Jack finds a loose red brick in some broken walling. Brushing off the cobwebs he reveals the maker's stamp: It was, "RAYNER: GEST-INGTHORPE".

"But what about the water?" I ask, of which there *is not a drop in sight.*

"The water from Belchamp Brook was diverted – into a great big reservoir or 'causey'", explains Jack, pointing to a steep bank. "But the 'causey' was nearly half a mile long, eight or nine feet deep – and seven or eight yards wide!"

Indeed it is this 'causey' that is really so extraordinary about Belchamp Walter. For this enormous reservoir was dug by hand. Then a stream was partly diverted. But most of all the levels were correctly calculated *on a plain* – where one feels that the water would almost have had to run uphill!

And it is not a facetious point. For whoever actually did engineer the levels – at least four centuries ago – was indeed supremely skilled.*

Fortunately we also have more recent recollections of the mill at work. For an existing contributor, retired farmworker Fred Chatters (b.1906) actually lived at the Mill house as a schoolboy. Today, he lives in the 'Old School House' at Borley, which has views across the open fields to both Brundon and Borley's erstwhile water mills. It was

*A map of 1605 in Essex Record Office clearly shows the mill and diverted mill stream. The mill which was rebuilt in Victorian times, had two pairs of stones – although only one pair could be used at any one time. As with many other country mills a small farm was attached to the Water Mill. In 1805 there was also a windmill not far from Belchamp Walter church. Older residents still refer to 'Windmill Hill'.

here, one cold, grey February day that I spent an engrossing afternoon recording his memories.

"When I was a boy Belchamp watermill was run by a Mr. Ruffle. But he also had Wickham St. Paul's windmill, so he left my father 'in charge' at Belchamp Walter, although he'd often ride over on his horse to see us."

"Could the water mill be kept going throughout the year?" I naturally wondered.

"Well, it was more full-time in the winter months. But by Dad's time, they also had a 'portable' steam engine which they could use to turn the grindstones if the causeway was too low in the summer. But there again, in the summer the horses and cattle were out on the meadows so the farmers didn't need so much grinding. One of father's main summertime jobs though, was to stop rats from burrowing in the bank of the 'causey'. Don't he'd soon have lost all his water!"

"What about the corn that farmers wanted grinding. When did they bring it to you?"

"They didn't! Well hardly ever. We generally did the collecting and delivering. It was a regular thing. You'd take out one week's grist [meal] and bring back their barley, wheat, beans or oats for grinding."

"Why didn't farmers collect it themselves?"

"On account of the First World War! There was a terrible shortage of horses. So father would go out in a four wheel miller's van, [a horse drawn cart]. He went right round Gestingthorpe up to Hill Farm and Delvyns' and even up Edeys Lane.

"One difficult place though was Goldingham Hall, Bulmer. I mean, it is only half a mile away – across the fields. But because of the Belchamp Brook it was nearly a five mile journey by road! So when theirs was ready, it was my job – as a boy – to run across and tell them. Then they'd send a cart and meet father halfway, at somewhere like Gestingthorpe crossroads or the 'Barracks'."

It was the same elsewhere:

"From Belchamp Otten windmill," declares the late 'Jute' Chatters, "ol' Henry Cornell would come round every week with a tumbril, and deliver half a dozen sacks of grist – and then collect six other sacks to grind for the following week. On the side of his cart was painted, 'HENRY CORNELL – GRIST FOR THE TRADE'."

Sitting in his home overlooking Alphamstone church, retired shepherd Eddie Tuffin recalls the larger establishment of Henny watermill – which also ground flour:

"There were FIVE horses kept in the stable! Two were used on the miller's van with one each for the smaller carts and baker's van. But they went round for miles – right up to Wickham St. Paul – before coming back along 'Broad Road', turning at Gentrys Farm and then coming down 'Watery Lane' to Henny."

Like all watermills those at Henny and Belchamp Walter faced problems from continuous heavy rain.

"So what happened when there were heavy storms and floods and the water began to rise?" I asked Fred Chatters, thinking of George Eliot's turbulent Mill on the Floss.

"Well in time you'd get so much pressure on the wheel that it could start the mill up in the middle of the night! We children could hear it creaking – it would even wake us up. So then Dad would have to get up and turn the brake on tighter. The other thing he could do – if he hadn't got too much grinding on – was to let some water out of the gates and take the pressure off that way. . ."

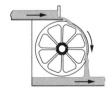

Overshot waterwheel

Undershot waterwheel

245

However if this was the response of an 'overshot' mill to rising water, what of the great majority which had 'undershot' wheels.

"If there was a flood on at Henny Mill" explains Eddie Tuffin, "they'd keep the mill going all night. You see if they once stopped, the water got too high on the other side of the wheel – and they couldn't start it no more! Ol' Chinnery used to do it and then the owner of the mill took over – he'd keep grinding all night!"

Alf Weavers – one time farmworker of Henny – but later soldier, and contributor to *The Khyber Connection*, further recalls:

"By my time they had an engine at Henny Mill. It was a lovely old engine it was too! But that's the reason he had it – to turn the grindstones when the river was too full."

. . . There was a pause whilst Alf looked at me wryly,

". . . But don't you start writing anything romantic about mills, Ashley! As far as I was concerned THEY WERE AS DUSTY AS HELL."

Sadly, Jimmy Theobald agrees.

"If I'm honest," he says, "I think it was the dust that actually killed my father. You take a job like grinding dry barley. There were times when you couldn't see across the mill floor for dust . . . and of course, there were no extractor fans or anything. I mean it hung around so long, that time of day."

But the dust presented other hazards – particularly when grinding oats.

"You certainly WOULD NOT go about with a lighted candle then!" exclaims Jimmy. "That dust would BANG like gunpowder – there'd be a heck of a flash!"

There were other, equally rigorous aspects. "Like the noise from the ol' oat crusher!" he exclaims, "You'd shout yourself hoarse trying to make yourself heard!"

246

Additionally there was the constant risk of catching Weil's disease – from the droves of rats which were drawn to the mills.

"At Belchamp Walter," says Fred Chatters, "there were *rows and rows* of rat tails nailed up on the wall of the 'engine shed' at the back of the mill. And there were other times you know, when there were so many rats running about on top of the water wheel that they'd almost start it off!!"

In addition to the rats, the unpleasant working conditions and the problems of floods and rising rivers, the mills were also involved in legal altercations.

"In Sudbury" reveal Messrs. Grimwood and Kay, "a bizarre dispute occurred when one windmill owner claimed that a newly built competitor had actually CAPTURED HIS WIND". (One was on the site of the Masonic Hall in North Street – and the other almost opposite.)

At Halstead, the 'Town Mill' was taken to court in 1826 for 'damming up' its water. (This prevented Box Mill – which was 'upstream' – from starting grinding until the Town Mill had been at work for a couple of hours.) Although it was thereafter prohibited from doing so, the fine was not exactly excessive. It was in fact ...precisely one shilling! (The 'Town Mill' is situated near today's Solar supermarket and is now a Craft and Antique centre.)

"The case is actually quite unusual," explains Colne Engaine's Harry Gilbert. "Because in a dry year it was normally the 'downstream' miller who was unable to grind – because the mills further up had not released their water. In a dry time, Langley Mill could not grind until Halstead Town Mill had made a start – and let some water go."

"And so," declares retired farmer Wally Twinn, of Alphamstone and Pentlow, "one little row would lead to another! Then the miller would tell you that you couldn't have the meal for your horses. But if you got frustrated he would just as soon reply, 'Well why the devil didn't you keep some in reserve!'"

Another contributor described a recurring source of mistrust:

"Farmers were always suspicious as to whether the correct amount of 'ground' barley and 'cracked' beans – which are both bulkier after grinding – actually came back. Particularly where a mill had a farm of its own!"

However as our oldest contributor, Edwin Partridge (1892-1993) explained:

"When we went to Layham or Raydon Mill, we'd take an extra sack. So if we wanted six sacks of grinding done, then we'd send a seventh sack for the little bit that they couldn't get in."

Another local farmer however, who also used to *sell* 'milling' wheat to the millers, was a little less diplomatic:

"Millers!" he quipped, "Huh! They were like a cart-load of monkeys!"

Even here the subject didn't close. For several weeks later a retired miller quietly recalled:

"In the great depression of the nineteen thirties, some of these farmers went months, years sometimes, without paying their bills. No, we just stood by them, and helped them out where we could."

There were other grievances. Many riverside farmers resented the water table being kept artificially high by the millers who had the water rights. As Witgar Hitchcock latterly of Bures Mill – where his family had lived since 1875 – helpfully explains:

"At Bures, what was right for the miller was bound to be wrong for the farmers – since it was necessary for the riverside meadows to be almost waterlogged for the mill to operate normally. Indeed the water was normally within a few inches of the tops of the banks."

"So the valleys had genuine water meadows?"

"Yes. The land was like a sponge and provided a wonderful reserve with which to keep the mill running in dry seasons. At Bures the mill owners could keep the level of their water at 61'11" above sea level."

"Are you saying that the level of the River Stour has actually been reduced?"

"Yes. At Bures by 3'11" since 1936. In part this explains why many water meadows have in fact become 'cultivatable' since World War Two. Also it makes it easier to understand why there was sufficient water to operate the most 'up stream' mills such as those at Belchamp Walter." (At Borley, for example, the river is 2'3" lower than in 1939).

Whilst water could be partially regulated – and reserves accumulated – the power which drove windmills was not remotely predictable and could never be stored. Consequently, as roads improved and motorised transport increased, it was usually the windmills which ceased operating before the watermills – even despite the addition of steam.

Windmills indeed, were inherently more vulnerable. During the nineteenth century five windmills were known to have operated in Halstead. Yet of these:

One was, 'rent in pieces by lightning' about 1800
East Mill was destroyed by fire on Christmas Eve 1862.
Box Mill blew down in 1882, whilst Frost's – or North Mill – was damaged by strong winds in 1867. (The latter subsequently added a steam engine although the sails continued to be used for several more decades.)

In Suffolk reveals Brian Flint, Boxford postmill was actually *blown over* in 1604. Then in 1795 a terrific gale blew down Cornard windmill – and savaged another at Ballingdon, whilst less than a week later Lavenham windmill was also destroyed.*

More recently, retired horseman 'Jute' Chatters recalled the problems encountered at Belchamp Otten windmill during the late nineteen twenties:

*From *Suffolk Windmills* by Brian Flint and *Essex Windmills* by Ken Farries. (During the hurricane of Friday, 26th November, 1703, more than 400 windmills in England were said to have been overset, broken or fired.)

"Times were hard enough as they were! But come the finish there was a hell of a gale and it blew the bloomin' sails off! As luck had it though, he already had an engine to help out. But before that, it was nothing unusual for old Henry Cornell to work all night – if he'd 'got some wind' after a 'still week'!"

Even when engines were installed hazards remained. At Wormingford in 1929 a fire developed from a 'crude oil' engine installed in the mill. In just three quarters of an hour the building was destroyed. So fierce was the conflagration reports Jimmy Theobald, "that burning timber landed over a quarter of a mile away!"

Then there were the seasonal concerns. "During the autumn gales at Borley," continues Jimmy,

"You could feel the whole mill sway and move! In fact the wooden floors and uprights weren't fixed tight – they deliberately had a little leeway so that the beams and uprights could move a bit. My father used to bellow out, 'if that didn't creak and bang then that 'ud blow us down boy!'."

Winter was little better.

The Mill-Bill.

"The 'mill-bill' was made of 'silver steel', which is so hard that it's impossible to cut with a hacksaw", explains Jimmy Theobald. "Now if the millstones weren't too bad you could do a pair of them in a couple of days. But if they'd got behind! Well they could take a couple of them in a couple of days EACH! That was eight hours to put the cracks in and eight hours for the furrows. And that 'mill-bill' weighed 5 1/2 lbs. Yes! That did – what you call 'make your wrists ache' after a day's work!"

"Oh Lord, that was cold! There were more draught holes than a little – I can tell you. There was only one warm place. And that was where the meal came off the mill-stones – but you darn't put your hands near there! Course winter was 'stone dressing' and 'repair time'. And you'd be laying on your side 'dressing the stones' with only a bag of bran to rest your elbow on – and your feet were frozen, and the only bit of you that was warm were your arms. And then first thing in the morning and last thing at night it would be dark – so you'd need an oil lamp or candle . . . Oh yes! You'd know what it was to look forward to your supper!"

As the weather got colder, so too came the likelihood of ice.

"If a waterwheel did ever break it would be in the winter. I mean occasionally a bucket (on the wheel) might split and you'd have to put on a spare one, but if ice got on the wheel and it became too heavy – well that *was* serious. I've known father turn it on Saturday evenings *and* Sundays – just to keep it free."

Slowly the months passed and summer arrived. But if it was too dry there would soon be new problems.
"It became a real art to keep the water up! And if you saw the slightest trickle coming out of the sides of the floodgates – well, you'd be down there right away with some cinder dirt to seal them up again. In fact they kept EVERY SINGLE BIT of cinder dirt from Borley Hall – just a purpose for it."

Jimmy's concern was a prime anxiety of all millers. In a letter to the artist John Constable, dated 7th July, 1808, his Mother wrote,

"Your Father . . . is now gone to Flatford and will I fear be vexed, as upon spending yesterday at the new floodgates there appears to be some unlucky leakage. But I trust it can be rectify'd without taking up the new water [and] detaining Barges, Gangs, etc."

(Constable's father owned mills at Flatford, Dedham and East Bergholt. Additionally he attended meetings of the Stour Navigation Committee at Sudbury.*

*From *John Constable's Correspondence*, Volume IV, edited by R. B. Beckett; published 1962 by Suffolk Records Society.

Not only were the millers alert and skilful but so too were the millwrights who actually built the structures and undertook the major repairs. As the late John Frost of Halstead's North Mill observed:

"The old millwrights were exceptionally skilful men. Part carpenters, builders, 'schemers', steeple jacks and mechanics. Think of them repairing a 'mill cap' sixty foot up in the air. Oh no. They deserve a place in any corn milling 'Roll of Honour'."

LOCAL DETAIL

Almost all parishes in our area had water or windmills at some point in the nineteenth century. (Gestingthorpe being an interesting exception. However there were nearby windmills at Castle Hedingham, Wickham St. Paul, and 'Cottonbury' in Belchamp Walter, the latter being situated between Gestingthorpe and Little Yeldham).

How different our landscape must have looked when windmills

WATERMILLS ALONG THE RIVER COLNE *c*.1880.

were so numerous! Three especially prominent structures were Armsey windmill, (at the brow of Ballingdon Hill), Highfield windmill, (near the Melford Road), and Batt Hall's smock windmill beside the Bulmer road into Sudbury. At the latter the base still stands. Similarly 'Frosts' or North Mill, must have had a dominating appearance on the hill-top skyline of the town. Yet the density of mills around both Sudbury and Halstead also testifies to something else. It is the sheer agricultural productivity of our area – and the standard of husbandry achieved in past centuries.

(The reference books mentioned earlier provide superb details and often photographs of most local mills.)

However not all water or windmills were agricultural. In 1824 a water mill was built at Glemsford for 'silk throwsting'; Courtauld's used water to power their silk mills at Halstead and Pebmarsh; whilst Halstead's 'North Windmill', relates John Frost, "once ground lavender for perfume." Similarly, in 1796 both Braintree and Wethersfield had cloth mills, whilst at Greenstead Green and Long Melford were mills for, "pounding rags into paper."

In medieval times, many 'wool fulling' mills had also existed along the Rivers Stour and Pant. More recently there was a 'malt-mill' at Clare; a 'sewage disposal' windmill at Colne Engaine, (from 1880 – 1884); and a 'tide mill' at Thorrington on the Colne estuary, (which ground up septaria cement stone). Finally, as noted in Chapter Seven, two local watermills – Alderford in Sible Hedingham and Bridge Street in Alpheton – generated and sold electricity in the nineteen twenties.

Yet whatever their purpose the erstwhile mills all share one unifying feature. The energy that drove them was entirely, 'Of the Furrow Born'.

THE LORE OF THE RIVER

"In front of the mill at Borley," recalls Jimmy Theobald, "there were three posts – which measured the height of the water. When it reached the highest one, it was all you were allowed – and you had to let some go. But sometimes, when the water fluctuated you were up and down that flood path a dozen times a day!

"'Course the next mill upstream could soon tell if you were 'heading up' water – because it would slow their wheel down! But as luck had it we got on well with Branwhites who were at Whithindale, above us. And downstream there was an experienced old hand who kept it right at Brundon."

Borley Mill as it is today.

"You know the very last thing you did at night, don't you? At ten o'clock you'd go and look at your water and check the levels were right. 'Course during a flood you might stay up the whole time – to make sure it didn't reach the mill bottom. In a bad flood you didn't go to bed . . ."

Jimmy Theobald

254

Chapter Sixteen

FURTHER DIARIES OF JOHN ROW
'Triumphs, Tribulations and Trials Work'

1888-1899

Although we left John Row in the depths of despondency, his diary provides a fascinating glimpse into local agriculture in late Victorian times. For Row was both a pioneering and progressive farmer. Indeed, at Kings Prentices and Highlanders Farm, in Long Melford, he even abandons the homely old field names for stark and efficient numbers. (Field numbers 1 to 9 are at Kings Prentices and 10 to 15 at Highlanders Farm). At Lower Hall Foxearth however the traditional appellations such as Bearlams, Pollards and Barn Field are retained. And of one of them he adventurously writes:

> 16th October 1897: "About twelve acres on Home Field,
> Foxearth – are *WHEAT AFTER WHEAT!*"

The following harvest he reveals – in prominent red ink;

> "Very excellent crop; all the goodness of two years
> White Clover layer has not been exhausted!"

A hundred years later there would be nothing exceptional in 'wheat after wheat'. Numerous fields in Bulmer, Gestingthorpe and the Belchamps have been 'continuous cereals' for the past two decades. Yet in 1897, with only cultural means of controlling weeds and a still tenuous understanding of plant nutrition, Row's field of 'wheat after wheat' was almost brazenly pioneering – if not slightly reckless. It is in fact, the only occasion in the ten year survey that he records a 'second' wheat. More surprisingly there is only one example of 'barley following barley'.

255

For Row was still governed by the limitations of his age with no chemical herbicides and only a few artificial fertilisers. As such, his rotation was designed to "clean the land" and restore fertility. Appropriately he commences his diary by intimating his intended programme.

> One fourth of the farm . . . Wheat
> One fourth of the farm . . . Barley and Oats
> One fourth of the farm . . . Leys; peas and beans
> One fourth of the farm . . . Roots or fallow.

Let us move forward then and slowly decipher the pages. We will need a magnifying glass and bright light .... And occasionally too we may wish that his hasty hand-writing had been just a little bit neater! We will read however of his triumphs and disasters; of the "lovely rain on the spring barley," of the "heavy storm on 'shocked-up' corn," and of his constant daily relationship with the weather and his Mother Earth.

January 1890, for example, had been, "Most unseasonable weather – more like May than January." The following year proved the reverse.

> 25th Nov 1890 . . . "Winter set in with a vengeance"
> January 1891 . . . "One of the most extraordinary frosts on record."
> February 1891 . . . "Driest February ever known."

– TWO WET AUTUMNS –

Eight months later our hero had to endure an abnormally wet October. A crop of red clover seed was COMPLETELY LOST and Row faced the gnawing anxiety that his crucial autumn drilling might not be accomplished. Once more the emotional aspect of farming is fully revealed:

October 8th 1891: "Tried to get seed clover at Highlanders cut, but rained more or less every day."

Week ending October 17: "Very wet and stormy until Saturday. No seed clover carted, and 3 acres still to cut. No chance of carting any mangolds yet."

256

Week ending October 25: "Dreadful wet week"

Week ending October 31st: "Wet early part of week. Weather changed on Thursday. Carted seed clover on Saturday – but it is <u>useless.</u> The seed is grown and straw rotten. Mr. Mills folded his sheep over the standing 3 acres. <u>Not a mangold carted, nor a single bean or kernel of wheat yet sown.</u>"
(Row's underlining was in red ink!).

The following year again produced another miserable wet season for drilling winter wheat. Again there were problems with 'puggled down', 'muddled in crops', as horses and farmworkers trudged across sodden fields. The following entry provides a graphic description of both the farmer's frustration – and conditions in the fields where the work was done!

12th November 1892 . . . "Tried to drill wheat on Field no. 14. Went in *very* badly. *Could only get in about 3 acres - in a whole day's work.* 4 horses on the drill but were scarcely able to pull it. *23 days* since the last wheat was sown."

. . . AND A DRY SPRING

The wet autumn of 1892 was followed by a compensatory dry March. Row's initial reaction however is of exultation: "Splendid weather," he wrote on both March 12th and the 19th, whilst on March 26th he records, "another marvellous week!" . . .

Today we can still visualize the farm operations of that Spring's work. We can picture the powerful heavy horses pulling the 'ducksfoot cultivators' across the ploughed land as the horsemen walked behind. We can imagine also a tumbril, laden with sacks of seed corn, being taken out onto the head-land. We can see the 'seed drill' being pulled, 'gun-barrel straight' across Row's fields – as the village of Long Melford stretched in the background. And finally we can envisage the later 'harrowing' and 'rolling', as the steady, dependable horsemen went about their work, with the special satisfaction of doing a job well – in a favourable season.

The spring corn had been drilled in perfect conditions. Row must have felt optimistic and thrilled. All he needed now was just a few 'good rains' to let the seed corn germinate . . .

But the dry weather continued. Some spring barley might have eventually emerged patchy and yellow but hardly vigorous. On April 15th Row quietly comments, "<u>Still</u> no rain."

With each additional dry day the possibility of achieving maximum yields diminished. With each succeeding dry week the sad likelihood increased that he would even struggle to reach 'farm average'. The joyous account of March's 'splendid weather and beautiful seedbeds' was all too quickly a bygone memory.

His entry for 22nd April 1893, audibly intones a farmer's concerned, plaintive voice:

"A cloudless sky but no rain: Want a good rain: Want it badly. Cannot sow small seeds of any kind." [e.g grass, clover, etc.]

But there was no respite to the dry weather. On April 29th his week's summary somberly reveals, "No rain again." For the follow-

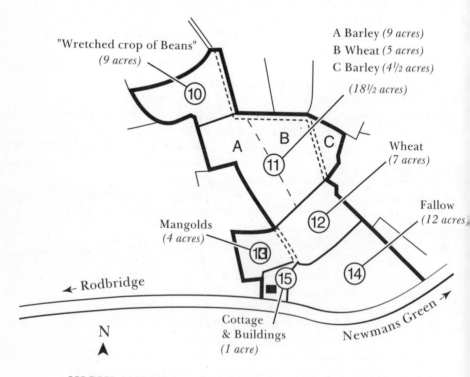

HIGHLANDERS FARM, LONG MELFORD, 1891–1892

258

ing three weeks, when his barley should have been vigorously growing, there was no real change.

May 6th: "A little rain. But only about an hour. Sowed clover seed – but doubt it can grow."

May 13th: "Another week without rain."

And then finally on May 20th, relief pours out of his pen as he joyfully scrawls:

"Proper rain at last! Five hours from 4.30 p.m. to 9.30 p.m."

Following the backward, mud-puggled seedbeds of the autumn and the drought-like spring, (and how we can imagine the knowing comments in the cart-shed about 'cuckoo barley'!), the harvest predictably produced,

"THE LIGHTEST CROPS ON RECORD."

But Row does not merely make impulsive statements. His accounts reveal that 1892 and 1893 were actually two of his poorest years. Additionally he records his *exact* yields and the daily details of each field's work. In 1893 for example, Field No. 10, at Highlanders was, 'wheat after beans'. During the autumn it had been:

"Ploughed, scarified, thoroughly cleaned and then part sown on October 20th – with the rest on November 26th."

But after harvest Row dismally wrote:

"Dreadful poor crop. About four coomb an acre." (9cwt/acre).*

Each year he drew a map of his farm in the diary. Within the outline of Field No. 14 he laconically noted the year's operations:

"Commenced sowing November 12th. Went in very badly — finished November 26th." (This is the field where only three acres were drilled in a whole day.)

*At the time many farmers would consider that, "Eight sack an acre was 'a good average' yield," and that, "Ten sack an acre was a very good crop." Row's words are sometimes slightly rephrased to improve clarity.

259

Then repudiating a local aphorism he resignedly comments:

"Sowed in a flood – but did not reap in a wood!"

On the facing page of the diary is the rough ink plan of Fields no. 6, 7 and 8 at Kings Prentices. Despite all being 'wheat after break crops' – which should have produced good yields – the dry weather had also affected them. For after harvest Row wrote across the maps, "Only about 6½ coombs per acre on these three fields." (About 14½ cwt/acre).

But the reality was worse. When the stack from these fields was finally threshed in the following spring – and the genuine weight established – Row objectively confessed in forceful red ink:

April 5th: "Only 85 coomb from Threshing Machine from Field Nos. 6, 7 and 8."

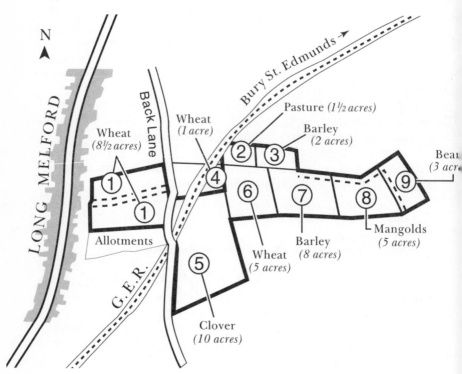

KINGS PRENTICES FARM, 1891–1892

Since he also included his field acreages – *to three decimal places* – his actual yield was a mere 5.61 coomb or 12.63 hundredweight an acre!

Yet even now – as so often with farming – the difficulties of one season, (in this case the drought), resurface in the next:
"7th October: had to sow extra grass seed on Field no. 13."
However Field No. 3 which had also been 'undersown' with grass was even worse. For Row had to resort to the 'ultimate solution':

"Ploughed it up," he scrawls, "and sowed the grass for a second time!"

As always the climate was the predominating influence on farm operations. And then – just as now – there were early seasons and late ones. So whilst Row was unable to finish sowing his wheat until December 17th in 1892, five years later he jubilantly wrote:

"October 16th: A most extraordinary month of marvellous weather. Most beautiful in every respect. All wheat sown by 16th October. *A record for us.*"

But apart from the winters without snow, and the summers without sun, as the mangolds were gathered and the fallow was 'ploughed back' and the interlocking, 'four course rotation' slowly revolved round the farm, there were also the moments of crisis and catastrophe.
November 24th, 1888 was one particularly fraught day. A threshing machine was at work on the farm at Kings Prentices, when:

"Some cinders from the traction engine, which had been raked out onto the ground in a grossly careless manner – with only a couple of pails of water put on them - SET FIRE to three surrounding stacks!
"Then the haystack caught fire. Great danger was felt by everyone that the flames might spread to the houses in the Street. But everyone – men, women and children worked with a will!"

Fortunately the fire was contained. Row moreover was insured, for on November 27th he writes:

"Mr. Gibbs from Messrs. C. H. Whites office came down and assessed the damage, making it £279.2s.0d."

From the hazards of threshing to the organisation of a traditional harvest, with its scything of headlands, 'bindering' or reaping of the fields; 'shocking up' of sheaves, loading of waggons and eventual building and thatching of stacks.

The incentive which induced so much laborious work to be accomplished was investigated in *The Long Furrow*. Here we explained how the harvest was 'let', (or contracted out), to a gang of workers who were led by the 'Lord of the Harvest' – or workers' foreman. Happily in 1891, Row corroborates our research for on 15th August he records:

"have 'let' the harvest to Bullock, Deeks, Wilby,
Martin, Munson and Reeve – Reeve to be the Lord."

Interestingly the harvest was 'taken' at, "12s-6d per acre (including the beans)"; whilst the farmer also agreed to pay:

"Reeve's boy and (indecipherable) into the bargain
for raking and driving . . ."

However the system could still lead to frustrations. In September 1897 Row noted:

"On August 23rd only needed about three days to finish Harvest. But the four men at the stacks would not help the four men in the field *'gather in'* the barley, and wet weather setting in! Just as it did last year. *The three days' work* was not finished until 3.0 p.m. September 2nd. Almost a repetition of last year. Ten days to do three days' work!" (The underlinings are Row's).

Yet some crops were still being harvested in the most primitive manner. On August 18th, Row noted, "Raining slightly – so 'pulled' beans." The following day he recorded:

19th August: "Wet morning – 'pulled beans'."

In other words *the whole plant* was physically removed from the ground and not even scythed. Yet I was even more surprised when my own father (b.1918) spontaneously declared:

"It was nothing unusual! They'd often be pulled if they were so short that the binder (or scythes) would miss the bottom pods – and of course it also reduces shattering."

Further corroboration comes from Gestingthorpe. Here both Bert and the late Stanley Surridge particularly recall beans being 'pulled' during the exceptionally severe drought of 1921. (In Row's situation however, one also wonders if it was a 'good way of using a wet day'? It is in fact the only reference Row makes to 'pulling beans'.)

But the diarist's preoccupation is not exclusively with crops. We read of 'Mr. Westropps's sheep grazing on a 'clover ley', and of 'turnips being sown for sheep feed'. We are reminded also of the importance of mangolds, (which provided crucial winter fodder), whilst on one occasion the writer cheerfully confides that pigs – which were then to be found on all local farms – were "selling pleasingly well." By comparison on 3rd June 1892, he thoughtfully ponders:

"The bullocks do not get on as I would wish."

Yet it was for the magnificent, 'heavy horses' – on which he depended for all his draught work – that Row felt the most affection. On 11th March 1893 he proudly announced:

"Kitty foaled. Beautiful bay horse foal. Named it 'Prince Charlie'."

But three weeks later, with a tight and convoluted script – much smaller than his usual scrawl – he scribbled tensely:

"April 1st. Poor old Boxer dropped down at plough in Field No. 11. Had him killed by Simpson. Feel sorry to lose the old horse."

A more mysterious death occurred on October 11th 1897, when Row reports:

"Found black cow dead in Horse Yard at home."

After which he writes a single word. It is placed in inverted commas and underlined. The word is "POISONED."
Had there been an altercation between the farmer and a stockman? Had a horseman been unfairly or summarily dismissed? Had

an insult or an injury long harboured finally been paid off? We are only at liberty to speculate, for Row stoically considers the matter closed – and never refers to it again.

Within the 'horse era of agriculture', fatalities and illness of the animals was a normal occurrence; but Row again seems genuinely affected – by more than financial considerations – in his entry of 23rd April, 1898.

> "Bad week. Prince, my best Melford Horse, bought in October 1897, was seized with inflammation of the kidneys at 3p.m. on Friday. Died in dreadful agony on Saturday at 8.0p.m. . . . Bad job."

✚　✚　✚　✚　✚

Despite the rural depression, seasonal anxieties and inevitable disappointments, Row obviously loved his farming and stewardship of the land. Additionally he was a thinking agriculturalist who enjoyed experimenting. On one field he applied Pure Dissolved Bones (presumably a form of phosphate), and later observed:

> "It far outyielded that part of the field where farmyard manure was applied."

Yet Row was already making *routine* applications of artificial fertiliser. For – as noted in our comments on coprolites – farming was already moving away from resources entirely 'Of the Furrow Born'.

> "27th February 1891 . . . got both fields in 'first class' order. Used 1 cwt Nitrate Soda and 1 cwt Super Phosphate per acre: harrowed in before sowing."

Yet we should not exaggerate. For the basis of Row's fertiliser programme still revolved around leguminous crops of clover and beans, 'Mr. Westropps's sheep' and traditional applications of farmyard manure – of which he notes in his journal:

> "For manure spreading and breaking: 2d per load is very good pay."

Other applications (and yields) for the same year include:

1890 - 1891 – KINGS PRENTICES, LONG MELFORD

Field No. 6   ....   "Put on 16 loads of Farm Yard Manure
(Barley after wheat)   per acre. Yielded 9½ coomb per
acre" (19cwt. an acre).

Field No. 8   ....   "1cwt Nitrate Soda per acre plus 1 cwt
(Oats after barley)   Triple Super Phosphate per acre.
Yielded 15 coomb/acre" (22½cwt. an acre).

Field No. 5   ....   "The yield of this field was VERY good
(Wheat after Clover)   – just under 13 coomb/acre"
(27cwt. an acre).

Field No. 9   ....   "21 loads 'Farm Yard' per acre and
(Mangolds)   (indecipherable) artifical. Yielded
about 25 tons an acre."

✢   ✢   ✢   ✢   ✢

Row also suffered some of the disease problems that we still encounter today. In 1891, Field No. 1 at Kings Prentices had looked like producing an exceptional "twelve coomb an acre of wheat" but had then got "very badly mildewed." Additionally, he also experienced 'Bean Sickness' or *Sclerotinia*. (Now known to be caused by growing beans too frequently on the same field). On part of Field No. 7, for example, an experiment was conducted using four bags of 'Special Bean Fertilizer'.

However, the scientific interest and keen enthusiasm was all to no avail. For Row later records:

"Beans 'went off' (died) in spring. Fallowed part of field and sowed swedes on rest."

This author, like many other local farmers, has also witnessed 'bean sickness', (although without quite such devastating consequences!) Intriguingly moreover, Row was consistently drilling his beans in the first week of October. Indeed in 1896 he even plants them on September 29th and 30th. By comparison a century later, local farmers are exhorted not to drill the crop until at least October 20th, (as a means of controlling another bean disease, 'Chocolate Spot'). One wonders how many more 'wet autumns' passed before it was noticed that later sowing produced better yields?

Row also discussed his cultivation techniques. On 'kinder soils', the fields destined for spring barley were sometimes ploughed twice – in both the autumn and early February. By comparison one field of winter wheat was typically:

"Ploughed, 'scarified' and thoroughly cleaned in September and October. Sown on October 19th."

('Scarifying is cultivating and exposes twitch rhyzomes to the wind and sun).

The importance of good weed control was paramount. 'Horse hoeing' and 'thistling' were crucial summer time jobs. On one occasion Row has four men *grassing* (i.e. forking out, "a lot of twitch grass and rubbish"). Yet even so, the battle against nature could still be lost: of one bean crop at Highlanders Farm in 1891, he laconically writes:

"Worst ever crop of beans! But a magnificent crop of weeds and thistles – although it was 'horse-hoed' twice *and* hand-hoed twice. Beans certainly not more than 2 coomb (or 4¾ hundredweight) an acre."

It would be tempting to suggest that Row didn't have much luck with beans! However we must record that in 1894 one 'very good crop' on Field No. 12 yielded ten coomb (or twenty five hundredweight) an acre, with "P.D. Bones outyielding the Farmyard manure."

One often wonders if a diarist like John Row has some inner perception that <u>one day</u> – years later – their jottings will be appreciated by a wider audience.

In deciphering his diary I have repeatedly felt that I have acquired a new friend. Someone who is older, wiser and more experienced but to whom I can always turn whenever I am most morose at the contrariness of contemporary farming: the perverseness of the weather, the fallibility of our modern machinery – or my own unfortunate decisions.

At those moments then – when the promising crop gets 'laid' at harvest; when the autumn seed beds are "too cloddy without rain" or when the price of wheat comes crashing down – as it has done in 1998 – then I turn to Row's diary again, and read it afresh, and imagine him saying, with such wisdom and understanding: "Ah, yes, young man! I felt the same as you in 1889 or 1894."

The emotions we share, beyond everything else – are still, ultimately, 'Of the Furrow Born'.

Chapter Seventeen

SOME CREATURES GREAT and SMALL

'Stockmen and Shepherds: Veterinary Memories'

"When father had Red House Farm, Boxford, he needed A QUARTER OF HIS LAND just to feed his working horses – and even more for all his other livestock. But it wasn't just the meadows and clover leys they needed! Some of his barley, oats and beans also went to feed the animals as did the mangolds as well!

"And if he had a poor ol' field that was all 'run down', he'd put it into mustard or turnips and then Bobby Partridge from Kersey would come and put his sheep on it, and so long as they were properly folded that land would grow two – or even three – good crops after that."

Claude Alleston (1912-1994)

Before the introduction of artificial fertilisers the farmyard manure which the animals produced was of inestimable value. However spreading the resultant manure – by hand – is still ruefully recalled by several contributors:

"At Jenkins Farm," declares Horace Elsey, "you were expected to load twenty tumbrils of muck each day – that was one man by himself! Well if you were getting it off a muck heap it was all right – but if it was in one of those poky old yards where those ol' bullocks had been stamping it down for the past year, then – oh my Lord! That could be tight! We'd have to cut it out sometimes – with an ol' straw trusser's knife – and you may depend on it – that did jolly well stink in those places!"

The old, low, dilapidated farm buildings to which Horace refers are also recalled by Long Melford butcher Freddy Ruse:

"I used to go and buy bullocks off farmers, and they'd take me to some dark, poky old places. The bullocks could barely see once they were brought into daylight!

"But when I bought bullocks on a farm years ago, there were no scales to weigh the animals – I just had to use my own judgement! But I soon learnt one lesson. Never value bullocks if you've got to look up at them. It makes them look bigger than they really are!"

"But what about the visits to Bury St. Edmunds market?," I wondered.

"Every Wednesday," continued Freddy, with a smile, "father or myself would take the ten o'clock train from Melford and go to Bury for the livestock market. 'Course it was a steam train in those days! And it was always a bit of an adventure because there would be several other butchers and farmers on the train, joking, playing cards or just going for a day's outing."

"How long did the journey take?"

"About an hour I suppose – but 'en route' we stopped at Lavenham, Cockfield and Great Welnetham. Once the market was over I would come home on the four o'clock train. But the cattle I purchased wouldn't arrive at the station until about 7.30 in the evening. Then two of us would take hurricane lamps, and with one behind, and one in front, we'd drive them along Melford Street back to our meadow . . ."

Another contributor also recalls droving bullocks.

"North Hill, Colchester?!" exclaims Claude Alleston, "Cuh. I've driven cattle up there and right through the town! We used to drive them from Boxford, through Colchester and right down to the marshes on Mersea island."

"How many did you take?"

"Oh, about thirty to forty. And there was only me and another

268

teenage boy, Herb Baker, who went with them! 'Course the first couple of miles were the worst. Those bullocks would be the devil of a trouble! . . . But later on, once they got tired – well they were much easier to control. And they would be tired, time they got to Colchester. 'Course if you meet a farm waggon on any of the narrow lanes about here, you'd just thread your way through. There was nothing unusual in it."

On a more routine level, Kathleen Grimwood (b.1901) of Sudbury, recalls dairy cattle,

"Coming over the bridge at the Croft from Sudbury's meadows, and then going down Curds Lane to be milked every morning at five o'clock for years and years. But do you know, not a single drop of milk now comes from Sudbury's meadows! But you'd often see farm animals in Sudbury. On one occasion my mother actually had to jump over a fence to get out of the way of some bullocks coming down Station Road!"

From cattle to pigs – which were also found on every traditional farm. At Twinstead, lifelong farmworker, the late Frank Turner (1903-1992), humorously recalled his very first day's work – with pigs – when he was just twelve years old.

"They were right keen to get you out of school that time of day – because the War was on. They were right short for a while! And I'll tell you about my first job. It was at Le Mote Farm in Pebmarsh and the foreman say, "take those pigs 'shacking' [foraging] on the bean land." Well the first time I took them, it was a bit of a struggle to drive 'em along the track to the field. But once they'd been there – and tasted those beans – cuh! It wasn't any trouble to get them there again! But that was suffen' hot that first day, and when I opened the gate to bring them back, those pigs saw the pond – AND AWAY THEY WENT!! Lord was I worried in case they should drown! But just then an old stockman came stumping along. 'They won't drown – boy!', he laughed. And they didn't either. But I was suffen' flustered for a moment!"

It is interesting that Frank refers to 'shacking'. This historic word is also associated with the Sudbury Common Lands where the Freeman had 'shackage rights' "to forage off the stubble" for many centuries. (See especially *Sudbury's Common Land* by John Wardman and *Suffolk Country Town* by Allan Berry).

But Frank is not alone in describing 'shacking'. On a fine autumn afternoon in 1997 I visited one of my favourite and most inspiring contributors of all – Alphamstone's delightfully warm-hearted retired shepherd and Church Warden, ninety-five year old Eddie Tuffin. Yet what makes our conversations so enjoyable is not just Eddie's personality – which remains cheerful despite personal sorrow – but his continuing interest in the activities of farming today. As he poured out a cup of tea, he quite naturally asked about the recent harvest.

Barley, I replied, had suffered in the drought but wheat had been good and winter beans exceptional – except that we had lost a lot when combining – because the crop was beginning to 'shale out'.

"You know what they'd have done years ago, don't you!" he exclaimed, "They'd have got the boy to drive the sow and pigs over them! "But I've also done it with sheep! They had a field of beans between Pebmarsh and Alphamstone one year, and our sheep were on the other side of the road near Dairy Wood so I took them onto those bean stubbles. But I'd only leave them on there for a quarter of an hour or so to begin with – on account of the sheep eating too many of them. Then perhaps in the afternoon and again the next day, I'd let them have another five minutes and slowly increase it like that."

"Would they eat other things?"

"Oh yes! They'd have conkers, acorns and crab apples. And they loved them too! But do you know, there was a programme on television the other night which made out they harm sheep – what damned rubbish!

"Where Rex Twinn lives, (in Alphamstone), there were three or four conker trees as we called them that time of day, and Mr. Stuck used to hire that meadow then, and at night when I brought the sheep back to the farm, I'd leave the gate to that meadow open, and next morning when I let the sheep out – AWAY THEY'D GO! Up the road, past the green and through the village to that meadow after those conkers! I didn't have to drive them! They'd go up the road like the devil! 'Course every day they cleared up what had fallen down the night before – so they never

had too many of them. But they'd also run for acorns and crab apples!

"And we also used to take sheep onto the wheat stubbles as well – especially if there was a lot left behind – but you mustn't stop too long, in case it made them 'blow'."

It was an era of 'waste not – want not'. Everything had a value in the traditional countryside. At Bulmer Brickyard, Tom Bird recalls hen houses being dragged out onto the stubbles of Wickham Hall, "so that the chickens could scratch about for any fallen ears or 'shaled out' grains laying about – especially in 'laid' places." It was a practice that was repeated on countless farms.

Then there was milk. As a Belchamp Walter schoolboy, Charlie Martin (b.1902) used to:

"Run down to the meadows and get Olly Pearson's cows up to Springate Farm ready for milking. In fact I'd even started to milk some of them myself – by hand of course – but that suffen made my wrists ache to begin with!"

At Halstead, Mary Downs described her days in the Land Army, at Armsey Farm, Bulmer – beside Ballingdon Hill. Here she helped to milk fifty Jersey cows by hand, starting at four o'clock in the morning. Later, she assisted in sterilising all the utensils and then filling up the milk bottles – from a jug – before putting on the cardboard 'bottle tops'. "But were there any nights out or high living?" I wondered.

"You must be JOKING!" came the jovial reply. "We were in bed every night by half past eight or nine!"

Yet mechanisation was slowly coming to dairy farms. As farmer's daughter the late Mary Brooks of Ashbocking, near Needham Market, recalls:

"In the 1920's my father was the first man in Suffolk – and possibly East Anglia – to have a proper milking machine. His name was John Brooks, and as he hadn't got any electricity it was driven by a 'Lister' petrol engine. But it was such an unimaginable advance that he actually received a letter from Yorkshire, simply addressed to, 'The Man with the Milking Machine – Somewhere in Suffolk'!"

However the old techniques and 'cures' were still sometimes called upon. At Long Melford, the late Charlie 'Pod' Martin spoke of a ewe which had suffered black garget and then 'gone off its food' when he was a shepherd at Goldingham Hall, Bulmer.

"She just wouldn't eat. I tried everything! But do you know what I finally did? I gave it a sprig of ivy. And she took it! I mean sheep loved ivy. I've even seen them scramble for it!"

A recurring problem to all shepherds was 'the fly' – whose maggots caused the sheep such distress – and which 'dipping' helps avoid. Eddie Tuffin recalls the process from the nineteen thirties:

"We used to drive our sheep along the roads from Alphamstone to John Nott's at Magnolia House, Pebmarsh. We had to be there at half past five in the morning, – before it got too hot – so you can see what time it was when we started out! But John Nott had a big flock. Getting on for a couple of hundred, so he'd be doing his first."

The sheep, which could only be dipped once a year, would be protected for two to three weeks.

"But it was after that," explains Eddie, "when the dip had begun to die off, that the flies would strike them. Especially on thundery days – when it comes out blazing hot. That's when the ol' maggots used to strike them. And all you could do was just wash them in weak carbolic . . .

"And if they'd got nipped by the shears and there was a bloody place, the flies would torment that damned bit. You'd have to keep putting something on. I've known people say they'd put a cobweb on – and that would help it to heal."

But possibly Eddie's most absorbing memories are of attending Haverhill Lamb Sale. For they remind us not merely of driving animals along roads – but also of the railway line between Sudbury and Haverhill.

"First off, we had to drive the lambs along the roads from Alphamstone here, down to Bures railway station. We'd set off at five o'clock in the morning. When we got to Bures we drove them up a little road – which led to the 'pound' – where we put the lambs. Then they got an ol' horse to pull a railway truck to this special place so we could load the lambs up. Then when the train came along they hooked you onto it . . . 'Course, when you got to Sudbury they did the same – as they did at Melford – where farmers like Brands and Paines put their sheep on as well.

"But when you got to Haverhill railway station, you had to mind what you were doing! Our blessed sheep got in the churchyard one year! They were devils for a while! But come the finish I managed to get them out."

"Where was the Lamb Sale held?"

"You went into the town and then turned sharp right – up the road to Bury – and then drove them up there to the meadow. But everybody else's lambs were there as well! You had to watch what you were doing! 'Course they were all 'dotted' with dye in case of muddles. Then once you'd got them in the meadow, they put hurdles round. Brand of Foxearth used to have some lovely lambs. If ever there was a prize awarded, he'd get it . . . But one year I did actually get a prize for getting a 'lamb and a half' from every ewe. I got ten shillings – that was the same as thirty or forty pounds today!"

Despite the best care and attention, accidents and illnesses invariably occur to farm animals which necessitates a visit from the vet. Locally however, the name of one veterinary surgeon has constantly recurred as I have spoken to older farmers and their stockmen. It is that of Jim Waters (b.1920) of Halstead, who together with his late father Wilfred, must have visited almost every single farm in our area – some of them on numerous occasions.

Although now retired, Jim still lives at 93 Head Street, beside premises that have been used for veterinary purposes since 1851. With a warm, friendly, rich voice, interspersed with engaging chuckles, I had two fascinating afternoons recording his memories.

Since interviewing him, moreover, Jim has actually published two delightful autobiographies, entitled *Animal Crackers* and *Animal Magic*. Both are an enchanting blend of personal anecdotes and animal recollections, whilst recreating a picture of life as it was for both farmer and veterinary surgeon. Indeed as principally 'farmers vets' both Jim and his father championed the cause of 'improving animal husbandry' that was so crucial in the days of food rationing after the Second World War.

"My biggest tuberculin test" recalls Jim, "was in Oliver Brand's Red Poll herd at Foxearth – and we did THREE HUNDRED AND TWENTY animals in a day! It meant starting at six in the morning and not finishing until about six at night!"

Yet as Jim explains:

"That was exceptional. Even until after the War many small farms in this area were still run in the old traditional way. These farmers had the odd sow or two, a few bullocks, a small herd of cows – which were milked by hand – and perhaps 200 chickens which the wife always considered to be laying eggs for her pocket money!"

Although new treatments were being developed, "you still had to be very diplomatic telling these older farmers, horsemen or cowmen what to do," recalls Jim – "especially if it involved new ideas!"

"Take milk fever in cattle," he continues. "Father would cure them with a 'shot of calcium'. But when I was a boy he also used 'pump up the udders with air' as well! You see that was the traditional remedy – and the older farmers didn't trust the new one!" (Blowing oxygen into the udder suppressed the milk supply allowing the cow to retain more calcium.)

Yet despite all the advances in veterinary science, one still detects a note of sadness as Jim compares the predominantly arable farming of today with the mixed agriculture of his earlier years, when every farm had an assortment of animals. Today, it is possible to pass through entire parishes without ever seeing a farm animal. As Jim points out, "In 1951 the practice dealt with 139 different dairy herds. By 1988 only nine were left."
An even more drastic decline has occurred to 'working horses'.

"When I was a lad," he continues, "I would often help my father to 'dose' horses which had colic. First however, the horse's head had to be pulled up to a beam in the stable with a plough line. It was then my job to crawl along this beam until I was over the horse's mouth and could pour in the 'medicine'. But when I looked down into the large mouth below me! I was terrified I would fall into the teeth! Some of those big Suffolk, Shires and Clydesdales stood 16 to 17 hands high – they were huge!"

Some years later when Jim was qualified, a particularly interesting case occurred with cattle:

"One Sunday some cows got into a field with a heap of sugar beet in one corner. But next day they were laying about all over the field. They were all drunk! The sugar beet was fermenting and causing alcoholism! We opened up the rumen of fifteen cows and emptied them out. Every two hours we had to inject them with a special drug which they use for human beings. But as we had about a hundred to do, it took a lot of material! Soon we had not only run out of the drug – but got as much as we could from other vets. So I had to go to Colchester Hospital and get their supply! Fortunately they only usually used it at the weekends – to dry out the drunks!"

Other conditions were more serious. Gravely so. For anthrax could still strike and both the pain of the animals – and distress of their owners – was clearly evident. What clearly emerges from talking to Jim is the arduous, no-nonsense nature of veterinary life – especially in his father's day before the Second World War. It was certainly not work for the squeamish.

Yet the challenging conditions endured by all rural vets, with their 'difficult animals', Christmas Day duties and unpleasant weather still continue.

"One of the hardest jobs to perform," explains Jim, "is a Caesarian in cattle. But in my first two cases it was snowing! One was at Strutt and Parker's farm at Thorpe Morieux. The other was for Tony Holmes at Chelmshoe Farm, Great Maplestead. But although I worked stripped to the waist for a couple of hours – with snow falling on my back – I never even felt the cold until I stopped! Then I was very glad of that whisky in the farmer's house!"

With these brief glimpses we bid Jim farewell. And if readers wish to know more of the occasion when he was left half-naked with a cow in a freezing field or the story of the .22 bullet in his father's pipe – they must turn to Jim's books in their entirety. And if they do, they will find a delightful portrayal of family life, wartime memories, and a lifetime's interest in veterinary work. Unquestionably they are the Sudbury-Halstead area's very own version of *All Creatures Great and Small*. We finish with one such typical story:

"At the outbreak of the Second World War, my father had just come out of hospital, so for a few months I drove him round in an old 'Ford Eight'.

"About eight o'clock one morning in October 1939, we had a call to go and see a Jersey cow with milk fever, which belonged to Mrs. Raymond at Belchamp Walter Hall. My mother immediately cooked breakfast, which we hurriedly ate. Then we rushed to Belchamp Walter. But after treating her cow Mrs. Raymond was so grateful that she asked us to come into the house. Two large plates awaited us! They were covered with fried bacon, sausages, and two fried eggs! She said she was so sorry to get us out before we had breakfast! We sat down and ate it all – never daring to mention we had had another breakfast before we came out!"*

Cutting hay from the stack for the farm animals . . . "You went down like slicing bread," recalls Tom Rowe.

Animal Crackers and *Animal Magic* are available from bookshops in Halstead, the Gainsborough Bookshop, Sudbury, the Red Lion Bookshop, Colchester, and Into Books at Hadleigh, price £5.00, or direct from the author at 93 Head Street, Halstead (plus £1.00 p&p). All profits from the publications are being donated to St. Andrew's Church, Halstead. Over £3,400 has already been raised from the sale of *Animal Crackers*.

Chapter Eighteen

HARVESTING TECHNIQUES

The Sickle, Scythe, Reaper and Binder

'Twas here the gangs at harvest mowed,
And young lads on the trace horse rode
And stacks were built and sheaves were tied,
In this our home, our countryside!"

This Countryside

In Chapter Thirteen we discussed the advent of the mechanical reaper and its introduction to the area from about 1851. Similarly we speculated whether the crop of wheat in the oil painting of *Mr. and Mrs. Robert Andrews,* commissioned about 1750, was harvested by sickle, 'reaping hook', or the scythe. Although somewhat inconclusive we do know that it was not until the middle of the *following century* that the scythe *finally* and irrevocably replaced the sickle for cutting wheat. (By which time it was fitted with a 'cradle' to lay the wheat more regularly).

Yet the subject had been discussed for many years. In his *Farmers' Kalender* of 1775 and 1805, Arthur Young argued that although mowing, (i.e. scything) of wheat, was cheaper than reaping with a sickle, the increased quantity of straw took longer to collect from the fields, and required bigger carts to convey it in. Similarly the 'barn space' (or stacks) needed to be larger. Moreover the sheaves were likely to contain more green weeds – as the corn was cut lower to the ground. "This objection," he noted, "has great weight in a bad harvest." Time, he admitted was saved in not having to haulm the crop. Yet this was more than offset by the increased effort of threshing the larger volume of straw. (As noted earlier the scythe was used earlier around London – where there was a greater demand for the straw. However in 1805 Young still estimated that "in more than three quarters of the county of Essex, wheat was cut by sickle or 'bagging hook'.")

In 1837 *British Husbandry* observed:

> "Although the mowing of wheat is increasing it requires a degree of expertness not necessary in reaping, *and is also the hardest of all agricultural labour.*" Additionally, "the scythe can not be efficiently employed on crops which are much laid and entangled, nor upon ground that is not perfectly even."

In July 1840 the *Hadleigh Farmers' Club* interestingly noted that:

> "Only ONE member was present who had practised to any extent the mowing of wheat. His evidence went to prove the advantage over reaping. Mowing was not only quicker but provided more straw – which is more valuable than haulm. Additionally the sheaves dried quicker after a rain – as they are not tied so tightly." (Slightly rephrased).*

The debate however continued. Although the increased bulk of straw created more manure, it also made threshing more difficult – until the development of machines. If threshing was still performed by flail observed the Royal Agricultural Society's Journal of 1848, "then mowing is rarely practised." Meanwhile the Ixworth Farmers' Club voiced concern that, "mowing left less for the gleaners – which has been allowed since time immemorial."†

Indeed at Jenkins Farm, Bulmer, the scythe was not used for harvesting wheat until about 1850. For in a fascinating hand-written memoir, the late Philip 'Tulip' Rowe reveals that Mr. Badham, the farmer, actually:

*Extracted from *The Report of the Annual Meeting of the Hadleigh Farmers' Club,* published 1840. Reprinted 1990 for the Club's 150th anniversary. (Ipswich and Ashbocking Farmers' Club discussed the issue in the same year and also recorded that scything of wheat had been "very little adopted by their members." Similarly one wonders whether Bear's exhibition of a reaper, "on wheat stubble," in October 1851 also followed a crop that was cut by sickle – since there was apparently enough straw for the demonstration to have been meaningful.)

†*Life and Tradition in Suffolk and North-east Essex*, by Norman Smedley, published by J.M. Dent, 1982.

"had a man come from Suffolk to demonstrate on the scythe and show how they did it. The Bulmer men started cutting wheat with the scythe and having got used to it, liked it. For it took a man, if a good hand, three days to cut an acre with a sickle. The men all had to get used to the heavy wheat rake on the Suffolk type of scythe." (By kind permission Robin Rowe).

The same source moreover, (who was born in 1861), even remembered sickles being used to harvest wheat on one final occasion. (It was on a small piece of land known as Little Gallows Field, not far from Bulmer Brickyard, and beside the footpath to Upper Houses). Even more helpfully he provides the reason:

". . . It was a mile or more from the home farm and not much wheat grew near the field that year. To get the machine there or to cut it with scythes would have meant having to horse-rake the field. A long way to go after such a small field of only three acres. Most of the men had used and knew how to use sickles. They thought it would be best in the long run as it was a showery time."*

The sickle which was slowly being replaced by the scythe, historically had a serrated edge to enable a gentle 'sawing off' action of the ears of corn which were held in the reaper's hand. (As previously noted the smooth edge sickle, or 'bagging hook', was originally only used in areas of laid corn – or to cut the stalks close to the ground). Yet despite all of the developments which have since occurred, the concept of the serrated edge has not been forgotten. In fact the 'cutter bar' of the most modern combine harvester, at work in the fields of East Anglia today, will also have 'serrated' sections on the 'knife' – which are a direct descendant of the 'serrated sickle' that was used for so many centuries!

With the scythe we are in the realm of genuine human memories. One memorable evening, as I sat in his thatched cottage at Lower Houses, Bulmer, researching *The Long Furrow*, the late Philip Rowe, (b.1900 – and one of 'Tulip's' sons), provided a vivid description of a scything gang at work:

"The men were led by the 'Lord of the Harvest' who set the pace. The Lord was principally the person who was best at scyth-

---

*From the reminiscences of Philip 'Tulip' Rowe. By kind permission of Robin Rowe.

ing. You see, a gang of mowers have the same formation as geese flying, so the man at the front has got to be a good one.

"What about the tying up? When was that done?"

"The wheat was tied up right behind the scythe, and it was always mowed into the standing corn, which would help to hold the cut wheat up, so the 'mower's mate' could tie it easier. There were always two. For every mower, there was one man tying up behind him. I can remember ten mowers going in a line and they all had their mates with them. Barley of course, might lay a day or two and be carted loose like hay."

As previously noted the first mechanical reapers were tried locally from about 1851. Usually they required a man to rake off the straw from the cutting platform. Later, however, this task was performed by revolving wooden 'sails' which deposited the corn in a quantity suitable for one sheaf. These machines are still recalled by older contributors:

"At Alphamstone," says Eddie Tuffin, "we carried on using an ol' sail reaper for years after most other people. I suppose Mr. Stuck was a bit old-fashioned. But come the finish three of the 'sails' were broken and the corn came off in such bloomin' big heaps that it was enough for two sheaves! But the 'reaper' had one main advantage over the binder. It didn't need so much effort to pull it. Two horses could work it nicely. When he did finally buy an Albion binder we needed four horses to pull it on some of this very hilly land . . .*

Yet even when the 'reaper' was replaced by the 'binder', (which both cut and tied the corn), the headlands of the wheat fields and entire fields of barley were still cut by scythe.

*Sail reapers commonly had four or five sails with the five sail versions being used in heavy crops on more fertile farms. One variation of the sail reaper, known as a 'Foot Engine', enabled the operator to activate the sails by pressing a pedal whenever he wished to discharge a bundle of corn.
Of local interest both Fred Chatters and Bert Surridge recall that at Gestingthorpe, the Downs family had five or six binders which they hired out from 'Foundry Corner'.

"We often mowed barley by hand," recalls Eddie Tuffin, "and then later we'd put two swarths together – by hand of course – with wooden hand rakes. We used to call it 'gathering'. But when we came to cart the loose barley that wasn't so nice! Cuh! Pitching and loading was a rotten job! Those avils! They'd get every-where!"

It was the same at Raydon and Layham, near Hadleigh, where Edwin Partridge (1892–1993) farmed. But why, I wondered, was barley still mowed with a scythe when wheat was entrusted to a binder?

"Barley was often 'undersown' with clover or grass you see," he explained shortly before his hundredth birthday. "So they would be all green when you cut the barley. Well they had to 'wilt down' first. And of course there were no weed killers that time of day. So if a crop was full of chickweed or cleavers or charlock – they'd need to 'wilt down' as well. Barley might even be 'turned' – just like hay before you carted it. But that barley straw with the clover in made wonderful feed for the cattle!

"Then in a dry year barley might not actually be tall enough to tie it into sheaves – so you had to cut it loose. And if it was for malting and you hadn't cut it by scythe, the maltsters might say that the binder had somehow damaged the barley! They would you know! Especially if there were a lot of weeds about – like charlock and bellbine – which might have 'heated up' in the stack and dam-aged the germination for malting.

"When I first came to Ponds Farm, Raydon there was a man worked here, and he was a good bit older than me, and he used to tell me about an old farmer that used to be here – and ALL his bar-ley had to be mown by scythe. Well this fellow used to tell me how many times he'd mown up this big field here before breakfast! And that was a big field as well!"

(At Gestingthorpe the late Charlie Chatters estimated that "one man could mow an acre of barley in a day".)

Yet although some barley continued to be cut by scythe, grass mower or 'reaper', the 'self-binder' slowly gained ascendancy. (There is interesting anecdotal evidence that a 'demonstration' of a binder occurred on Manor Farm, Elmsett, as early as 1879 and in Bulmer in 1882). Typical of our contributors however, Jack Wallace of

Wethersfield and later Lavenham, records his father buying their first self-binder in about 1907-08. At Layham, Edwin Partridge was eight years old (i.e. it was in 1901), when his own father made a similar purchase; John Row certainly had a binder by 1898; Harry Winch believes that at Bulmer the first binder was used commercially in about 1908, "although the Auberies Home Farm didn't have one until about 1915."

Yet the question which needs to be asked – however elementary it may seem – is this. How did a farmer know when to begin harvest – when it was performed by scythe or binder?

Indeed it was with some embarrassment that I put the question to older contributors. For today – with an electronic moisture meter and combine harvester – the process is quite simple. The farmer waits until he thinks the grain is sufficiently dry, checks it with a 'moisture meter' – and if satisfactory, begins harvesting.

We still, of course, walk through crops, rub out ears in our hands – and then bite the grains between our teeth – which provides a good indication of the moisture. But what criteria did a Bulmer or Gestingthorpe farmer use before the Second World War – when the wheat was still cut by binder, the sheaves 'shocked up' and then pitched onto waggons before being built into stacks?

At High Barn Hall, Halstead, veteran farmer Bill Waters explains:

"We used to start bindering when the wheat ears were just turning colour – while the actual straw was still a bit green. But you then had to let it ripen in the sheaf properly – before you could build your stacks. On one occasion a wheat stack actually 'got hot' – because the straw wasn't properly ripe when they built the stacks – and the men had to turn it over to 'let the heat out'! But I should think that when we started bindering the kernels of wheat would be getting on for 25 to 30% moisture. You could still press your thumb nail into it. And I think we sometimes did lose yield by starting too early. When I had my first combine we reckoned that we harvested almost a sack an acre more."

(With combines and 'grain driers' one might typically start harvesting at about fifteen to twenty per cent moisture.)

"But even if you started the first fields with a binder when the grains were soft," continues Bill, "by the time you finished all your cutting and 'shocking up', the last fields might well be completely ripe. So if you didn't make a start in good time you'd never have got done. In a bad time the weather would have beaten you at the other end!"

"So how much sooner would you start harvest with a binder than with a combine?" I asked my own father:

"On average I should think about ten days. When we bought our first combine in 1936, some of our neighbours *had almost finished* bindering before we started combining! They though we were ABSOLUTELY DAFT for having a machine that prevented us getting on sooner. They said we must be mad for trying to thresh and harvest together!"

At Whatfield, our 'Tithe War hero', John Waspe continues:

"We used to start almost a fortnight earlier with a binder than your grandfather did with a combine! We used to start as soon as the wheat got 'yellow necks'. It didn't matter if all the corn wasn't ripe. It would ripen in the sheaf. And the earlier it was cut the tougher the straw became – which for thatching the stacks was all the better!"

At Bulmer, Tom Rowe continues:

"There was a man from Pentlow by the name of Brand who used to farm Pannells Ash and Paines Manor. And he always used to cut his wheat when the straw was still *very* green. 'Course when we went 'straw tying' we used to make straw bands out of it. Well I should think a bit no thicker than your finger would pull a ton!! But he told Father that the wheat was always all right; and he was the first to start cutting round these parts!"

Frank Billimore provides an interesting comment on oats:

"When I was a lad I worked at Stanchells Farm, Hengrave. Well the first thing we generally cut were oats and likely as not, he'd want us to do it on August Bank Holiday Monday, (then at the beginning of August). But sometimes he carted it home too quickly

– before the straw had dried out in the 'shocks'. Oh yes. I've had to turn stacks of oats over because they were heating up."

In any chapter which researches bygone harvests, wet and difficult seasons will inevitably be remembered. Of the steep hillocks and small fields of Alphamstone Eddie Tuffin spontaneously provides one example:

"Down 'Back Lane', he'd got a field of oats, and they went as flat as a penny! Anyway he cut them with a grass mower and we had to tie them up. He could only cut them 'one way' because they were so laid, and then he 'slipped back' to the other end, time we were tying that swarth up. But of course it didn't lay the straw like a reaper did – and those oats were FULL OF THISTLES! . . . So we'd got to gather them up into 'traves' (sheaves) and then tie them up with bands made out of the oat straw with all those thistles in! There was five acres of that. Cuh! I was glad to see the back of that job!"

Wet weather additionally compounded the work load. On September 14th, 1888 for example, John Rowe, "Had all the wheat (sheaves) in Field No. 1 'thrown down' to enable them to dry." Retired horseman, Fred Chatters (b.1906) who for many years worked on the fields of Eyston hall, Belchamp Walter continues:

"You'd set the sheaves up in shocks of six or seven together. You had to stand them on the ground pretty firm mind. But then in a wet time, you'd have to move them onto fresh ground and then turn them round again – to expose a different side to the sun. Then in a windy time they'd all get blown over – so you'd have to go and set them all up again!"

Like many others, Fred recalls "pitching sheaves beneath a harvest moon," and explains:

"The thing was this. You made the bargain as to how much you'd do the harvest for. Before the First World War it used to be five pounds – and then you'd want to get it done in a month 'to do yourself any good'. So wet weather was no good to you – or the farmer. If it dragged on too long you'd have to draw some money – just to live on – so the longer it took, the less there was as a 'bonus'. (When farmworkers wages were twelve shillings a week if they could do the harvest in four weeks it was the equivalent to double wages – although of course for longer hours.)

Although Fred recalls "One dreadful wet harvest which wasn't finished until the day they turned the clocks back," Eddie Tuffin provides an equally epic story from Alphamstone.

"We had some wheat that had got wet in the sheaves. We turned them round, and moved them heaps of times – but they WOULD NOT get dry. Come the finish we did finally bring them home – but after it was threshed this wheat still wasn't right and it began to 'heat up'. So Mr. Stuck told me to tip it out into a tumbril, and then take it onto a meadow – and shovel it out of the back – just to get rid of it. But do you know? It was so hot that I couldn't even stand in the cart!"

Although wet weather caused anxiety to the farmer, and protracted the harvest for the gang who had 'taken' the work on a contract basis, there were also summers which were intensely hot. (I often think how exhausting scything must have been – when I emerge from the 'air-conditioned' cab of our combine on days of rocketing temperatures.)

"When I was about fifteen," recalls Frank Billimore (b.1912), it was so hot in the harvest fields for a few days that the men stopped work from about mid-day until about five o'clock. The farmers wouldn't let them work. It was a killing sort of heat. Mind you they'd start early in the morning and carry on late at night!"

At Parkgate Farm, Gestingthorpe, Bert Surridge similarly remembers:
"It was terrifically hot one year when we were pitching sheaves by the Hedingham road. There were hares sheltering under the shocks of wheat. But if the waggon came along and we pitched those sheaves up, it was so bloomin' hot that they would only just limp to the next shock three or four yards away."

Whatever the weather there could still be problems in transporting the waggon loads of sheaves from the field to the farm as Eddie Tuffin recalls:

"It is steep around here – as well we know! Well we were loading sheaves on a hilly field down the back here one Saturday afternoon and were all hoping to get off early. But when he turned the waggon round to come back the other way we started to 'lose' the sheaves. Off they came! You can tell what happened to getting off early then can't you!"

John Waspe continues:

"I've quite often known the side of a stack to begin to slip out – if it wasn't built correctly – and have to be 'shored up' with wooden posts. Oats were especially slippery – and you could easily lose half your load coming home on the cart ways, because they weren't level like today! Barley could be a bit of a problem – because it hadn't got the length. But wheat straw was all right – because you could put another sheaf cross-ways."

In 'The Long Furrow' we discussed the bygone traditions of a horse era harvest with its 'wetting of the scythe', Lord of the Harvest, 'Hen Beer', sale of harvest rabbits, 'largesse for the horkey', and interesting custom of placing an oak bough on the final waggon load of sheaves at the end of harvest. To the author's delight this last archaic practice was also remembered by some new contributors to this book, Edwin Partridge of Hadleigh, Pat Morton of Henny, Fred Chatters of Belchamp Walter and Eddie Tuffin of Alphamstone.

"When I was a boy," the latter typically explains, "I was working with an old man at the end of the harvest – well when we'd loaded up the last sheaves onto the waggon – he went off to the hedge, and cut off a small branch from an oak tree, and put it atop of this waggon. Mind you that was only done when we were with one of these older men."

Another interesting custom – not included in the first book – was described for us by retired farmer, the late Jack Wallace of Lavenham. Sitting in his retirement bungalow, one May evening, he recalled his youth at Nortofts Farm, Wethersfield:

"When barley was cut with a scythe it was sometimes put loose in the barn and then trodden down with a horse! Only with a quiet ol' horse of course. But I actually did that job when I was a boy! And sometimes I stayed up there, riding that horse about until I could touch the rafters of the barn! 'Course getting the horse down, could then be a bit of a problem. So first of all, a ramp of barley straw was built up one side, and then a rope was put onto the horse's tail. But they'd lay a good quantity of straw down so that the horse didn't hurt itself . . . We used to call it 'riding the goof'."

In *The Farm and the Village*, author George Ewart Evans explains that the side bays of a barn were known as the gof or goafstead. (Gof apparently means corn that is still in the ear or stack before being threshed.) As Evans points out, although the horse's principal purpose was to compress the corn down, which enabled more to be stored indoors, the trampling also began to dislodge the grains from the ear prior to being flailed or mechanically threshed.

Whether the corn was stored in a fine old East Anglian barn or in stacks – and then thatched against bad weather – the harvest was ultimately brought home. (However getting the stacks thatched in good time was also of importance – as our illustration from Far From the Madding Crowd on Page 145 reminds us!)

More recently Phyllis Golding of Sudbury recalls some wheat that had got 'unusually wet' in World War Two:

"Some boats which were full of wheat had been sunk by German bombers in the River Thames. Because of rationing and the shortage of food they tried to salvage it and then brought some of it up to Mr. McQuae's brickyard beside Gallows Hill. To try and save it they actually put it on the floors of the long sheds where they dried out the bricks. But whilst it was there that place swarmed with flies – and it smelt pretty funny as well!" (Peter Minter confirms that another consignment went to Bulmer Brickyard.)

Yet amongst the long hours of hard work, the exigencies of the weather, and the inevitable anxieties of every harvest, it was for the rural children of the time, an unforgettable experience. At Bulmer, farmworker's daughter Hilda Dixey (b.1912) graphically recalls the harvests of her own childhood at Applecroft Farm, Henny:

"Every afternoon at four o'clock, we took a bottle of cold tea, and a bit of bread and cheese into the fields for my dad, and stopped there while he had it and then we'd bring the empty bottle back; but sometimes we'd take a little sandwich for ourselves and that used to be lovely, sitting there in the sun . . .

"Sometimes we'd ride to the fields in the waggons, or ride on the horses home and dad would walk beside. And when the binder went round the fields, we'd take our sticks and try and catch a rabbit. I've even known people from Sudbury walk up to the harvest fields at Henny to get a rabbit or see the binders and horses . . .

"'Course father and the other men would carry on working until dark. And even when they'd finished, he still had his horses to attend to; he had to bring them home, water them, brush them down and feed them – all before he could have his tea!"

But we must never fall into the temptation of being too nostalgic. Frank Billimore recalls the harvesting of another crop – in the worst of weathers:

"Don't forget sugar beet! Thousands and thousands of acres were 'pulled, knocked and topped' by hand – until the nineteen forties and fifties! And it was in the middle of winter – in all the freezing cold and rain. And if you went home because it was too wet – you didn't get any pay! But when we saw Catchpole's first beet harvester – in the late thirties – we thought it made a *wonderful* job."

Another similar crop was mangolds – which were fed to the livestock on a traditional farm. At Gestingthorpe the late Bert Surridge instantly exclaimed:

"For harvesting mangolds you wanted big ol' hands! Little ol' hands aren't any good – they couldn't get round the mangolds when you were chopping the tops off! I mean some of 'em were almost as big as footballs! 'Course we had turnips as well – just a few for the sheep – and after the sheep gnawed what they could, the shepherd would 'spud out' the rest."

Eddie Tuffin provided a similarly spontaneous memory about mangolds:

"Every Tuesday John Stuck, who I worked for, went to Halstead market by pony and trap. He used to go to the *Rose and Crown*. But one week Harry Buckle who farmed at Pebmarsh and John Stuck had a bet – about who had grown the biggest mangold! So the following week Johnny took his mangold into the *Rose and Crown* – and then Harry came in and saw John's mangold – but he never bothered to bring his in then!"

Chapter Nineteen

THRESHING MACHINES and TRACTION ENGINES
– A BRIEF RESUME –

"During the thirties when times were hard, you'd hear farm-
ers say to Whites – who did the threshing round here – that they
wanted some threshing done, to 'get some chaff and straw for the
horses'. 'Huh!' he say; 'the real reason is a bit different. They
want to sell some corn – to get some money!'"

the late Edwin Partridge of Hadleigh (1892–1993)

The thought of threshing machines evokes a nostalgic picture. Of men with string tied round their trouser legs, pitching sheaves from the stack to the threshing 'drum', accompanied by the latter's rhythmic rattle, and the traction engine's steady chuff. Yet we should not be too sentimental. As Bulmer's, Freddie Hunt declares "Threshing machines! Huh! Dustiest things ever invented!"

"What's more," exclaims threshing contractor, Jack Cornell, "the driver had to keep the fire in over the weekend, and probably bike over on Sunday afternoons to stoke it up! But he also needed to arrive early in the mornings to 'take the hat off', (from the engine's chimney), and build up steam ready for work."

Additionally the entire procession of traction engine, threshing drum and straw elevator were lengthy, cumbersome and awkward to manoeuvre – especially on the narrow lanes that are so typical of the Suffolk-Essex border.

"If you want to know about trouble!" continues Jack, whose threshing tackle was based in Bulmer, "Just about the worst place of all was getting up to Eyston Lodge in Foxearth – up that long narrow lane. There were plenty of places where the wheels touched the banks of both sides. But worst of all was the gateway being so close to the road. It was a devil of a job! You hadn't got any room to manoeuvre. I was FIVE HOURS going up to Eyston Lodge and getting in that field one year – and that lane can't be much more than half a mile long!"

But eventually the threshing machine would reach its destination. The late Douglas Hasler (b. 1918) of Gestingthorpe continues:

"To everyone in the village young or old, the threshing machine was known as the 'sheen', and the whole operation was called 'sheening'. So in those days before television and when only very few people had radios, it was of real interest to hear someone say, 'the sheen has gone to Delvyns'. It also meant a few days work for a few unemployed men in the village."

The arrival of the threshing machine also engendered great excitement amongst the village children for whom it represented both an interesting spectacle – and the chance to go 'ratting'. As one older contributor exclaimed:

"Years ago there wasn't any Disney World or Theme Parks for children! We had to make our own amusement that time of day. But if the 'sheen' turned up so we could go ratting, then we had some 'real fun'. That was our 'Disney World'!"

Douglas Hasler continues with a typical recollection from the Gestingthorpe of the nineteen thirties:

"One day, when I was a lad, they were 'sheening' at Foundry Farm (near the cross-roads and Downs's previous works), so I put my Sealyham dog under my arm and biked down there. By the time I arrived there was only about four feet of the stack left to do – and the rats were running everywhere! Mrs. Oates's farm manager, a Mr. Stevens, was delighted because my dog immediately started to kill the rats. We must have got at least twenty! But after the stack was finished we blotted our copybook, because my dog now discovered he'd got nothing left to fight. So he went and attacked Mr. Stevens' dog instead! 'Take that damned dog home,

Ginger!' he yelled at me. And that was all the thanks we got. But my dog and I went home well satisfied with the sport!"

The threshing contractors would naturally attempt to thresh as much as possible each day. The older men on the farm however might be, 'a little less enthusiastic'. Jack Cornell commented wryly that the chute, where the 'chaff' came off the threshing drum, could sometimes 'cause problems':

"If that was a hell of a hot afternoon and everyone was as tired and dusty as hell, you might see one of the old farm men go to this chute – a bit on the sly – and hold his hand there for a few moments – until that blocked up and brought everything to a halt! When I was a boy I did it by accident near the Belchamp Otten *Windmill* once and one old man grunted, "Huh Boy!" he say, "That's the first good thing you've done all day long!"

The threshing process itself required a team of about ten people. At the end of an arduous, dusty day's work they might have successfully threshed some ten to twelve tons. As an example of the devastating trans-formation that has occurred to farming, the same amount today would be threshed <u>and harvested</u> in just thirty or forty minutes by a modern combine harvester.

Yet even when the stacks were threshed, the corn taken to the barn and the threshing contractor departed for another destination, the hard work was not over.

"Why were the sacks of corn sometimes tipped out onto the floor – when they were brought to the barn from the threshing machine?" I wondered, thinking of the laborious effort required to 'sack it' up yet again.

"So we could put it through the 'hand dresser'!" exclaims Eddie Tuffin, "and then dress it all again! I've done days and days in the barn like that. You see it was still pretty 'chobby' after it came off the threshing machine. So one of us would turn the handle of the 'dresser', and another bushel the corn up – from the heap on the floor – and put it into the 'dresser'. Then as it came out of the dresser you had to shovel it away, and when you'd done all that you'd bushel it all into sacks again!"

✝ ✝ ✝ ✝ ✝

The steam engines which drove the threshing machines required both skill to drive and considerable mechanical expertise to maintain and repair. One passionate steam enthusiast is retired farmworker and engineer Bunny Brown of Castle Hedingham, who has not only built his own model of a Fowler 'portable' steam engine but vividly recalls his own days working with 'traction' engines at Parkgate Farm, Gestingthorpe. As he proudly showed me his own beautifully crafted model – which took him ten years to build – he recalled one particularly difficult maintenance job on a 'full-sized' engine many years ago.

"There are long tubes in a steam engine, (to heat up the water), but they used to get 'furred in' – and it was a heck of a job to get them tubes out to be repaired. When I worked for Mr. Ruffell at Parkgate Farm, he had an engine and we took it over to a place at Ridgewell – where 'Blythe and Pawsey' are now, and they put all new tubes in. It was there nine weeks. There used to be a bloke there called Wilson what used to shoe horses and do all sorts of other work. But once the tubes were out, I had to go in, through a hole, to chip off all the scale and clear out all the slime and mud. And I could only just get through the hole you know! I put one arm in first, then my head, and then my other arm. And once I was in, it was just like the inside of a kettle – with fur about an eighth of an inch thick. I had an ol' chipping hammer, and I laid in that 'mud hole' A WHOLE WEEK chipping off fur and cleaning out the mud with only a candle for light!"

Noticing the beautifully made 'governors' which Bunny had made for his model, I asked him if he could explain both their function – and how they worked.

"It's like this. Every time you put a sheaf in the threshing machine the 'governors' on the engine opened up – to release more power – so that the threshing drum kept working at a constant speed – to prevent 'unthreshed heads'. But you'd still hear the engine 'whoosh'. You'd hear it go 'chuff chuff, CHUFF! chuff, chuff.

"But one day when we were threshing at Priestfields Farm this

294

'ere belt broke – and cuh! The engine went full throttle and the drum started going faster and faster! You'd think it would have shaken the threshing machine all to bits – but thankfully the main drive belt came off so the drum then stopped! . . . But we were worried for a minute or two!"

"Was it a full time job to be 'the driver' – if you were threshing?"

"My uncle used to drive one at Kirby Hall (Castle Hedingham), but it was a portable mind – so you hadn't got to keep hopping up steps to get on it or anything – and he used to put a shovel of coal on the fire, and then take a sack of corn off the threshing drum. He could just work it like that!"

"What about the water?"

"He could set the pump so it would just draw water in at the same pace as the engine boiled it away . . . 'Course he had to keep an eye on it mind – but that's how fine he could set it."

"How many horses did it require to pull a portable engine?"

"I've seen ten horses pulling it!"

"Dudley Paine at Kirby Hall had a big ol' Ransome's portable steam engine and I've seen TEN horses pulling it! My grandfather used to drive it, and I've seen it come up to the top farm at Rushley Green up the hill there with these five pairs of horses pulling it!"

"I've heard that some of the farmers needed a bit of 'reassurance' as to how much coal was burnt," I said coyly. (The farmers provided the coal and replenished the supply when they left the farm. Inevitably however – in the austere years of the 'great depression' – it provided a natural temptation for the hard up or unemployed.)

"Oh yes," chuckled Bunny. "Take ol' Whitholm, who had Brundon Hall and Fowes Farm up at Belchamp. Well he actually had his own ploughing engines. But he actually used to paint whitewash over his heaps of coal – so he could see if any was taken or not!"

Chapter Twenty

SEEDTIME, PLOUGHING & EARLY COMBINES

*"The following account of the 'blackgrass' of Essex – shows not only
that 'certain weeds are apt to be predominant on certain lands
but that the occupiers of such lands are, or have been
UNPARDONABLE SLOVENS.*

*"The plant is the curse of the fine pale impalpable loams of
Bradfield, Wix, Ramsey and the Oakleys, etc . . . By eighteen
month fallows, preserved with, any farm may be freed from this
and every other troublesome weed."*

Arthur Young, Secretary to the Board of Agriculture:
Report on the County of Essex circa 1800

As we have seen from John Row's diaries, autumn ploughing
immediately succeeded harvest. In turn this was followed by the cultivating, scarifying and 'thorough cleansing' of fields due to be sown
with winter wheat.

Before drilling however, the wheat had to be chemically 'dressed'
against seed-borne diseases – a process which has been conducted for
over 300 years – and still continues today. (Robert Andrews, we
recall, used aresenic). Salt water however was also used. "This was
first practised," explains *The Royal Agricultural Society Journal* of 1848,
"about the year 1660, when a vessel of wheat was sunk near Bristol."
After being salvaged the wheat was used for seed, and was then,
"found to be free from disease at the following harvest."

*'Seed dressings' are still of importance to local farmers. (Indeed it was
not until 1992 that mercurial dressings were prohibited). Today however
a 'mobile seed dresser' arrives on the farm in early September operated by
Steve Warner of Anglia Grain Services. The half day each year that his*

297

three man team are on the farm, dressing our thirty odd tons of seed corn makes a pleasant, cheery break from the insular routine of tractor driving. It is – in effect – a little like the arrival of the threshing machine in bygone years. An opportunity to meet fresh faces, share a joke and swap gossip about the yields and varieties that they have witnessed on other farms.

At Bulmer Tye, Horace Elsey provides a more typical memory from 'the horse era', when the product used was copper sulphate – better known as 'blue vitriol'.

"You couldn't just go off drilling like you do nowadays, and do about sixty or seventy acres a day! Oh no! On the night before you'd have to mix this Blue Vitriol with water, and then tip your seed corn out on the barn floor, pour on this Blue Vitriol and then stir it all over. Then next morning you'd sack it all up again and take it to the field in a tumbril. We used to call it 'wetting the wheat'."

Gestingthorpe's Les Smith ruefully adds:

"Do you know, my Father lost his hair – every single strand of it and he was sure it was because of Blue Vitriol. You see when he was drilling with horses he couldn't get right back into the corners of the fields, so he'd take his cap off, and fill it with seed and broadcast it there instead."

At Whatfield in mid-Suffolk our 'tithe war hero' – John Waspe, reveals an even more archaic practice – with seed beans:

"First off we'd flail them in the barn – because they used to reckon too many would get cracked if they put them through the threshing machine. But if there were two or three of you together, and you could get into your stride, flailing used to sound right nice – especially beating on a barn floor. But once you'd finished you'd still have to sort the split ones out. Oh yes, we've been up night after night sitting in the barn – with an ol' oil lamp – and with a tray of beans on our laps picking the cracked ones out!"

Other crops such as trefoil and clover seed were also 'sieved' in the barn. Often these 'small seeds' were sown with a 'fiddle', (which was hung round the neck), or with a 'seed box' which was carried on a frame like a wheelbarrow. However Eddie Tuffin proudly exclaims:

"Ol' Mr. Stuck could sow turnip and clover seed – by hand! I reckon that was remarkable! I mean you don't need more than about two pounds an acre of wild white clover seed – so you couldn't put much on every step – just a bit between your finger and thumb, but he'd sow clover like that!

"But I'll tell you something else though. When he got older – and he lived to be a hundred – he'd sow his turnip and clover seed as he sat on the back of a horse!"

After I had visited Eddie, spring work and then harvest halted any further research on this Chapter for a further six months – until I had finished my own autumn drilling. It was only then – when I came to write up my notes that I perceived the full significance of his comments about, 'sowing from horseback'. But had I understood him correctly? When I visited him again, in October 1997, I was keen to check the details. "Last time I came to see you," I began, "you told me that Mr. Stuck had sowed turnip and clover seed from horse back . . ."

"Yes, he did! And that's the truth!"

"But did he have a 'fiddle' to sow it with?"

"No. He just sat on the horse. He had one hand on the rein – but of course there was no 'collar' on the horse or anything. He might have had a saddle – but I don't say he always did – and there'd be a bowl with the seed in between his legs. And then with the rein in one hand, he'd sow it with his other hand. 'Course he'd use one of the cart horses. He had a lovely old mare called Blossom. And he always said that turnips wanted sowing first thing in the morning: he'd sometimes be finishing a field when we came to work at six o'clock. And do you know, he always got a lovely plant."

"What about the other crops you grew years ago – like mangolds?" I asked.

"When he drilled the mangolds," replied Eddie, "he drilled just ONE ROW AT A TIME! Cuh! That wouldn't be quick enough now! Whatever would they think! Still I expect your own seed drill is pretty wide?"

"Yes. Twenty feet," I murmured, before quickly attempting to return the conversation to the agriculture of years ago. (A constant problem where Eddie is concerned, for at the age of ninety five, he is simply so 'young at heart' that he takes almost as much interest in the author's contemporary farming, as I do in his memories of the 'horse era' husbandry!) "So how did you make the ridges for mangolds?" I continued.

"We ploughed two 'thoroughs' (furrows) together to make a ridge. Then it was rolled down with a flat roll, and then he'd come with the drill; and the horse walked up the 'thorough' – one row at a time!"

With most other crops straightness was of paramount importance – for it enabled the fields to be weeded by 'horse-hoeing'.

"The drilling had to be dead straight – like a 'gun barrel'," recalls Bunny Brown of his days at Parkgate Farm, Gestingthorpe. "If it wasn't the horse hoe would damage the crop. Cuh! You'd hear about it! We used to 'horse hoe' sugar beet and beans with a single horse. But we've also 'horse-hoed' corn. The hoe used to have a steerage device on it. So there'd be two men go with it; one to drive the horses and the other to steer."

Horace Elsey similarly describes 'horse-hoeing' at Jenkins Farm, Bulmer Tye. Moreover we can easily imagine him doing the job, for the fields on which he worked lie alongside the Hedingham road, almost as far as Bulmer Brickyard and then up to the rear of Bulmer School:

"With beans we might do about three acres a day with a 'Cottis hoe'," he explains, "But if you'd got a really good horse it would-n't need leading. A good horse could walk between the plants – just as gentle as a kitten. And it was the same when you were drilling. You had three horses in front, but the one in the wheel mark would keep in that line and you'd hardly ever need touch that 'plough cord'. It would follow that line like you did."

"So did you mark a field out before you started drilling?"

"When we started drilling at Jenkins, we'd often have one wheel in the furrow of a 'stetch' – because they never got properly filled in – and of course the ploughing was always straight. But where they drilled 'over wart', [at right angles to the direction of the ploughing], they'd probably go across the field with an *empty* drill first."

Like numerous others, Horace had used a Smythe Steerage drill – which as noted earlier , was made at Peasenhall in Suffolk.

"There was generally two of you went drilling. One man would steer it. He had to keep the wheel in the 'wheel mark' from the last bout – dead straight of course! But the other man walked behind the drill, and kept his eye on the coulters – to make sure they didn't block. Then at the end he had to pull a lever – to lift the drill out of work – and then put the press on when you started drilling again. At Jenkins we'd swap over on the headland.

"How much could you do in a day?" I wondered.

"We used to reckon on doing ten acres a day – but you had to keep going mind. First you had to take your seed corn out and stand it on the headland in those big 'coomb sacks'. And then you'd have to bushel it into the drill. But drilling could be hard work for the horses as well, especially in the autumn when the land was all wet and puggy, and you had the 'press' on hard. On a winter's day you couldn't hardly see the horses for the steam coming off them."

"It often amazes me that you could get 'seed beds' on heavy land with such limited equipment."

"We didn't! In wet autumns it was like putting wheat into a lot of plaster – it's a b_____ wonder it ever grew at all really. There weren't any clods – it was just like dough. Ol' Ernie Lott used to come behind me with the harrows – and there were times when he never moved anything! You'd just see where the teeth had knocked off the ringes a bit – and if you looked across the field you'd see all this wheat just lying in the groove what the coulters made.

"I said to ol' Driver at Clapps Farm one spring time, "that's suffen' thin on this field!" "Ho!" he say, "that'll be all right – so long as there's one plant every time you put your foot down – that'll do." And do you know, some of it branched out to have six or seven tillers and that was a good ol' bit of wheat."

Then there was ploughing. Although discussed in Chapter Thirteen, the subject is of such importance to traditional farming, that the following notes are also included. John Waspe, recalls his own days of horse ploughing at the legendary Woodlands Farm, Ringshall:

"The head horseman did the marking out," he explains. "That was the most difficult job. The first furrows had to be perfectly parallel to each other – even on hilly fields – otherwise you'd get unlevel land . . . At Woodlands Farm we used to plough on an eighteen yard stetch. We'd do so many rounds 'gathering' and so many rounds 'splitting' and we'd have a furrow every 18 yards. But on several farms, they did it on a 3 yard stetch. That matched the drill – so the horses could walk up the furrow when they drilled."

"Is it right that some of the old horsemen could control their horses just by talking to them – and didn't ever need to touch the 'plough line' – and still plough dead straight?"

"Yes it is! There used to be a man at Furneaux Farm, Whatfield. His name was Mowles. He was a very kind man. He didn't shout or make any noise. But he could talk his horses round . . . 'Course they were quiet, steady horses."

At Jenkins Farm, Bulmer, it was the same:

"Old Bill Toatley could plough all day without a line," recalls Horace Elsey, "just by talking to the horses – and when I first started I thought that was wonderful. But do you know – I could do the same in time!"

302

With the enormous power of modern tractors and ploughs, which now enable us to 'widen our furrow widths' when 'on the move', I was naturally interested in the width and depth of ploughing in past years. (Most local farmers now plough about eight inches deep for cereals with furrows from twelve to twenty inches wide.)

"So how wide were the furrows on a horse drawn plough – and how deep did you plough?" I asked Horace.

"We used to plough about four to five inches deep for cereals and perhaps seven for mangolds," he explained, "But we never had a furrow wider than 9 inches. However when I worked at Ferriers Farm, Bures, the ol' farmer said, "That ol' field look suffen' wet – we'd better plough it with furrows only *six inches wide.*" But from what I could see it didn't seem to make a lot of difference. And around the Colnes, the 'stetches' were only seven feet apart! That was like 'ridge and furrow' and was reckoned to let the water off better. But that was very close."

In *The Long Furrow* we recorded how the horsemen were expected to plough 'an acre a day' on average land – and sometimes less on 'really heavy' soil – where the horses would require more time to rest. One interesting memory is provided by Eddie Tuffin:

"At Kings Farm, Pebmarsh, the men could leave off a little sooner than we did – because there were some long fields there! I expect they got to know how many bouts made an acre. On some of those big fields I dare say they could get done half an hour before we did!"

At Whatfield John Waspe provides one typical – if amusing – exchange from the 'horse era':

"They were in the stable one wet day at Furneaux Farm here, four or five horsemen ready to go to plough, and ol' Fairweather the farmer came round, and he say, 'Men, aren't you going to plough today!'

"'Well boss', one of them say, 'it's still a raining – look at the pond.'

"'Well' he say, 'You ain't got to go and plough the pond, have ye!'"

Yet today many farmers have an even greater preoccupation than ploughing. It is this. How does one get a 'good seedbed' for winter corn on the roughly, nubbly outcrops of raw clay that surface 'on the tops of hills' along our Suffolk-Essex border? And how on earth did our farming predecessors cope with these difficult raw seams?

One wet Sunday afternoon in late October I visited another of my most respected 'oracles' of traditional farming, the late Bert Surridge who lived in a cottage near the Gestingthorpe 'Pheasant', to ask this very question. Firstly however I had to confess that my own autumn work was 'a bit behind schedule'!

"H'aint you done drilling yet!," he teased me. "Blast, Tony Self said they'd finished Delvyns and all up Yeldham a week or more ago. Everyone else is finished. What ever have you been doing, Ashley!"

"We were messing about on our Hilly Field nearly all week," I interjected before conversationally adding,, "Some of the heavy soil there is so difficult to work – it's enough to break a man's heart."

"You don't need to tell me!" he exclaimed. "At the back of the Leys Wood (Gestingthorpe), we had some terrible heavy, yellow ol' clay, and when you were at plough, and it was a bit sticky, you might as well say it would just bloomin' well *turn round and laugh at ye.*"

(Until my dying day I will never forget Bert's brilliant definition. Hours with a Thesaurus could never provide anything as pertinent!).

"But how on earth," I was bursting to know, "did you ever get land ready for a 'winter wheat seedbed' – when you only had horses to do the work?"

"We got over half of it ready before harvest! We'd plough up the hay ground in June or July, there'd be some which was fallow, and then some other land after trefoil seed – so they could all 'weather' and crumble down in good time. I mean if it was a fallow we'd plough it FIVE TIMES – to kill weeds! But you know the real secret of difficult ol' clay land don't you?"

If only I did!!

"Get your farming so you only have to plough some of it every two years! Undersow it with clover or grass seed. On your very worst land try and get two crops – for only one seedbed!"

As indicated fallowing provided an excellent opportunity to 'clean fields' of weeds such as couch grass, wild oats and blackgrass. (It is however of interest that the technique – which Arthur Young so attempted to avoid in the eighteenth century – had actually become 'cost effective' in the depressed agriculture of the 1930's).

"The whole of your farming," explains Harold Cooper (b.1918), "was based on weed control; that was your greatest problem – your greatest adversary.

"And the real expert farmers, like Charlie Gardiner, at Little Yeldham were always walking over their fallowed fields, to see if blackgrass had 'chitted'. As soon as it emerged, they'd start to plough it back. But they had to start soon enough – because it might take a week to plough a field with horses . . . In my first year at Hill Farm in 1946 I grew peas on one field of fifteen acres. But they were so infested with wild oats that after harvest I was actually able to sell them! There were six to seven TONS of wild oats!"

We have already mentioned the coming of tractors. But it was on wet, compacted land that their introduction had the most immediate, visible impact. Despite being a skilled horseman, Horace Elsey graphically recalls:

"When Driver took on Clapps Farm, (Bulmer), the land wasn't all that special to start with. It was a bit run down and very compacted. I mean they never ploughed more than about three inches deep with horses there. But after Driver took it we started to plough to a proper depth. And especially after he'd got a tractor and we could go that bit deeper, it used to grow good crops! In those days if you got 10 sacks an acre (20–22½ cwt/acre) it was a good crop – and a lot of the time you never got more than seven to eight sacks an acre. Now you get four tons – it doesn't seem possible really!"

305

As we have hinted, the early tractors – whilst welcomed for the beneficial effects that they had on the soil – also had their own 'peculiarities'.

"The first Fordsons came to Gestingthorpe about 1921," says Bert Surridge, "but on the one we had, the bloomin' worm that drove the cogs in the 'back axle' kept busting!"

Starting them was a principal frustration:

"You didn't just get in like you do now," exclaims Bert, "and then just turn a key! There was nothing on our first tractors! No bloomin' magneto, no bloomin' self-starter, no cab, no nothing. Only a handle in the front! There was just a commutator and coil box; and it might start first thing – on the other hand it might not start until the middle of the afternoon!"

Others provide similar memories:

"You'd swing your bloomin' arms off trying to start them!" declares Dennis Holland who purchased his first Fordson Tractor about 1924; "You'd swing your guts out!" recalls Horace Elsey; whilst Fred Chatters exclaims,

"They were devils! The gear oil was like tar, and as for the handle! You could hardly move it! Oh no! In the winter you'd half kill yourself trying to start it – swinging it over and over again – and then when you had finally got it running you'd almost freeze to death while you sat on top driving it!"

In the summer there were other exigencies – as Dennis Holland recalls:

"Those early Fords didn't really have any mud guards and if it was dry and windy and you were cultivating or harrowing – Cuh! The dust was enough to cut your eyes out!"

However we should not be too dismissive for as Horace Elsey quips:

"I've got to say I thought it was right nice to sit down and ride – in the warm weather at least!"

Some tractors however had special idiosyncrasies. Both the Lanz Bulldog and Field Marshall had single cylinder engines. Quite frequently when starting them up the engines would 'run backwards'.

"There was a young bloke up here one day," recalls Bunny Brown, "when Charlie Williams was farming and he hadn't got much experience, and he started this 'ere single cylinder tractor up – but I don't think he knew much – and when he got on he say, 'Cuh! I've got three reverse gears – but only one forward!'"

Despite the inevitable frustrations there was an overall perception that tractors not only improved soil structure, but additionally relieved horses of their most strenuous activities. Farmer Colin Cracknell of Henny continues:

"Father bought his first tractor in the mid nineteen thirties. Well the very first job he used it for was to pull the binder at harvest. That was a rotten job for horses – especially on steep, hilly land round here."

In 1934, Edwin Partridge purchased his first tractor,
"a Fordson on 'spade-lug' wheels. It cost me £120, when a good horse was thirty guineas. But the next thing I bought was a 'Boby' Mill – so I could do my own grinding." (Much the same occurred at Parkgate Farm in Gestingthorpe – contributing to the decline of the rural grist mills).

An era of devastating change was underway. In 1936 the author's Grandfather, had – almost foolhardily – obtained one of the first combines to be used in Suffolk. (A Case 'Model Q' combine which was pulled by a Lanz Bulldog tractor). So great was the interest that over 200 people came to watch it at Manor Farm, Elmsett – on one day alone – in its first season's work. So popular an attraction was it, that a collection was taken for the Red Cross in aid of Ipswich Hospital.
But why did the combine generate so much interest?
Essentially because in the great Depression of the 1930's, when the price of wheat was lower than it had been for over two hundred years, it replaced at least ten operations. (For example, scything round the headlands, bindering, 'shocking up' the sheaves, pitching the sheaves onto the waggon, building and then thatching the corn stacks, threshing, taking away the chaff and corn etc., etc.)

By comparison, the 1936 Case Model Q reduced the process to just two operations. Combine harvesting and taking the corn to the barn.

Again we must not be too simplistic. If threshing machines were the, "dustiest things ever invented," combines must occupy second place. By the 1960's both they – and the operator were frequently surrounded by engulfing masses of black dust. Not only did combines become exceptionally unpleasant to drive, but great problems were incurred in keeping the combine's radiator and air breather clean.

From the mid-1970's cabs were fitted to combines. The transformation in driver comfort has been beyond our wildest dreams.

With the coming of the combine, the increase in tractors and a general drift away from mixed farming came a new phenomenon. The burning of straw.

Purely coincidentally the introduction and demise of widescale straw burning coincides with the beginning and the end of the 'Golden Era' of Suffolk's twentieth century farming: when the 'great campaign' of land reclamation and food production instigated in World War Two was described as nothing less than an 'heroic achievement' by the *Encyclopaedia Britannica,* and was followed by another forty years of prosperity, experimentation and reinvestment resulting in three – and sometimes four-fold increases in yield.

It is again purely coincidental that the straw burning ban of Autumn 1992 – which was eventually welcomed by almost everybody – was immediately followed by the very first year of compulsory 'set aside'. For the land of the Suffolk-Essex border a new phase was to begin.

But what of the farms themselves? And their occupiers – the contemporary farmers of Bulmer and Gestingthorpe, Hadleigh and

Halstead? Are they a last gathering; a final mustering in falling redoubt? Each year we are fewer in number. Family farms are steadily – inexorably disappearing.

Within another thirty or forty years will most larger 'commercial' farms be operated by national corporations? (Despite the land itself being privately owned.) If they are – as seems increasingly likely – who then will have the greatest love, the truest affection – for the land, its seasons, its behaviour and the minutiae of its soils?

It will be those with the smaller acreages. To them then – who are so often 'immigrants' from the 'City' or elsewhere – with their holdings of sheep and ponies, organic gardens, woodlands and wildlife reserves will pass the baton of loving the land, and of tending it, and of knowing it intimately, and of cherishing within it, all the finest and most ancient emotions of those who before them were more truly, 'Of the Furrow Born'.

Chapter Twenty One

OF THE FURROW BORN

Farming has been changing and evolving for the past five hundred years. The history of farming is underwritten by change. Throughout the seventeenth century, the 'heavy horse' increasingly replaced oxen for draught work, whilst in the eighteenth century the 'four course rotation', horse-hoeing and 'seed drills' were pioneered, as crops such as clover, turnips, carrots and parsnips were introduced from the continent. More surprisingly, in 1790 even potatoes, were still regarded as a new crop in Suffolk. "For," reported Arthur Young, "they have not been cultivated in the county to within a few years." Indeed one of Young's correspondents – a Rev. Nesfield of Wickhambrook declared:

"I have been earnestly pressing upon my parishioners for nearly forty years to grow them – with as little effect as if it (the advice) had been delivered from the pulpit."

Ten years later however, Young himself observes that there are now, "ten times more acres as ten years ago – the two scarcities have operated powerfully in this respect."

More recently linseed, flax, borage – and in the 1970's oilseed rape have been re-introduced to our countryside. Yet as noticed, innovative crops are not a new phenomenon. In 1924 when farmworker Cecil Smith of Wickham St. Paul returned to England after service in India with the Suffolk Regiment he saw a strange crop. "'What the darvil are those things?' he wondered."

The 'new' crop was sugar beet. Yet sugar beet had actually been grown in England in the nineteenth century. For at Lavenham a small factory was built and operated from about 1865 to 1868 –

before having to close in the face of Caribbean competition. Four decades later however the crop was again attempted. In 1912 the famous Cantley Beet Factory was established in Norfolk, and in 1925 the Bury St. Edmunds factory was built.

"But when the Bury beet factory first opened," explains Claude Alleston, "there were no quotas or acreage limits – so once the factory had enough you just had to feed them to your livestock!"

Yet as cereal prices plummeted, the crop was soon to be the salvation of many an East Anglian farmer. But it was not just crops which were pioneered. In about 1835 the first consignment of Peruvian guano (a nitrogen fertilizer), and batches of nitrate soda were applied to Britain's crops; whilst in 1843 Lawes of Rothamstead took out a patent for the manufacture of Super Phosphate fertilizer – evinced locally in the use of coprolites. In 1849 one local farmer from Hundon named Snell, enthusiastically declared:

"In my opinion nothing can compete with Peruvian Guano. At £9 a ton I think it is the cheapest artificial fertilizer we can buy, especially for heavy land, and its use is certainly very much on the increase."

But the changes were to continue. The local varieties of wheat such as 'Pettit', 'Copdock' and 'Essex White', would give way to selective breeding of which our 'grand old man of farming', Cyril Philp of Castle Hedingham, perceptively declared:

"It used to be an achievement to get one ton an acre – and now three tons is a poor crop. The farmer is doing what he has always done with a little schooling – but I think the plant breeder has done more than anybody; I mean crops will now stand four or five times as much fertiliser!"

Today, the 'plant breeder's' role is more vital than ever. For as new environmental pressures arise – and consumer needs dictate – so too are new strains being developed. Already varieties of cereals – which receive *no fungicide* – can produce significantly higher yields than three decades ago.

Throughout this book we have emphasised one thing: the land;

311

our Mother Earth and the use of our natural resources. We have looked at wind and water mills, local brickyards, and most of all our farming countryside.

In cherishing and caring for the land today, we are confronted with two principal threats. That of global pollution and a giddy espousal of 'free market forces'.

Yet, as is so patently obvious, the whole ecological infrastructure is sustained by a nigh-on miraculous interdependence between species and organisms.

Those who seek to remove all support from agriculture should indeed be careful. For history has taught us something crucial. That politicians – in time of plenty – take our 'Mother Earth' for granted.

In both 1914 and 1939 they were bluntly reawakened. On the next occasion it may not be military aggression which creates shortages. Climate change, industrial pollution, (e.g. another Chernobyl), population growth or European economic malaise, (by comparison with wealthier economies elsewhere), could all act as catalysts for a shortage of food on our supermarket shelves.

"Yet to justify fiscal support agriculture must be increasingly sensitive to the environment." Thirty years ago such a statement would have been provocatively radical. Since then a change of attitude – another in farming's long history – has been quietly taking place. It was pioneered almost three decades ago by the, 'Farming and Wildlife Advisory Groups'. It has been continued more recently by government inducements.

For this is the crux. We, the entire human race – are the custodians of our planet – our Mother Earth. Economic assistance for the countryside is not a call to support one small vested interest. It is something far wider.

An appreciation that at the end of the day our environment is under perilous threat. And that our entire society is ultimately, totally, 'Of the Furrow Born'.

Epilogue

"At tumbled farms in times of yore,
The ewes were lambed in pens of straw,
In woods swine fed, and kine were reared,
Cows milched by hand, and sheep were sheared,

By hardy men, who weather-tanned
By storms and gales yet worked the land,
And hunched 'gainst autumn's driving sleet,
Yet drilled the field and 'pulled' the beet,

As empires, fashions, waxed and waned
These men each year a harvest gained –
Til thanks in village Church is cried,
Praise God for food! This countryside!"

This Countryside

CONTEMPORARY FARM DIARIES:
THE CONTINUING SAGA

HILL FARM, GESTINGTHORPE

19th August 1983:   Accident with Combine Harvester. Local electrician Les Hayes rushes author's father to West Suffolk Hospital, Bury St. Edmunds.

26th August 1983:   Huge outcry as smuts from 'straw burning' blow through Sudbury.

August 1984:   Extraordinary, wonderful harvest! Best ever experienced! Begin 'ploughing in straw' on majority of land.

August 1987:   May, June, July were almost continuously wet. Meadows around Sudbury constantly flooded.

September 1987:   Disastrous harvest. Poorest yields since drought of 1976. Do not finish combining winter beans until September 25th.

October 14th 1987:   October continues wet. So far have only got 25 acres of winter wheat drilled.

October 16th: Hurricane during the night causes immense damage to rooves of barns, farmhouse and cottages. Seventy 'hedgerow trees' blown down around farm. 300 cricket bat willows destroyed.

November 1987:   Unable to complete autumn drilling. Revert to spring barley.

(As a consequence of both the 1987 harvest and a trend towards larger farms, approximately one quarter of the 'holdings' in the Sudbury-Halstead area either changed hands or amalgamated over the following two to three years).

May 1989: Winter wheat variety *Slepjner* 'breaks down' to yellow rust.
Finally clear willow tree plantation of all ruined trees after hurricane. Majority of cracked and strained trees sell for a pittance. £2.00 each. (Compared with the 1998 price of £200 per good tree).

1990: Dry summer. Ponds low, clear them out after harvest.

1991: Good, pleasing harvest.

1992: 'Straw Burning' banned from after this year. Autumn sees the beginning of 'set-aside'. (17 1/2 % of farmed land).
Several neighbours try crops of 'industrial' rape and linseed.

April 1993: Huge panic as we try to fill in I.A.C.S. forms for set-aside payments! Long queues outside Heffers Bookshop in Cambridge to get the correct maps!

May 1993: Farm looks filthy. Blackgrass everywhere!

June 1993: New threat. Orange blossom midge.

February 1994: Huge pressure on grain trade. Sell wheat for May at £97.50 ton.

May 1994: Wheat rockets to £120/tonne. Shame I've got none left to sell!

December 1994: Watch Ken Leech's men lifting fruit trees in Bulmer.
Despite gales and rain storms they tenaciously keep at it.

July 1995: World shortage of grain looms. Set-aside to be reduced to 5%.

6th August 1995:	Lose 34 acres of standing wheat on Church Field, when a fire sweeps behind Bulmer Street and heads for Lower Houses. Gary Rooney, David Sears, "and many others work with a great will." (Repeating John Rowe's remarks 107 years earlier!).
March 20th 1996:	Terrible alarm about B.S.E. Beef market in pandemonium. Friends and relatives exceptionally concerned.
Harvest 1996:	Intense drought. Poorest yields of wheat since 1987. Land ploughs beautifully. Prices quite favourable.
December:	'Normal winter work'. Visit accountant Jim Leggett in Friars Street, Sudbury; solicitor, Geoff Challacombe at Steed & Steed, Gainsborough Street, and Patrick Scrivens, manager at Lloyds Bank. (Feel a bit like John Rowe in 1898).
May:	Wheat prices crash. Sell last load for £82 per tonne.
	Very dry spring. Despite regular watering many of our young Cricket Bat Willow trees die.

Following a succession of dry years with below average rainfall, the meadows beside the Belchamp Brook that in 1970 were too wet for arable farming, are now really too dry for Bat Willows. Is this a very local example of climate change, we wonder?

November 10th 1997:	Meet Ken Leech. Half of the fruit farmers to whom he supplied trees fifteen years ago have grubbed up their orchards. He blames supermarkets and continental governments. How much longer will we be able to buy British apples?

316

December 1997:	Strong pound depresses grain trade and most other sectors of British agriculture – including milk, sheep and pigs. Beef farmers desperate about cheap imports and B.S.E. restrictions.
March 1st 1998:	Countryside March in London. Over 250,000 turn up including many friends and neighbours from the Suffolk-Essex border.
March 31:	Sell wheat for £70 per ton.
August 12th 1998:	Pig producers in dire straights. Eight local vets write to the *East Anglian Daily Times* to point out anomalous situation where British farmers have complied with new animal welfare schemes but some supermarkets are buying from non-complying sources abroad.
August 22nd:	Finish harvest. One of our best ever! Wheat yields excellent.
September 30th:	Tidal wave of depression hits sheep farmers as ewes 'sell' for less than six pounds each in the Midlands and Wales.
October 9th, 1998:	Got half of farm drilled by September 26th. Then fortnight's wet weather . . . Enables me to finish this book! Exactly the same as with *The Long Furrow* sixteen years ago!
	The saga continues. What will happen next? Who will survive? Which crops will be growing in 2020?

Appendix

A FEW OF THE ENGLISH FARMING IMMIGRANTS
TO EAST ANGLIA 1880–1940

From Devon, came the Westren family to Elmsett Hall in 1884, the Crook's to the Earls Colne and the well known Haylock family, (who still farm near Haverhill). In 1900 Rider Haggard similarly recorded, "a Devon farmer adjoining the Melford Hall estate who made butter and cream after the Devon fashion."

From Somerset came the Padfields – a descendant of whom was a recent chairman of Essex N.F.U., whilst from Cheshire came Brooks to Ashbocking (1908) and Robinsons to Thetford (1934). Neighbouring Lancashire provided Colleys (who came in 1917), together with Bradleys, Chamleys and Bainses – who came to Pebmarsh and Wakes Colne in the nineteen twenties and early thirties. The latter families are related and now also farm at Fordham, Tolleshunt D'Arcy, White Colne and Chappel. Also from Lancashire are the Loftus family (now near Braintree) and Craystons (in 1901) – who today farm at Earls Colne and Witham, whilst the Roberts family migrated from Liverpool to Ashen and later to Livermere near Bury St. Edmunds.

Another contingent came from Northumberland, "and soon established a reputation for taking good sheep farms." Locally, Pickerings came to Leavenheath and Nayland, (one of whom later became Muriel Pickerings' husband), the Lennox's to Layer-de-la-Haye and Wilsons to Gestingthorpe.

Two well known Suffolk farming families, the Lawsons (in 1875) and Stennetts migrated to East Anglia from Lincolnshire, whilst the Rows moved to Nowton Hall, (near Bury St. Edmunds) from Shropshire in 1929 and the Fluxs' came to Long Melford from Hampshire about 1940.

The Brooks family who today farm at Assington moved to Edwardstone from Norfolk in about 1912. Even the Gardiner family who have played such a fundamental role in our local agrarian history, and who still farm at Little Yeldham, originally came from Radlett in Hertfordshire in the nineteenth century.

Finally, as described in 'The Khyber Connection', many semi-retired ex-colonials and army officers started fruit farming in the area when land was still cheap after World War Two. Fruit farming was particularly appropriate, since only a small acreage was needed and required expertise in 'man management'. The following all became fruit farmers after 'coming home':

Hugh Moule	Henny & Bulmer
John Irving	Assington
Ted Spencer	Wickham St. Paul
David Tippets	Earls Colne
Jim Macpherson	Polstead
Archibald Maskell	Newton Green
Gerald Bourne	Assington
Brigadier Heany	Wakes Colne
Jim Irving	Assington

A FEW OF THE LOCAL FARMERS
WHO CAME FROM SCOTLAND

Farmer's son, journalist and clergyman, the late Rev. Philip Wright, provided the following list – which are not merely Scottish names – but very much working *Essex* farmers.

Addison, Barron, Calderwood, Currie, Drummond, Gemmells, (from Ayrshire to Ongar), Hodge, McLaren, McCauley, McDonald, McTurk, Nesbitt, Torrance, Ritchie and Wilson, and the ancestors of well known farmer, writer and broadcaster, Hew Watt of Orsett.

Similarly, previous A.D.A.S. officer, John Llewellin, told of:

"Davidsons at Peldon, Grays at Little Wigborough;
McCready's at Little Clacton and Tolleshunt Major;

MacDonalds at Great Bromley, MacFarlane's at Peasenhall, McGregor's at Milden, Rayne and Lindsey; McKenny at Clare, MacLean at Stanway and Baine's in villages such as Great Wigborough and Tendring and Melroses at Easthorpe."

Butcher Freddie Ruse of Long Melford recalled some who moved to the Sudbury area:

"There were the Millars who came to Cuckoo Tye Farm, Acton in about 1910, the Cristals to Lavenham, the Alstons to Assington Hall (in the mid 1920's), the Cutlers to Long Melford and Alan Steele to Assington."

From a variety of sources we noted the Kiddy family – now at Halstead – who are believed to have come down in the early nineteenth century; the Stratherns who came to Birch and later moved to Layer Marney, and James Craig who came to Halstead in approximately 1895-96. (He later farmed at Spoons Hall, Pebmarsh and finally Bennetts Park, Halstead.)

To Stisted came the McMillan family, whilst in 1902 came William Johnston first to Pattiswick and then Greenstead Hall. Similarly the Morton family who today farm at Henny and Belchamp Walter, record that, "Grandad was born in Cambridge – but we think that great grandfather came down from Scotland – perhaps about 1890."

To Hintlesham, near Hadleigh came the Bryce family, to Preston the Knoxs' whilst to Bacton, migrated David Black in 1898. Two other prominent Suffolk farmers of Scottish descent are the Kerrs of Letheringham – who also run the famous Easton Farm Park, and past chairman of Suffolk N.F.U. John Wallace of Colney Weston. Closer to home, Bob Letham of Bulmer records:

"Around Halstead nearly all the farmers on the Courtauld family estate were Scottish. At Knights Farm, Colne Engaine, there was William Steele and then at Harmas Farm, Gosfield, there was my uncle, Tommy Letham.

"On the Halstead estate there was Jim Craig (already noted), Alex Anderson who came to Hepworth Hall, Jim Bowie at Bentalls, and my father (Adam Letham), at Slough Farm. In fact when dad came down in 1931, the farm was actually let, 'rent free' for three years. But a lot of my father's family also moved down, and took farms in Wethersfield, Stratford St. Mary and Elmstead Market."

Elsewhere there were Camerons at Assington and Wiers at Tendring Hall, whilst an Ian Davidson Barron came to Bures in 1924 before moving to Wethersfield in 1928. As already noted, Coll Bain came to Goldingham Hall, Bulmer in 1936, whilst the Wallaces, latterly of Lavenham, 'came down' sometime in the nineteenth century.

Finally, in 1958 Messrs. Gray and Dale came to Great Yeldham Hall, representing – we think – the valedictory wave of 'the great migration'.

DOUBTLESS SOME READERS CAN EXTEND THIS LIST!!!

For readers with an especial interest in the subject, a book entitled, *'From the Glens to the Lowlands'* by George Murray Anderson, (b.1894), records the author's own migration to Hall Farm, Stanton in 1925, together with reminiscences of his fellow Scotsmen in Suffolk.

Finally, farmer Dennis Holland of Lavenham refers to that well-known Scottish characteristic, euphemistically known as 'thrift'.

"I've heard say," he laughs, "that a Scottish 'shepherd' accepted a job down here – but only on condition that the farmer would bring his furniture down on his truck. Well, the farmer agreed, but the 'shepherd' had to sit out in the open – on the back of the truck – even though it was bitterly cold weather. Apparently it was perishing – but he sat there all the way from Glasgow to Wickham Market . . . Anyway he did about three months work for this farmer and then he said, 'I'm off now – I've bought a farm near Ipswich' . . . All he'd ever wanted was a free lift down for his furniture!"

Bibliography

OUR MOTHER EARTH

The Land of England: Dorothy Hartley. Published 1979 by Macdonald and Jane's Ltd., London.

Life and Tradition in Suffolk and North East Essex: Normal Smedley. Published by J. M. Dent & Sons Ltd., London. 1980.

A Pictorial History of Sible Hedingham: Adrian Corder-Birch, F.Inst.L.Ex.,M.I.C.M. Published by Halstead and District Local History Society. 1988

Figures in a Wessex Landscape: Edited by Joanna Cullen-Brown. Published by W. H. Allen & Co. Ltd., 1988.

British Husbandry: Published 1837.

Trees and Woodland in the British Landscape: Oliver Rackham. Published by J. M. Dent & Sons Ltd., 1976.

People at Work in Halstead and District: Doreen Potts. Published by Halstead and District Local History Society.

The Diary of Ralph Josselin 1616 - 1683: Edited by Alan Macfarlane. Published by Oxford University Press, 1976.

Cato & Varro: De Re Rustia: Translated by W. Hooper and H. B. Ash. Published by Loeb Classical Library, 1967.

The Discovery of Britain: Jack Lindsay. Published by Merlin Press, 1958.

The English Dairy Farm 1500–1900: G. E. Fussell. Published London 1966.

Meagre Harvest: Arthur Brown. Published by Essex Record Office (E.R.O. No. 106), 1990.

Wills of the Archdeaconary of Sudbury: Edited by Nesta Evans. Published by Suffolk Records Office.

Let's Git up Agin the Table: Basil Slaughter. Published by Essex Federation of the Essex W.E.A., 1992.

General View of the Agriculture of Essex, 1807: Arthury Young, 1807.

Farmers Tour through the East of England: Arthur Young, 1770.

General View of the Agriculture of Suffolk: Arthur Young, reprinted 1813. Reprinted by Augustus M. Kelley, New York, 1969.

The Maplesteads: Then and Now: Published by Maplestead W.E.A., 1986.

Victoria County History of Essex.

Essex Brewers: Ian P. Peaty. Published by the Brewery Society, 1992.

Eighteenth Century Sudbury: Allan W. Berry. Published by Suffolk County Council Arts & Libraries, 1992.

Sudbury and District News 1875–1930: Stephen Bixley. Published privately.

Land of My Fathers: Wickham St. Paul 1750–1850: Marion Turp. Published privately.

MIGRATIONS AND THE TITHE WAR

Bulmer; Then and Now: Edited by Basil Slaughter. Published by Bulmer W.E.A. Second edition published 1990 by Simon Harris.

The Maplesteads: Then and Now: 1881–1986. Published by Maplestead W.E.A., 1986.

Chartism in Essex and Suffolk: Dr. Arthur Brown. Published Essex Record Office No. 87, 1982.

Wickham St. Paul: Some Items Towards Its Story 1662–1980: Published by Bulmer W.E.A.

Where Beards Wag All: George Ewart Evans. Published by Faber and Faber, 1970.

Meagre Harvest: Arthur Brown. Published by Essex Record Office. (E.R.O. No. 106), 1990.

Colne Engaine – The Story of an Essex Village: Published by Colne Engaine History Society, 1992.

The Tithe War: Doreen Wallace. Published by Victor Gollancz Ltd., 1934.

Agricultural Records A.D. 220 - 1977: J. M. Stratton. Published by John Baker, 1978.

The Report of the Annual Meeting of the Hadleigh Farmers' Club: December 1840. Reprinted 1990 for the Club's 150th anniversary.

Country Padre: Philip Wright. Published by Egon Publishers, 1980.

A Guide to St. Andrew's Church, Bulmer: Richard Slaughter, 1987.

Chelsworth: Geoffrey Pocklington. Republished by Bernard Quinland, 1994.

OF THE FURROW BORN: MORE OF THE LONG FURROW

The Farmers' Tools: G. E. Fussell. Published by Bloomsbury Books, London, 1985.

Farming Technique from the historic to Modern Times: G. E. Fussell. Published by the Commonwealth and International Library, 1965.

A History of Great Yeldham: Adrian Corder-Birch. Published by Halstead and District Local History Society, 1994.

A Stroll through the Century: Earls Colne Parish Council Centenery Publications, 1994.

Garrett Diesel Tractors: Robert A. Whitehead. Published by R. A. Whitehead & Partners, 1994.

The Agriculture of Suffolk: W. & H. Raynbird, 1849.

History of the Borough of Sudbury: C. G. Grimwood and S. A. Kay. Published locally, 1952.

Industries of the Eastern Counties Business Review: 1888–1890: Reprinted by Essex Libraries, 1992.

Halstead's Heritage: Doreen Potts. Published by Halstead and District Local History Society, 1989.

White's Directory: 1844 & 1863.

Essex and the Industrial Revolution: John Bocker. Published by Essex County Council, 1974. (Essex Record Office Publication No. 66).

A Walk Through Clare: Penny Parker. Published by Clare Parish Council.

Suffolk Windmills: Brian Flint. Published by the Boydell Press, 1979.

Essex Windmills, Millers & Millwrights: Kenneth Farries. Published by Charles Skilton Ltd., London, 1981.

Some Essex Watermills: Hervey Benham. Published by Essex County Newspapers, 1976.

John Constable's Correspondence Vol. IV: Edited by R. B. Beckett. Published 1962 by Suffolk Records Society.

Overshot Mill, Colne Engaine: Jane Greatorex, 1991. Available locally.

INDEX OF LOCAL PARISHES

(Roman numerals relate to centre section.)

Acton 90.
Alphamstone 55, 58, 89. 101,121, 150, 151, 153, 169, 175, 220, 245, 270, 273, 285–287, 299.
Alpheton 154.
Ashbocking 179, 272.
Ashen 189, 217.
Assington 112, 154, 236.

Bacton 178.
Ballingdon 23, 25, 76, 110, 112, 213, 214, 249.
Ballingdon Grove Brickworks 23, 29, 34.
Ballingdon Bridge xi.
Ballingdon Hill 33.
Belchamp St. Allbrights 186.
Belchamp Brook 14, 31, 243.
Belchamp Otten 89, 102, 106, 110, 148, 162, 186, 221, 237, 245, 249, 293, 294.
Belchamp St. Pauls 84, 89, 124, 178–179, 189, 220, 237, 240.
Belchamp Walter 17, 51, 53, 61, 68, 69, 85–89, 103, 108–109, 115, 139, 152, 153, 168, 189, 215, 252, 276, 285, xxix.
Watermill 238, 242–247.
The Belchamps 36.
Bildeston 148.
Birdbrook 124, xxv.
Bocking 115, 124, 126.
Borley 17, 51, 106, 112, 186, 190, 220, 235, 239–241, 243, 250–251, 253–254, xxiv.
Boxford 148, 182, 233, 234, 249.
Bradfield Combust 81, 116, xxvi.
Bradfield St. George 163.
Brandon 50.
Braintree 48, 59, 108, 124, 174, 178, 253, xxv.
Brent Eleigh 71, 154.
Brettenham 121.
Brundon 186.
Bulmer – mentioned repeatedly see especially:–
Andrews (Robert) vi–xxi, 185, 297.
Brickyard 23, 26, 32–34, 49, 58, 111, 280, 288.
Cock and Blackbirds xxx.
Fox Public House 104.
Hilly Field 14, 31 108, iv.
Limekiln 37, iv.
Plough Inn xi.
Bures 23, 60, 76, 81, 99, 146, 224, 225, 235, 248.
Railway line to Haverhill 273.
Bury St. Edmunds 56, 224, 225, 236, 237, 311.

Buxhall 53, 72.

Cambridge 119.
Castle Hedingham 20, 23, 29, 62–72, 89, 91, 94, 99, 149, 156, 165, 204, 221, 226, 228, 252, 294–296, 311, viii, xxii–xxvi.
Bell Public House 73.
Railway Station 30.
Rising Sun 158.
Cavendish 23, 71, 79, 123, 143, 154, 236.
Chappel 23.
Chelmsford 61.
Chelsworth 154, 237.
Chilton 20, 23, 71, 90, 112, 122.
Brickfield and Lime Works 41, 47.
Clare 23, 119, 142, 143, 225, 236, 253.
Cockfield 106.
Coggeshall 119, 149.
Colchester 49, 53, 58.
Castle 40, 49.
Castle Museum 61, 65.
The Colnes 236, 303.
Colne Engaine 17, 20, 23, 69, 171, 253.
Colne Valley Railway 21.
Combs 35, 72.
Cornard (Brickyard, Heath and Mere) 110–112, 236.
Culford 35.
Culford Heath 151.

Dagworth 72.
Debenham 81.
Dedham 251.
Diss 191.
Dunmow 61, 117.

Earls Colne 23, 69, 71, 86, 99, 117, 118, 123, 167, 185, 217.
Earl Soham 81.
East Bergholt 18, 251.
Edwardstone 71, 73, 236.
Elmsett 84, 90, 147–148, 180, 184, 192–193, 211, 241, 282, 307.

Farnham 68.
Felsham 114.
Felstead 126.
Finborough 72.
Finchingfield 51, 153, 237.
Flatford 251.
Foxearth 15, 16, 37, 89, 110, 115, 152, 157, 169, 185, 274, 292.
John Row's diaries 128–135, 255–267.
Framlingham (Castle) 49.

325

Gestingthorpe – mentioned repeatedly see especially
  Brickyard 22, 23, 25–31.
  Church 20, 38, 49, 57.
  Iron Foundry 140, 214–217.
  Pottery 58–62.
  Roman Settlement 36, 50.
  Tithe dispute 193–194.
Glemsford 23, 52, 54, 71, 75, 104, 123, 152, 159, 253.
Gosfield 19*, 20, 87, 99, 124, 126, 168, 237, xxviii.
Great Bricett 126.
Great Cornard 44, 49, 71, 90, 112, 238, 241, 249.
Great Henny 35, 71, 151–153, 241, 245, 246.
Great Maplestead 51, 70, 71, 89, 112, 124, 168, 189, 241, 276, iv.
Great Waldingfield 71, 154, 186.
Great Yeldham 19*, 23, 71, 92, 94, 95, 119, 189, 225, 236.
Greenstead Green 217, 253.
Groton 73, 126.

Hadleigh (Suffolk) 20, 90, 99, 148, 182, 236, 291.
  Farmers Club 279.
Halstead 23, 48, 51, 57–60, 71, 72, 76, 90, 112, 114–118, 165, 247, 274, 283, ii, xxvii.
  Rose and Crown 290.
  water and wind mills 236, 247, 249, 252–253.
Halstead Rural District 101.
Hartest 58, 90, 112, 154, 237.
Harwich 49.
Haughley 72, 194.
Haverhill 107, 27, 273.
Hedinghams 19, xxviii
  brickyards 30.
Helions Bumpstead 20, 107.
Hengrave 284.
Henny 89, 98, 115, 288, 307.
Hinckford Hundred 153.
Hintlesham vii.
Hitcham 50.
Honnington 78.
Hundon 53, 90, 154.

Ickworth 97.
Ingatestone 174.
Ipswich 76, 160.
  Farmers' Club 279.
Ixworth (Farmers Club) 279.

Kersey 71, 76, 90, 154, 233, 236.
Kirton 230.

Lamarsh 76, 82, 89, 161.
Lavenham 48, 71, 83, 126, 182, 236, 310.
Lawford 218.

Layham 248.
Leiston 228.
Liston 20, 97, 160.
Little Cornard 23, 54, 58, 71, 79, 90, 154.
Little Henny 143.
Little Horkesley 173.
Little Maplestead 48, 71, 73, 112, 124, 151, 153, 156, 160, xxvii.
  Cock Public House 102.
Little Waldingfield 90, 123.
Little Yeldham 25, 88, 96, 124, 147, 168, 169, 237.
Long Melford 20, 23, 45, 51, 71, 75, 76, 92, 93, 99, 114, 143, 169, 170, 186, 217, 236, 253, 273.
  John Row's Farm Diaries 128–135, 255–267.
  Withindale Mill 254.
Long Melford to Hedingham Railway 30, 31, 151.
Luton 86.

Manningtree 147.
The Maplesteads 69.
Middleton 27, 121, 150, 152, 189, vi.
Milden 236.
Monks Eleigh 119.
Mount Bures 58, 189.
Museum of Rural Life (Stowmarket) 50.

Nayland 182.
Newmarket 119.
Newton 126, 143, 154, 158, 167.
Nettlestead 174.

Oakley 297.

Peasenhall 225–226.
Pebmarsh 20, 71, 126, 153, 189, 219, 242, 253, 303.
Pentlow 75, 89, 153, 241, 284.
Polstead 119, 126.
Poslingford 90, 154.

Rattlesden 179.
Raydon 18, 248, 282.
Ridgewell 76, 89, 124, 126, 153, 294.
Ringshall 194–204, 302, xxxii.
Rugby 63.

Sible Hedingham 23, 27, 58, 68, 76, 89, 101, 126, 189, 231, 241, 253.
Sicklesmere 58.
Southminster 47.
Stambourne 23, 89, 168.
Stanningfield 58.
Stansfield 195, 214.
Stanton 230.
Steeple Bumpstead 81, 168.
Stisted viii.
Stoke By Clare 90, 191, 195.

Stoke By Nayland 49, 71, 103, 149.
  Church 20.
River Stour 52.
  Navigation: barges 19.
Stour Navigation 251.
Stowmarket 72, 186, 196.
Sturmer 20, 124, xv.
Sudbury 23, 35, 45, 48, 88, 90, 93, 96, 98,
  101, 110, 111, 122, 238, 247, 288, 314,
  iv, vi.
  Cornard Road Chalk Pit 40, 41, 45, 46.
  Clovers Mill 238, 241.
  Gas Works 99.
  'Clovers Mill' (Mill Hotel) 238, 241.
  Kings Head 239.
  Middleton Road Lime Pit 35, 38, 39.
  Station Road 12.
  St. Peters Church 49.
  Quay Theatre 25.
Suffolk (cheese) 79.
      (butter) 82.

Tendring Hundred 172.
Terling 107.

Thorrington 253.
Thorpe Morieux 276.
Tilbury-Juxta-Clare 20, 89.
Tiptree 47.
Toppesfield 20, 50, 119, 126, 146, 151, 158,
  159, 237.
Twinstead 20, 75, 89, 150, 219.

Waldingfield 48.
Wattisfield 58.
Wattisham 121.
West Stow 58.
Wethersfield 51, 69–72, 83, 126, 156, 253,
  283, 287.
Whatfield 284, 302, 303.
Wickhambrook 189, 230, 310.
Wickham St. Pauls 16, 20, 62, 74–77, 79–81,
  107, 114, 149–153, 157, 186–188, 234,
  237, 244, 245, 252, 310.
Wortham 195.
Wix 297.
Wixoe 90.
Wormingford 250.

*　　*　　*

GENEAOLOGISTS

See especially list of local Brickmakers on pages 23–24; Hop Growers page 69; Cornish Immigrants　page 168; Farming visitors to Bulmer demonstration of 1851 on page 210; Footnotes on pages 138, 141, 144, 210 and Appendix on pages 318–321.

*　　*　　*

QUOTED NOVELS AND POEMS

Anna Karenina 208.
A Tale of Two Cities 87, 91.
Emma 208.
Far From the Madding Crowd 83.
  Illustration on page 14.
Oliver Twist 87.

Pride and Prejudice 184.
Tess of the D'Urbervilles 208.
The Farmers Boy 78.
The Mayor of Casterbridge 92.
The Shepherd's Year 177.
The Woodlanders 77.

INDEX OF SUBJECT MATTER

Agricultural Depression 142–144, 174–175, 190.
Ancient Woodlands 123–126.
  grubbing up 124.
Andrews (Robert) vi–xxi, 185, 297.
Animal cures 83.
Australian Gold Rush 158.
Australia 156, 157, 163.

Bark pelling 72.
Basket making 121.
Bingham (Edward) 62–67, 70, 91, 158.
Blackgrass 297, 301.
Blackshirts 205.
Brickyards and brickmaking 17–35.
Brick & Tile Tax 91, 92.
Bullace Plums 121–122.

Canada 158–162.
Carraway & Coriander 73–74.
Chalk 35–50.
Cheese (locally made) 77–81.
  (poor reputation & decline)
Churches with brick towers 20–21.
Clodburning 50.
'Clay lump' buildings 53–55.
Combine harvesters 310.

Depopulation of villages 17, 150–155.

Earth spreading 55.
Emigration – from Suffolk and Essex 146–164.
Ergot 121.

Fallowing 304–305.
Flax 74–75.
Flint 50.

Garrett diesel tractor 229.
Gas works (locally) 99–100.

Harvest customs 287, xv.
Harvesting techniques 278–284, xii–xv.
Haverhill Lamb Sale 273.
Hay trussing 92–97.
Herbal remedies 114–121.
Hops 68–73.
Horsemen's powers 84, 85.

Immigration (of farmers from Scotland, North of England, Cornwall, etc.) 15–16, 164–181.

Light 98–101.
Lime kilns 37–47.

Marl 50.
Migrations to London 16, 147.
  to north of England 148.
  to Australia, Canada 156–163.

National Agricultural Labourers Union (N.A.L.U.) 155, 156.
Non-Conformists (problem with farm tenancies) 165.

Orchids 108–110.

Ploughing with horses 218–222, 302–303.
Plough from Gestingthorpe 214-215.
Potteries (local) 57–68.
Potash manufacture 126.

Rat catchers 123.
Reaping machines 209–214, 281.

Sand 51.
Scrophulous diseases 114–121.
Scottish drovers coming to Suffolk 177.
Seed dressings 297, xx, xxi.
Seed drills 225–226, 299–301, vi–viii, xxiii–xxv.
Septaria stone 20, 49.
Shepherds recollections 270, 272, 273.
Sickles and scythes xii–xv, 278–283.
Steam cultivation 226–228.
Stockmens memories 82, 83, 269–272.
Straw plaiting 86–91.
Straw tieing 92–94.

Tanning and tanyards 76–79.
Teasels 73.
Threshing machines 291–293.
Tithe 184–206.
  (Lay Tithe) 185.
Traction engines 294–296.
Tractors – early models 230–234, 306–307.
Tuberculosis 114.
Typhoid 107.

vallus 210, 230.
Veterinary reminiscences 274–277.

Wells 103–107.
'White' Blackbird 122.
Windjammers 159.
Windmills & watermills 234–253.
Wildflowers 111–113.

Young (Arthur) 36, 51, 71–75, 81, 87, 91, 92, 278, 310. See especially vi–xxviii.

BOOKS BY ASHLEY COOPER

(see next page)

Further copies of all Ashley Cooper's books are available via book sellers using Whittakers 'Tele-ordering' system. Please add £1.20 for postage and packing.

N.B. Despatch of books may sometimes be delayed due to farm work. Books are not usually available in August or September; otherwise allow 3–4 weeks for delivery. For direct orders write to Hill Farm, Gestingthorpe, Halstead, Essex, CO9 3BL.

The Long Furrow

'Two thousand years of rural history along the Suffolk-Essex border'

Complete with the memories of the horsemen, shepherds, drovers, blacksmiths and threshing contractors of a bygone era. Additionally included are chapters on Roman Gestingthorpe; medieval agriculture, rural characters; seedtime and harvest, 'village life and horkeys', the Tithe war, the Great Depression, Horse era agriculture, the coming of tractors and a special section devoted to wildflowers and wildlife.

The Long Furrow is Ashley Cooper's first book and was largely quoted in *The Reaper's Year*, a play written and performed by the Eastern Angles Touring Theatre Company.

Fifth print now available. ISBN 0 900 227-82-6

Price £6.95

THE LONG FURROW
– Brief Subject Index –

Ancient woodland 17, 200–203.
Ash whistles 211.

Baking, brewing 72–73.
Birds:
    (populations and memories) 218–222.
Blacksmiths 150–154.

Combines 190.
Coppicing and Pollarding 204, 205.

Domesday Book 28.
Droving 127–130.

Elephants, Hippopotamus, Lion
    (bones discovered) 15*.

Farmworkers strike:
    at Belchamp Walter 50–54.
Ferreting 60.
Fruit trees 195, 232–234.

Gleaning 107.
Great Depression
    (and derelict land, etc.) 167–172.

Harvest customs 91–93.
Harvesting:
    (with scythes, binders, etc.) 96–98.
'Home Guard' 184.
Home-made wine 78.
Horsemen's memories 137–150.
    Head horseman's position 139.
    Horse cures and potions 144–148.
Humour 63–66.
Hurdlemaking 132.

Ice Ages 15.
India 59.

Manor Courts 31.

Oxen – used for ploughing 37.

Peasants Revolt 30.
Pigs and chickens 195–197.
Pig 'Up the chimney' 73.
'Pop Gun' manufacture 212.

Rabbiting 29, 76.
Roman Agriculture:
    Crops and vegetables 23–24.
Rotations 191–192.

Shepherding 124–126.
Steam ploughing 109.
Stour Navigation:
    (strong man at Pitmire Loch) 80.

Thatching 102–103.
Threshing machines 155–165.
Tithe War 173.
    Gestingthorpe case 174–181.
Tractors (early models) 185–189.

Village cricket 67–68.

Wild Flowers
    –Nicknames and uses 212–217.
'Withe making' 221.
Wool 32–33.
World War One 59.

Young (Arthur) in Bulmer and Belchamp 41–46.

The Khyber Connection
'Connections betweeen Suffolk, Essex . . . and India!'

After an extraordinary series of accidental meetings the author interviewed over 70 local people from the Suffolk-Essex border who had served in India. Privates from the local regiments, Gurkha officers, retired tea planters and railway officials all describe their lives.

But the book is not all nostalgia. A complete section is devoted to local men who served in the **BURMA CAMPAIGN** of World War Two.

Many other connections between India and the Suffolk-Essex area are also unearthed. Finally the reader is taken on a 7000 mile journey from the coasts of Kerela to the snow peaked Himalayas and the rugged boulders of the Khyber Pass as India is explored again.

ISBN 0-900 227-81-8

Price £5.95

KHYBER CONNECTION
– Brief Subject Index –

Belchamp Walter:
  'Mutiny Shawl' 39.
  'Tipu Sultan' 23–24.
Bildeston, mutiny death 32.
Bulmer:
  Afghan War 44.
  Cock and Blackbirds 162.
Butler (*R.A.B*) 153, 207.
Burma Campaign 120–145.
Bury St. Edmunds 34, 43, 52, 124.
  (Barracks and Church)
Children:
  – Long absences from parents 74–79.
Coconut Fibre Mats:
  Sudbury and Glemsford 47.
Darjeeling 188–200.
Delhi 164–166.
Earls Colne (Church) 24, 223.
  Exports 46.
'Elephant Plough' 46.
  (Ransomes of Ipswich).
Essex Regiment 26, 54, 55, 138, 158, 212.
Farmworkers in Uniform 56–73.
  Reservations, lives, pets, practical jokes, humour, restrictions.
'Forgotten Army'
  Arakan Campaign 125–129.
  Malaria 129.
  Boredom, humour, jungle life, frustrations 131–136.
  Separations from families 149.
  Reunions 149, 222.
  Tribute 150.

Greenstead Green:
  (Medical missionary) 83.
Great Maplestead (Church) 90.
Gurkas 106, 143, 201.
Henny (Barnardiston Diaries) 21, 111.
Hadleigh: Mutiny death 32.
Indian Mutiny: Church Collections: 34, 35.
  (Assington, Bury St. Edmunds, Castle Hedingham, Edwardstone, Hundon, Milden, Sudbury, Wickham St. Pauls.)
Indian Mutiny: Lectures:
  Gestingthorpe 35 (and 'new' national anthem).
  Castle Hedingham, Coggeshall, Halstead, Sudbury 36.*
Kohima 138–141.
Liston: Mutiny Memorial 32.
Madras 184–186.
Maharaja Duleep Singh (at Elvedon) 41.
North West Frontier 205–215.
Oates (Captain) in India 230–231.
Ootacamund 178.
Rajastan 167–169.
Skinners Horse 109, 110.
Sudbury: Corrupt election 25.
Suffolk Regiment 42–44, 52–59, 137, 175–176, 184–185.
Tea planting 97–102.
Troopships 122.
Witnesham (Victoria Cross) 37.
Womens lives: 80–88.
  Contribution in war 131.
  Early deaths, Hadleigh Church, etc. 84.

331

Heart of Our History
'500 years of village history along the Suffolk-Essex border'

Including the recollections of ninety people in the Sudbury-Halstead area, and Record Office material from sixty local parishes, this book explores village life from the era of the 'sovereign parish' with its Overseers, Surveyors, Constables and workhouse, to more recent memories of village schools, 'Big Houses', being 'in service', first bicycles, early buses, rural childhood, public houses, village cricket, 'Dad's Army' and local wildlife.

The book contains valuable resource material for the student of social history. Parish perambulations, local charities, and school Log Books are all examined, together with research on civilian life during World War Two, and a chapter on the evolving role of both the parish Church and non conformist Chapels.

270 pages plus 24 pages photographs and illustrations by Benjamin Perkins.

Third print now available.
ISBN 0 9524 778-0-7
Price £6.95

HEART OF OUR HISTORY
– Brief Subject Index –

Airfields (wartime) 235.
'Acorning' 105.
'Beating the bounds' 38.
Breadmaking 144.
Breweries (local) 179.
'Big Houses' 149.
Butlers' memories 162.
Chapel 266.
'Coppers' 136.
Constables (parish) 69.
'Dad's Army' 218.
Early bicycles 92.
Fire engines 84.
Food rationing 225.
Football 208.
Funerals 79.
Gamekeeping 210.
Gleaning 142.
Greengages 257.
Harvest 106.
'Higglers' 75.
Home Guard 253.
Housemaid's duties 151.
Ice houses 166.
Kersey 58.
Kentwell Hall 160.

Land Girls 244.
Manorial courts 14.
Mischief 118.
Non-conformism 266.
Oates (Captain) 149.
Olivers Brewery 180.
Overseers 21.
Parish boundaries (map); perambulations 41.
Postmen's huts 76.
Public houses 169.
Riots 35.
'Bluffy' Rippingale 94.
Schools 103.
'Settlements' 31.
Smallpox 22.
Stagecoaches 182.
Stone picking 60.
"Surveyors of highways" 56.
Twinstead "hand hearse" 80.
Vestry meeting 25.
Village cricket 195.
Walking to weddings 83.
Walnuts 258.
'War-Ag' 249.
Wildflowers 262.
Workhouses 51.

Countryside Journey

Part Three of Ashley Cooper's *Heart of Our History* trilogy brings all the diverse threads of his previous volumes into a historical travelogue around the Suffolk-Essex border. The book will be a combination of historical research and rich rural anecdotes giving a new perspective to every village and by-road in our area.

Publication in due course.

*   *   *

FICTION

Tales of Woodland & Harvest

In *Tales of Woodland & Harvest*, Ashley Cooper writes with humour and great feeling of the contemporary East Anglian countryside.

They are fictitious stories of love – love of the land and the seasons, of the seedtimes and harvests; of the woodland and fields and of the people with whom the experience is shared. They range from his immortal portrayal of Curley – a retired farm mechanic – and also include wily gamekeepers and poachers, the hero of a rural 'who-done-it' and an ageing horseman whom we enchantingly meet in a moment of true village cricket.

Each story is delightfully illustrated with the countryside drawings of Elizabeth Martland.

Second print now available.
ISBN 0-900 227-84-2
Price £4.95

More Tales of Woodland & Harvest

Publication in due course.

*Ten horses pulling Dudley Paine's Ransomes portable steam engine
at Kirby Hall, Castle Hedingham.*

Born at Gestingthorpe in 1952, Ashley Cooper is a working farmer with a passionate interest in local history. His first book, *The Long Furrow* has been reprinted four times and was followed by *The Khyber Connection, Heart of our History* and the fictitious *Tales of Woodland & Harvest*.

For ten years he hosted an 'experimental trials centre' on his farm and in 1991 was awarded the *Farming News* prize for combining "a high standard of cereal husbandry with advanced conservation practice." He is the Honorary Patron of Gestingthorpe Cricket Club, President Elect of the Sudbury branch of the Parkinson Disease Society, and Chairman of the Gestingthorpe Educational Foundation and Bulmer History Group.

A lifelong passion for natural history and art resulted in estate manager Benjamin Perkins devoting his life fully to painting and writing in 1978. His definitive book *Trees* was graced with a foreword by the Duke of Edinburgh, although his best known work is undoubtedly *A Secret Landscape* – which in prose, colour paintings and illustrations recounts the 'wildlife year' of a group of isolated meadows along the Suffolk-Essex border.